Groups
at Work

Techniques in
Training and Performance Development
━━━━━━ Series ━━━━━━

Groups at Work

Oscar G. Mink
Professor, Human Resources Development
University of Texas at Austin

Barbara P. Mink
President, OHRD Associates
Austin, Texas

Keith Q. Owen
Director and Chairman, Human Development
Austin Community College
Senior Vice-President, OHRD Associates
Austin, Texas

with contributions from
Phil Jones, Barbara Peek Loftin,
David McKay, and Barbara J. Zechner
OHRD Associates

Joseph W. Arwady
Series Developer and Editor

Educational Technology Publications
Englewood Cliffs, New Jersey 07632

Library of Congress Cataloging-in-Publication Data

Mink, Oscar G.
    Groups at work.

    (Techniques in training and performance development series)
    Bibliography: p.
    Includes index.
    1. Work groups. 2. Group relations training.
I. Mink, Barbara P., 1945-   II. Owen, Keith Q.
III. Title. IV. Series.
HD66.M55   1987   658.4'036   87-9081
ISBN 0-87778-196-6

Printed in the United States of America.

Library of Congress Catalog Card Number: 87-9081.

International Standard Book Number: 0-87778-196-6.

First Printing: June, 1987.
Second Printing: October, 1990.

DEDICATION

We are grateful to Gordon Lippitt for his enlightened leadership of Human Resource practitioners these past thirty years. No mentor was better equipped to improve the human condition. His colleagues and students know this and will rely on Gordon's legacy to carve out improvements in organizational change, growth, and performance.

Both Gordon and Barbara have made a difference—Gordon in the limelight, Barbara in the shadows—both have made the world a better place for others.

EDITOR'S PREFACE

This book began with inquiries to George Odiorne and the late Gordon Lippitt as to who in the group process field was best able to write about the *practical management* of group activity in performance-based environments. Group process had acquired so many reputations and labels that I was hesitant to offer the project to anyone without first collecting third-party endorsements and evidence of their approach *vis-a-vis* earlier published works. This had to be a book about performance-based group process, not a collection of "nice-to-have" activities.

At any rate, all roads led to Oscar and Barbara Mink, he of the University of Texas at Austin and both principals in OHRD Associates, a management consulting firm specializing, not coincidentally, in organization and human resource development. In "The Minks," as they were affectionately referred to throughout the manuscript development cycle, I felt we had found people with a near-perfect blend of reputation, know-how, and approach.

First, they are well-known and respected nationally for their work with groups, especially in the organizational development area. Oscar Mink, in particular, is a "household" name as a result of his 100-plus publications and years of association with the national HRD movement.

Second, Gordon Lippitt's endorsement focused on the Minks' range of expertise and experience. He was particularly sensitive to my insistence that we identify individuals who could address the realities of *group performance in the world of work*, where resources, time, politics, and structure are regular mitigating factors. His original list of eight who "could write the book" dwindled to two and eventually to The Minks after interviews and an analysis of earlier work.

Third, and of critical importance, was the approach or philosophy the potential author(s) would unavoidably lend to the selection and description of individual techniques. The intent with every book in the series, including this one, was to ensure that readers be provided with practical ideas and techniques they would *want to use* in their own work environments. This was difficult with *Groups at Work* because group process, by nature, requires *extended* activity to permit a collection of individuals to function as a group or team. Processes that take time to complete are not readily viewed as practical and easy to use. This notwithstanding, the authors managed to identify numerous techniques which they consider both representative and useful based on their own repeated applications with client groups. I find the related contextual material equally useful in improving my grip on the group process and the considerations that can affect its destiny.

Themselves true believers in the value of group effort, Oscar and Barbara included Keith Owen as a third co-author and Barbara Zechner, David McKay, Phil Jones, and Barbara Loftin as contributors. Each person played a distinct role in producing the book, underscoring the fact that when groups work well they do so because individual members retain accountability. Fortunately, Oscar, Barbara, and their group recognize this and have embedded the concept throughout the book.

One final morsel of perspective: With at least 80,000 people starting new jobs every day in the United States alone, costing untold billions in separation, relocation, recruitment, and legal fees, there is merit in investigating the extent to which group process is either perpetuating or controlling the level of job dissatisfaction felt by employees *before* they pursue new opportunities. Oscar Mink was really making a statement about this issue when he suggested a modification of the book's preliminary title, *Working with Groups*, to *Groups at Work*. The book and the techniques it contains are not intended for isolated use, i.e., self-help, small-group counseling. The aim is to draw the relationships between organizational development and financial performance, to see the big picture, and then to address the underlying group process issues. For just as certainly as individuals should ultimately be held accountable for their work performance, group dynamics can inhibit or enhance the capacity of the individual to perform and to derive satisfaction from that performance.

We've derived considerable satisfaction from our combined work on this book. Now, it's your turn, as readers, to indicate at what level we've performed.

Joseph W. Arwady

PREFACE

We are pleased to share our thoughts on groups and the techniques and instruments contained here. We thought it worthwhile to write this book because in group literature one rarely sees process concepts linked to useful exercises. Perhaps this unique approach will aid human resource practitioners and line managers.

We have not stressed theory. The process model is one Oscar first heard described by Sam Culbert during the summer of 1969 in Bethel, Maine. Sam Culbert was one of our mentors. He supplied the National Training Lab (NTL) interns with an early draft of his paper on task phase interventions in T-groups. The six-phase progression model—*trust, individual differences, feedback, individual problem solving, group problem solving*, and *celebration*—reflects elements common to the thinking of Carl Rogers, Jack and Lorraine Gibb, Talcot Parsons, Lee Bradford, Ron Lippitt, Bill Schutz, and others. The text and exercises follow Culbert's six-phase progression model.

We also appreciate good tools—exercises, instruments, and designs—and find a certain romance in developing new ones.

The discovery of the alphabet led to later blessings of classification and communication of knowledge and thought. But it would have had little value to mankind without the time to think, create, and build. The person who first put an iron shear on a wooden plow, enabling one person to feed ten, provided conditions for seeking ways to feed the mind and spirit as well. The maker of the metal plow shear contributed as much to the beauty and complexity of life as the inventor of the alphabet. Both were tool makers—both searchers of ways to create a more valuable future for mankind by extending human potential. We find it exciting and rewarding to take part in tool making.

Working with the minds and energies of three or more persons, collected to work at a common purpose, provides ample challenge for the brightest and most skilled person. Techniques and insight into the functioning of groups enable groups to improve performance, provide much with which to work, and at the same time, leave many questions to be answered, suggesting a myriad of tools still to be developed. This book may be useful to both tool users and tool makers. We hope these pages will invite creative thinking about groups.

Many good books exist which report research, explain principles, share cases, and describe exercises to enlighten persons working in or with groups. One can question the need for yet another document encouraging group work and engaging the reader in a lexicon of principles and techniques. Yet, in group life, the whole is greater than the sum of the parts. We find a scarcity of works that depict the total dimensions of life in groups.

We hope to make a unique contribution here by sharing models which reflect ideas in a clear and practical way. Recent works describing new paradigms of how organizations work—development and renewal—also emphasize the growing importance of groups. Below is a list of system outputs (or desired results) that may be achieved through groups:

- generating new ideas
- creating and developing new products
- achieving productivity and high quality in manufacturing
- satisfying customers through better service
- improving relationships with vendors
- achieving a high quality of work life within more informal information structures
- achieving higher utilization of human resources in a world of rapidly advancing technology
- renewing organization [substance] vision, mission, goals, shared values and management philosophy, and varying structure to accomplish mission.

Oscar G. Mink
Barbara P. Mink
Keith Q. Owen

TABLE OF CONTENTS

Groups at Work

1

PERSPECTIVE
A History of Group Theory:
Past, Present, and Future

> Now all the evidence of psychiatry . . . shows that membership in a group sustains a man, enables him to maintain his equilibrium under the ordinary shocks of life, and helps him to bring up children who will in turn be happy and resilient. If his group is shattered around him, if he leaves a group in which he was a valued member, and if, above all, he finds no new group to which he can relate himself, he will under stress develop disorders of thought, feeling, and behavior. . . . The cycle is vicious; loss of group membership in one generation may make men less capable of group membership in the next. The civilization that, by its very process of growth, shatters small group life will leave men and women lonely and unhappy.
>
> George C. Homans, *The Human Group*
> (also found in Ouchi and Jaeger, 1977)

What Does a Backward Glance Tell Us About Groups?

The earliest writings on group dynamics tell of the teachings imparted to kings and emperors about leadership. The most important of these is the *Hitopadesa* (translated from the Sanskrit, 1896), an Indian classic that uses fables and quotations from other writings to teach a king's son. Another example is *The Instruction of PTAH-HOTEP* (translated from the Egyptian, 1909), in which human and thoughtful leadership is encouraged. A gracious leader is greatly desired because his conduct is without defect and encourages open communication among his supplicants.

The greatest emphasis on leadership lies in politics and military tactics. The leadership viewpoint is most often stressed because teamwork is not considered as essential as leadership in a military situation. However, the Chinese philosopher Sun Tzu (500 B.C.) took exception to that point of view in his *Art of War* (translated from the Chinese, 1963), the oldest military treatise in the world. Sun Tzu wrote about military leadership in terms of the philosophy of group dynamics.

Confucius wrote much about leadership in the life of a moral man. His primary concern was the place of moral man in the interwoven fabric of society. In *The Wisdom of Confucius* (Ed., Lin Yutang, 1938) he states:

> In a high position he (moral man) does not domineer over his subordinates. In a subordinate position he does not court the favors of his superiors. He puts in order his own personal conduct and seeks nothing from others; hence he has no complaint to make. He complains not against God, nor rails against men.

If one were to follow the advice of Confucius on the role of the leader, one would avoid the pain and low productivity which occur in a basic assumption mental state of dependency (Bion, 1961, p. 66).

The more common attitude of the ancients was that of the leader as protector, advisor, and tactician. The men under his command were *dependent* on the leader as an exemplary model and trusted superior. Marcus Aurelius wrote at some length about the qualifications, duties, and responsibilities of leadership. In Book Five of his *Meditations* (translation, 1957), he encouraged communication and feedback as responsibilities of the leader in dealing with men.

> ... fellow is endowed with reason, and he is perfectly able to understand ... if he gives any thought to it. Well and good: but you yourself are also endowed with reason; so apply your reasonableness to move him to a like reasonableness; expound, admonish. If he pays attention, you have worked a cure, and there will be no need for passion; ...

Writings of the Middle Ages emphasized theology. Again, the view of philosophers centered around leadership, and the populace was dependent upon its leaders.

During the Renaissance, Machiavelli was the primary writer on leadership principles. A proponent of intrigue in dealing with the governance of people, he used a strong dose of such, along with a liberal sprinkling of suggestions for correcting leadership defects.

He believed strongly in aiding states and countries in gaining freedom from oppressors, but just as strongly that a leader, once entrenched in the workings of government, must not permit the government and its people to gain control of themselves (*The Discourses*, translation, 1940).

After the Renaissance, a period of three centuries passed during which world thought was supplied with theory based on the natural law of group dynamics. The natural law was derived from political situations that were tested against historical outcomes.

Philosopher Otto Gierke summarized the writings of that era in the fourth volume of *Das Deutsche Genossenschaftsrecht* (translation, 1957). He described the theory of sovereignty, the ruler, and the ruled. Within this theory, many avenues of thought developed. One was *usefruct*, in which the ruler has the use of the fruits of the property of the ruled. From this concept other theories of political science and group dynamics theory evolved.

In essence, although there was some balance in ideas, the subtleties of dependency emerged. Leaders carried off many of their followers' gains in the form of money, property, and other perks. The followers seemed able to accept this exploitation within vaguely defined limits. The power granted the leader was like an invisible line of credit. At various points in history, leaders have run out of credit, and followers have invited them to step down by whatever means were needed. Often the course of events led to revolution, as in Eighteenth Century France and America. In Twentieth Century America, however, Mr. Nixon was simply forced to resign. He and his advisers had used up their line of credit.

Obviously, the emphasis on leader-centered groups, although challenged from time to time by such thinkers as Confucius, seems to have prevailed to the present. Leaders still have more perks and power than nonleaders and create more dependency than their enterprises can afford. Although the Youth Movement of the 1960s focused some thought upon the interdependent nature of ecological and human systems, the necessary revolution in thought was slow to occur. The dependency mode is so thoroughly imbedded in world culture that changes in the ways that leadership functions are not easy to discern.

What Are Some Recent Views of Groups?

Curiously, the primary focus of group literature emphasizes process and interpersonal relationships within process—cohesiveness, conflict, high and low communication rates, group maintenance, conflict. It seems that context-purpose (vision, mission, goals, and tasks), shared values, leadership philosophy, and structure of a group are less significant. In short, the group literature appears to focus upon what is possible within more closed, bureaucratic, hierarchical systems rather than upon the system in the context of a larger system—both of which are organic, holistic, and changing.

One view of the issue of what seems addressable in a work group is illustrated here (see Figure 1.1).

Much of what is described in group literature focuses upon Items 3 and 4 in Figure 1.1. This includes typical team building events, conflict resolution, third party consultation, human relations groups, T-groups, and basic encounter groups. Several issues need to be examined, for example: (1) the assumption that people and their processes are at fault; (2) the exclusion of substantive issues like (a) strategic analysis of the business in relationship to environmental context, and (b) the collective vision of the current stakeholders; (3) the limited perspective of the closed system because of any constraints or forces affecting the group's ability to manage input (skill, energy, resources) and process to achieve desired outputs. With these thoughts, let us review some widely held assumptions about groups.

What Are Some Key Concepts About Groups?

Perhaps the most influential person operating on the frontiers of group dynamics was Kurt Lewin. Lewin (1951) was a field theorist. He believed that the whole was greater than the sum of its parts. He was concerned with unity, the whole, and differentiation—looking at the parts and their interrelationships. One of his notions was that any social phenomenon could be viewed as existing in a quasi-stationary state (Lewin, 1947). He believed in context and studying whole/part relationships.

> The basic statements of field theory are that (a) behavior has to
> be derived from a totality of coexisting facts, (b) these coexisting

Participation in/by Current Constituents	Topic

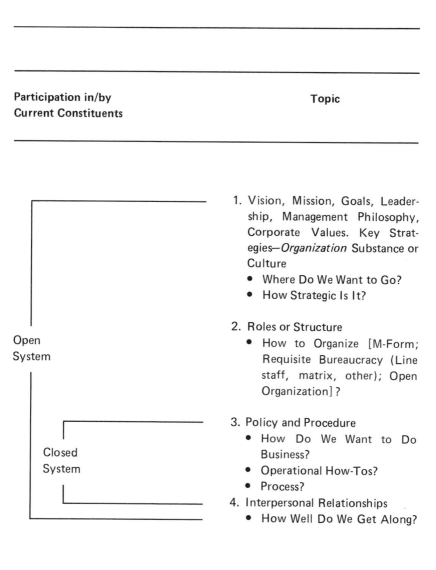

1. Vision, Mission, Goals, Leadership, Management Philosophy, Corporate Values. Key Strategies—*Organization* Substance or Culture
   - Where Do We Want to Go?
   - How Strategic Is It?

2. Roles or Structure
   - How to Organize [M-Form; Requisite Bureaucracy (Line staff, matrix, other); Open Organization]?

3. Policy and Procedure
   - How Do We Want to Do Business?
   - Operational How-Tos?
   - Process?

4. Interpersonal Relationships
   - How Well Do We Get Along?

Open
System

Closed
System

Figure 1.1. A View of Open and Closed Systems.

> facts have the character of a "dynamic field" in so far as the state
> of any part of this field depends on every other part of the field.
> (Lewin, 1951, p. 25.)

Later in the same work he laid the theoretical foundation for the
Force Field Analysis Technique described in the chapter on
Problem Solving. He stated,

> To predict which changes in conditions will have what result, we
> have to conceive of the life of the group as the result of specific
> constellations of forces within a larger setting. (Lewin, 1951, p.
> 174.)

Some of his early thinking on part/whole relationships can be
found in an article on Aristotelian and Galilean thinking (Lewin,
1930). Basically, Lewin did not subscribe to Aristotle's notion
that a rock falls because of the nature of the rock. Lewin believed
in the Galilean proposition that rocks move in relationship to
larger and smaller masses.

In 1939, he and two of his students published an article, now a
classic, on the effect of various "social climates" (authoritarian,
democratic, and laissez-faire) on the aggressive behavior of groups
of boys. His early thinking about groups appeared to be clearly
focused upon the larger, more holistic or "systems" context.
Results of these studies were interpreted in such terms as
"tension," "restricted spans of free movement," "rigidity of group
structure," and "culture." (Lewin *et al.*, 1939, pp. 271-299.)

In the summer of 1947, a group of social psychologists and
others studying leaderless groups in Bethel, Maine, became
intrigued with the processes occurring in these groups. They
initiated what became known as T-group and laboratory method,
which tended to focus upon the re-education of individuals. They
established the National Training Laboratory in Applied Behavioral Science (NTL). Over the years they have trained and educated
many able people in T-group methodology and related theory,
which contributed substantially to the humanistic psychology
movement of the 1960's. T-group methodology, applied in the
organization setting, was added to action research as a second
organization development methodology. T-group work led to team
development and other activities. For a complete history of this
movement, refer to: Bradford, Benne, and Gibb (1964).

The T-group movement, unfortunately, tended to drift away from much of the substantive, holistic work of Lewin. T-group methodology soon focused almost exclusively upon process and individual member behavior. At the same time, much useful information about how to facilitate group process came from persons affiliated with NTL. The Tavistock Institute in England seemed to adhere to more holistic notions, and there was a healthy cross-breeding of ideas with NTL affiliates.

Among the many contributions made to group work in the last 40 years, we have found three sets of ideas especially useful to management groups. These are: (1) The thinking of W.C. Schutz and his three-dimensional theory of interpersonal behavior; (2) the Menninger Morale Curve; and (3) Cog's Ladder (Charrier, 1965).

Schutz (1958) postulated that:

> People need people to receive from and to give to—inclusion, control, and affection. These interpersonal needs are viewed as being analogous to biological needs.

The literature supporting the reasonableness of postulating these three interpersonal needs and the FIRO-B (*F*undamental *I*nterpersonal *R*elations *O*rientation-*B*ehavior) instrument as a tool to measure individual characteristics of these needs is compelling. Potential for group member compatibility can be predicted from FIRO-B* scores.

Schutz postulated a group development sequence: First, the inclusion issue; second, the control issue; and last, the development of affection. (Schutz's sequence is shown in Figure 1.2.) Work subsequent to these early beginnings is reflected in descriptions of instruments recommended in Chapter 5, on *Individual Differences*.

The Menninger Morale Curve was developed by a psychiatrist observing the training of Peace Corps volunteers. He noted the sequence depicted in Figure 1.3—the Menninger Curve. Menninger's observations are very similar to the sequence of phases set forth by Schutz. For a more complete discussion, see Seashore in References.

---

*Schutz has recently integrated the FIRO-B with other of his instruments into "An Integrated System for Assessing Elements of Awareness."

**Issues in Life of Group
Sequence or Order**

EARLY	Inclusion	(Am I included? Accepted?) (Do I include others?)
LATER	Control	(How influential am I going to be?) (Do I need to control others?) (Do I need to be controlled?)
LAST	Affection*	(How close are we going to be?) (Will you express acceptance and affection toward me?) (Will I express acceptance and affection toward you?)

*Recently Schutz has relabeled this dimension "Openness."

Figure 1.2. The Schutz Group Development Sequence.

Charrier (1965) produced a model of group maturation which we believe reflects some issues that support some of the open systems thinking covered in detail in the following pages and underlying this complete text.

Charrier depicts the *stages of group development* in Figure 1.4.

Systems Theory and Organization Functioning

Any organization has three major subsystems, all of which must be kept in balance. These are (1) organization substance, (2) human, and (3) technical. Figure 1.5 illustrates one way this balance might be viewed.

These subsystems intricately interrelate to form a total organism called the organization. Any change in one part of the system will affect other parts. In any given business, in the process of providing *what* to *whom*, the organization, as pictured in Figure 1.5, exchanges vital energy with a larger socioeconomic system.

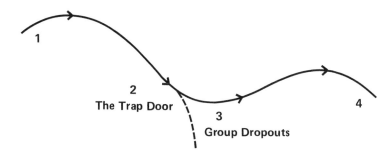

Four Key Crises on Curve

1. Crisis of *entrance*. Getting Started. Apprehension.
2. Crisis of *involvement*. a. Early peak based on false expectations and fantasies. b. Realities start surfacing. Control issues arise. c. People drop out.
3. Crisis of *acceptance* of realities of situation and acceptance of self. "Let's see if we can get something out of this experience." People start taking responsibility for self. Person feels accepted by others.
4. Crisis of *separation*. Coping with leaving the group.

Actually there is a series of smaller curves along the main curve.

Figure 1.3. Menninger Morale Curve

When Argyris (1957) published his first work on the theme of the dysfunctional relationship between a mature human being and a bureaucratic organization, he addressed the need for a different and more organic focus. An organic system is alive and growing, adaptable and open. Learning must extend to understanding values and sharing them among people within the work setting. Through a series of works culminating in 1978, Argyris (and later Argyris and Schön) pointed out the compelling need to extend learning about the organization to the values and substances of it in order to optimize the relationship between the healthy, open person and the organization.

Mink, Shultz, and Mink (1979) addressed the issues and dimensions of the relationships between the person, the group,

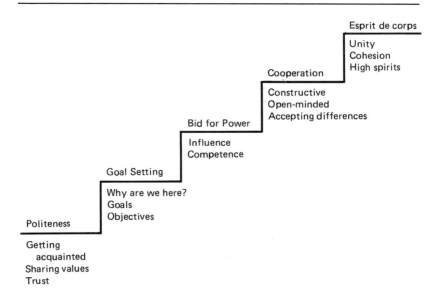

Figure 1.4. Cog's Ladder: Stages of Group Development.

Figure 1.5. The Three Major Subsystems of an Organization.

and the organization. They identified three key properties of healthy human systems. These are (1) unity (which forms around a compelling purpose), (2) internal responsiveness (exchanging energy between components), and (3) external responsiveness (exchanging energy with the environment).

Openness and closedness are points on a continuum reflecting an ability to maintain intelligent or adaptable behavior similar to that of a healthy human being. The more open the system, the more the principle of open organizations deemphasizes structure as a static phenomenon. A more closed system would tend to maintain a single, static, layered structure. We believe that purpose and function determine what the structure needs to be. In an organization that focuses on vision and purpose, needed functions interact to produce roles and structure.

Unity is the process of centering. It is the organizing dimension of any biological life or physical form—the nucleus of an amoeba, the eye of a hurricane. Psychologists, physicians, and clergy have assigned many labels to dimensions of the psychological centering process—self-concept, ego identity, perceived self, ego, ego states, self, selfhood, persona, personhood, and personality. From our perspective, these terms overlap and represent various descriptions of the way a person organizes consistent, unifying, and purposive behavior in varying environmental settings. To be a unified whole, one need not be fragmented internally or closed to one's outside environment. Unity both permits and promotes awareness of self and components and awareness of the external world of events, things, and people.

In examining a healthy human being as an open system, one observes awareness, responsiveness, spontaneity, autonomy, and congruence among feeling, saying, and doing. This *internal responsiveness* accompanies a healthy personality. An open system is not fragmented. Like the healthy human body, all parts are responsive and functionally interdependent. No part is a rigid, isolated empire. The parts of an open system are themselves open systems, exchanging elements of organic functioning (life or energy). In contrast, a tumor in the body, a neurotic fixation in a personality, or an isolated blood clot in a vein or artery constitutes a nonresponsive part. The nonresponsive parts dissipate and diffuse energy to the point of organismic death. An unhealthy body is a good metaphor either for an unhealthy group with a closed, belligerent member or for an unhealthy neurotic organization with closed, defensive departments or subgroups. For all practical purposes, an "unhealthy" organization or organization component spends its time in nonwork states and is in fact "terminated" as a contributor to the next higher unit served.

Finally, for a system to be truly open *external responsiveness* must be achieved. At the interfaces with other systems, exchanges of activity, data, and energy will occur. Such interchange is not passive but consists of an ongoing series of transactions—between the individual and all other systems that can influence person-hood. Truly, in the context of General Systems Theory, no person is an island. Interdependence is the hallmark of the universe.

The open system, then, does not achieve its centeredness by fencing itself off from the outside. Unlike the fanatic who becomes unified by a closed, oversimplified world view, the open system is both centered *and* exchanging energy. This energy exchange takes place both internally and externally.

Figure 1.6 depicts open systems of various sizes, from the minisystem of the person to the maxisystem of mankind. The first three columns describe the characteristics which, when simul-taneously present, make up openness. The fourth defines the overall degree of openness. The labels in the cells represent only one set of possibilities. You may experiment with labels that might have more meaning for you.

––––––

References

Argyris, C. (1957). *Personality and Organization: The Conflict Between the System and the Individual.* New York: Harper.

Argyris, C., and Schon, D.A. (1978). *Organizational Learning: A Theory of Action Perspective.* Reading, MA: Addison-Wesley.

Aurelius, M. (1967). *Meditations.* Translated by A.S.L. Farquharson. In Everyman's Library, Volume 9. New York: Dutton.

Bion, W.R. (1961). *Experiences in Groups.* London: Tavistock Publications.

Bradford, L.P., Benne, K.D., and Gibb, J.R. (1964) (Eds.). *T-Group Theory and Laboratory Method: Innovation in Re-education.* New York: Wiley.

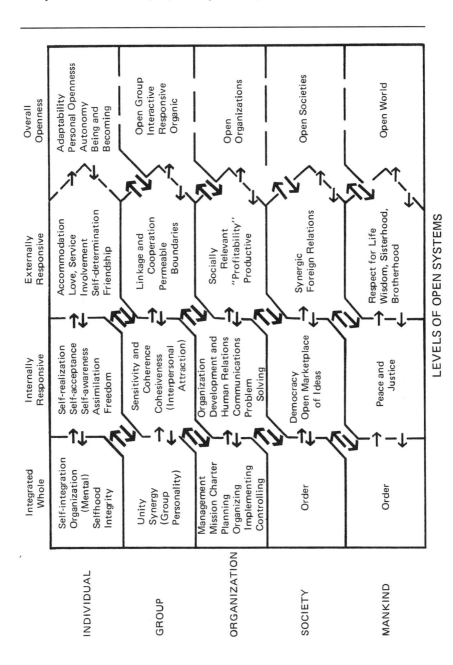

Figure 1.6. Defining Characteristics of Open Systems.

Charrier, G.C. (1965). *Cog's Ladder: A Model of Group Growth.* (Unpublished paper at Proctor and Gamble Co.)

Gierke, O.F. von. (1950). "Das Deutsche Genossenschaftsrecht." Volume 4. Translated by Ernest Barker. In *Natural Law and Theory of Society.* Cambridge: Cambridge University Press.

Hitopadesa: The Book of Good Counsels. (1896). (Sir Edwin Arnold, trans.). London: W.H. Allen.

Homans, G.C. (1950). *The Human Group.* New York: Harcourt, Brace, and World.

The Instruction of Ptah-Hotep. (1909). (Battiscombe G. Gunn, trans.) London: J. Murray.

Lewin, K. (January-October, 1930). The Conflict Between Aristotelian and Galilean Modes of Thought in Contemporary Psychology. *Journal of General Psychology, 5,* 141-177.

Lewin, K. (1947). Frontiers in Group Dynamics: Concept, Method, and Reality in Social Science: Social Equilibria and Social Change. *Human Relations, 1*(1), 5-41.

Lewin, K. (1951). *Field Theory in Social Science.* New York: Harper & Brothers.

Lewin, K., Lippitt, R., and White, R.K. (1939). Patterns of Aggressive Behavior in Experimentally Created "Social Climates." *Journal of Social Psychology, 10,* 271-299.

Machiavelli, N. (1940). *The Prince and The Discourses.* New York: Modern Library, Random House.

Mink, O., Schultz, J., and Mink, B. (1979). *Developing and Managing Open Organizations: A Model and Methods for Maximizing Organizational Potential.* Austin, Texas: OHRD Associates.

Ouchi, W.S., and Jaeger, A. (1977). Type Z Organizations: A Corporate Alternative to Village Life. *Stanford Business School Alumni Bulletin,* 46, 1.

Seashore, C. (No date). *In Grave Danger of Growing.* Arlington, VA: National Training Laboratories.

Schutz, W.C. (1958). *FIRO: A 3-Dimensional Theory of Inter-Personal Behavior.* New York: Rinehart.

Sun Tzu, *The Art of War* (1963). Translated with an introduction by Samuel Griffith, Oxford University Press, London.

Yutang. L. (Ed.) (1938). *The Wisdom of Confucius.* New York: Modern Library, Random House.

2

THE PURPOSE AND CONTEXT
FOR SUCCESS IN GROUPS

What is honored in a country is cultivated there.

—Plato

It is not enough to be busy, the question is What are we busy about?

—Thoreau

Ideals are like stars: You will not succeed in touching them with your hands, but like the seafaring man on the desert of waters, you choose them as your guides and following them you reach your destiny.

—Carl Schutz

What Is a Group?

Groups are three or more persons in a combination of mental energy. For discussion purposes, we define groups as three or more persons joined together to work toward a common goal or purpose. In short, groups form to engage in a task—to work. The work defines the group.

Not all groups function alike. Mature groups resemble mature people. They work and contribute toward a valuable future for the next larger human system served, for their own members, for other individuals, and for similar groups.

The discrepancy between the purpose of the group and the present state of the group provides the energy for work, and provides two key components of the problem solving and action planning process—the visualized outcomes and the analysis of the current situation. These form necessary but not sufficient conditions for the conscious direction and control of work. Conditions needed for problem solving, action planning, and implementation are (1) gathering, analyzing, and clarifying data; (2) constructing practical action plans; and (3) securing commitment to those plans from the system that must make them work. Meeting these conditions does not guarantee success in controlling work, but failure to meet them greatly increases the probability of failure and nonwork.

Do Groups Form a Collective Subconscious?

How does a group consciously control work? Groups form on the level of psychic activity. This phenomenon may represent the least noted but most important dimension of groups. Group practitioners and managers who fail to note the formation of mental energy in groups and work with it probably face more failures and frustrations than necessary. A compelling argument for groups is the notion of synergy, borrowed from the fields of pharmacy and ecology. Pharmacists learned that the effects of some combinations of drugs on the human body exceeded the impact to be expected otherwise from the same drugs administered separately, i.e., the sum of the part. Group potential (mental energy) is greater than the total mental energy of the individuals of the group. Understanding and successfully developing group potential means enhancing the conditions within which synergy can form and can be consciously directed toward control over the work.

As we assume the existence of a group subconscious with individuals, we also assume that groups may experience as Bion (1961) called it, a basic assumption mental state,* these mental states represent nonwork (or work avoidance) conditions if or when they control the group process or the collective mental energy. Just as a person can malfunction because of the interference of repressed material with rational functions, so too can a group misfire! The role of the subconscious in creating interference with conscious

---

*We refer to this concept at other places in this book. Basically, it refers to the group's nonwork or off-task state, due to subconscious assumptions of group members.

functioning was Sigmund Freud's great contribution to psychology (Freud 1953a; Freud 1953b). We argue that groups malfunction for similar reasons.

The basic assumption mental state, or "nonwork mentality," presents an enormous challenge to any attempt at purposive behavior. This negative momentum has the following effects:

- Members devote creative capacity to self-defeating ends
- Self-esteem decreases
- Drive, commitment, persistence, and dedication in the face of constraints produced by subconscious mental states serve only to create frustration and burnout in highly motivated and committed individuals
- Foresight becomes hindsight
- Predictive capacity decreases
- Thoroughness and quality decrease
- The work climate deteriorates
- Perception narrows
- Manual support systems deteriorate

Under the foregoing conditions, negative feelings rule and problem solving becomes incomplete and inadequate. Group members collude to avoid work. (See Figure 2.1 for BAM's characteristics and Figure 2.2 for a brief summary of Bion's assumptions and ideas.)

Three authors besides Bion have described similar phenomena interfering with task. Berne (1964) believes that much group time is spent off-task in playing psychological games. These games are very systematic and occur outside of conscious awareness. Berne defines a game as ". . . an ongoing series of complementary ulterior transactions which progress to a well-defined predictable outcome." (Basically two or more people are saying one thing and meaning another). Berne is referring to communications with double meaning that involve two or more people and end in bad feelings for the persons involved. It has been estimated that some groups spend as much as 90 percent of their time in the game process.

Jerry Harvey (1974) describes a phenomenon in which people agree but experience conflicts out of fear of sharing feelings.

---

*high level of disorganization
*low creativity
*resistance to learning and change
*low or poor rate of task completion
*low productivity
*high levels of anxiety impeding change
*lingering and unresolved discontent
*little or no personal development
*authority rests with leader
*communication not sensible
*inability of people to listen
*increased incidence of mental rehearsal prior to speaking
*negative feelings prevalent
*low time management quotient; team controlled by time
*recycling of items or events
*ongoing conflicts created by low harmony among roles
*formation of many sub-groups

Figure 2.1. Characteristics of Basic Assumption Mental States

---

Harvey calls this process the Abilene Paradox. Symptoms are: (1) members agree privately about a situation and what should be done; (2) members collude to keep real opinions hidden; (3) the group makes decisions and acts against what members want; (4) counterproductive action leads to anger, blame, and phony conflict.

The basic cause of the Abilene Paradox is fear of separation from the group. Ironically, real separation from the group, as well as a waste of group resources, often results from "trips to Abilene." This is discussed further in Chapter 4 of this book.

Finally, Janis (1972) describes a similar phenomenon called "groupthink." Members of a group seek to maintain group harmony at the expense of sound decision-making. When a group member raises a minority opinion, other members tend to overpower him and the minority opinion is not heard. This process, like the others, leads to poor decisions and poor outcomes. Group members suppress individual judgments for the sake of group cohesion. This is usually a function of prolonged or intermittent stress. Again, anxiety seems to overrule task.

1. People are "herd animals."

2. Groups use group members in very special ways. We are all cast in roles (generally outside of our conscious awareness) in the process of living up to the group's expectations. Therefore, *ALL BEHAVIOR IS GROUP BEHAVIOR* and must be relative to the group's expectations.

3. *Individuality* thrusts are not tolerated very well.

4. If individual, group, or organization *anxiety* gets high (security is threatened or rejection becomes a possibility), a "subconscious mental state" takes over and can be observed behaviorally in the individual, group, or organization.

5. This collective subconscious mental state is called technically a group's "Basic Assumption Mental State" and is really a collaboration among the members to not work.

6. There are three kinds of BAMs:

   A. *Fight/Flight.* The purpose of choosing this group is to fight or run away from some perceived threat.

   B. *Dependency.* The focus is on leadership. Until the leader does, decides, or acts, everybody waits. Meanwhile, the leader sits and says, "When will somebody down there do something?" The purpose of choosing this group is to obtain security from one individual on whom they depend.

   C. *Fracturing.* People form pairs (subgroups) for purposes of union but not necessarily task. Some new entity (usually a nonwork pairing) will derive from that union. Typically, these subgroups bicker with each other and finger-point. Meanwhile, customers needing service are on hold and the work to be done is at a standstill.

Figure 2.2. Bion's "Basic Assumption Mental States."

On the surface, the singleness of group purpose may seem to be served. In reality, task accomplishment suffers. (See Figure 2.3.)

Where Do Groups Get Energy and Motivation?

We have traced the two key sources of energy in a group forming to *work*. First, there is a unique, often synergistic, combination of mental energy. Second, the difference between the goals to be accomplished and the actual situation, when identified, provides energy, direction, and focus for group members, as they strive to close the gap between the real and the ideal. It also increases the potential for synergy to form.

Groups have the potential of appealing to the three key motives of individuals in working environments. These were originally identified by David McClelland (1965). They stem from three psychological needs—for achievement, affiliation, and power. A *good* group can help a person meet all of these needs. When all group members actively participate to establish work goals, they begin to meet their affiliation needs. More affiliation needs are met as members reach consensus and cooperate to achieve their goals. The cooperative setting of work goals also appeals to both dimensions of power needs—individualized (for self-aggrandizement) and social (for common good). Individual achievement needs are met through actual accomplishment of group goals as long as members of the group align themselves with the group goals.

Achievement of group goals set through participation releases motivational energy. The actual achievement of group goals provides the group—individually and collectively—with an increasing awareness that skill plus effort will achieve results. Experience with success gives the work group an ever-increasing will and sense of confidence, and each success increases group strength and the "success expectancy of the group."

In a healthy, open group, member roles will change in response to the actual task. More closed groups stress particular roles, develop stereotypical behavior, and may attempt the same rote solution to differing problems. For routine tasks, closed groups may be very efficient. For changing environments and non-routine

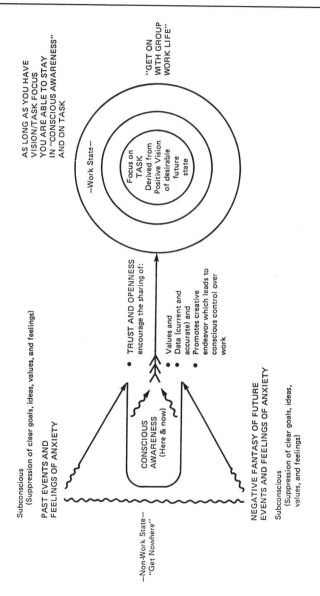

Figure 2.3. An Illustration of the Relationship Between Non-Work and Work States and Task.

tasks, closed groups may act like a neurotic person, repeating ineffectual or self-defeating behavior in pursuit of an inappropriate plan.

What Are the Conditions for Effective Groups?

We have said all groups form for a *purpose*. For example, a family forms when two persons join to achieve common goals in an atmosphere of love and intimacy. Families contribute a valuable future to the society when they raise children. Individual family members gain permanence in a meaningful relationship, in sharing work. So types of groups vary, as do the purposes of groups, but all groups form to achieve goals and maintain themselves. Nonwork states are by definition destructive of the group's reason for existing. On the other hand, natural phases in a group's process contribute to its maintenance. Any group that is in a "normal" process phase cannot be defined as being in a nonwork state.

Essentially, when groups are on task or in a natural process phase that enables task achievement, they have the potential for being effective. However, task achievement does not occur in a vacuum. Tasks occur in the context of a culture or environment; different tasks. are required to be effective in different contexts. The group activity necessary for success will be relevant to the environment. If two or more persons are present, the activity— searching for food on a lush South Pacific Island, for instance—will lead to interactions (around coconut trees, fishing, digging for roots). The activity in turn will create the conditions within which sentiment or interpersonal attraction begins to form. As feelings form, the social structure—norms, taboos, etc.—will form (Homans, 1950). These sentiments then become the culture, and the culture becomes the context for further interaction.

Much current writing focuses on the relationship between an organization's performance and culture.* A stream of good

*See particularly: Deal, Terrence E., and Kennedy, Allan A. (1982). *Corporate Cultures*. Reading, MA: Addison-Wesley Publishing Company. Peters, Thomas, J., and Waterman, Jr. Robert H. (1982). *In Search of Excellence*. New York: Harper and Row, Inc.; Hickman, Craig, R., and Silva, Michael A. (1984). *Creating Excellence: Managing Corporate Culture, Strategy, and Change in the New Age*. New York: New American Library.

information and research on this relationship has been produced for well over 25 years. Unfortunately, the more holistic the approach to the study of the human work group, the more difficult it is to examine.

The problem of establishing empirical support for holistic theories cannot be used as a reason either for refuting or for believing a theory. We need a conceptual context or theory as a framework for working with groups. Open systems theory is the best context available for working with and observing groups at work. One can observe in a group the same major dimensions that one observes in a personality—*unity* (the wholeness of the person); *internal responsiveness* (self-awareness); and *external responsiveness* (involvement with others in truthful, open, and honest ways). The fundamental condition for a group is the common task or purpose.

Certainly, without work to do, a group would not form. Problems for groups begin after they have formed. Then the group establishes its preservation as a purpose. Paradoxically, when the group devotes itself chiefly to its own preservation, it ensures its own demise. The manager or group practitioner who fails to clarify the purpose of the group in terms of the work to be done will fail to bring the group or team into a state of conscious control over task. Intervening in group process through exercises and instrumentation, in the absence of clear purpose, is as futile as was the rearranging of the deck furniture on the Titanic after it hit the iceberg.

The *unity* of the group forms around the purpose of the group—its work. The many within-group interactions around tasks that lead to the formation of norms and interpersonal attraction (also called cohesiveness) make up *internal responsiveness*. The linkages of the group with other groups, individuals, and human organizations best depict the *external responsiveness* of the group, the group's contribution to a valuable future for other human systems. Thus, a condition for any effective group, second only to the work to be done, is linkage with the context or the social structure within which the work must occur.

In a business, organization structure is determined by the assigned roles of individuals and subgroups, which are in turn defined by the functions or operations to be performed. For example, a sales group may link with engineering, manufacturing, and parts and service. The sales group may simultaneously interact effectively (doing the right things) with the marketplace and its fluctuations. Constantly examining the question *"Who sells what to whom?"* becomes one of the key external responsiveness or linking functions of the sales team. At the same time, the efforts of this sales team must be aligned with the vision, mission, and goals of the total organization as it interfaces with the total business environment—economy, government, social conditions, etc.

In summary, environmental conditions form the context of group functioning—clarity about and commitment to the job to be done, and relevant interchanges with the contextual forces that can influence success or failure in these tasks may create successful work groups.

How Do We Revitalize an Existing Group?

The purpose of renewing group effort is to get the group back on task. The group may be viewed as a system that needs to renew focus on purpose. An open system renews and grows by exchanging energy with the task and related systems. The relative strength of any group or human system naturally varies in its ability to cope with energy surges from the environment.

The goal of group development is to improve the group's strength and work. To become a more open system, a group needs a method of moving from the starting point to the goal. Several rules of thumb are important to remember:

1. Change needs boundaries and direction. Refer to open systems theory, Figure 1.6 (p. 15).
2. Change must be based on the commitment of individuals to group purpose (task).
3. Change must involve all facets of the existing structure.
4. Planned change must use the existing power sources—formal and informal. Group leaders must employ the formal structure as well as the unofficial power structure (the powerful "outs") in establishing support for increased task orientation.

5. Change can be first-order (like accelerating as you drive your car, or changing individual role assignments within a group), or change may be second-order (like shifting gears, giving yourself a whole new range of speeds to choose from, or reorganizing a group around a new vision and mission) (Watzlawick, Weakland, and Fisch, 1974).

6. Open systems are capable of second-order change. Basically, they receive energy from outside sources on which they are dependent. Then they distribute the energy through their system components.* Managed second-order change requires someone external to the group to go through the change with the group. Preferably this external person would be directly linked and working with the group leader.

7. Since force external to an organization can cause second-order change, changes in the economic cycle, corporate raiders, new technology, mergers, and so forth *can* and *do effect significant change.*

Whoever you are, wherever you are, and whatever your system may be, renewal must be a process of change, a movement toward a goal (ideal) different from where you are now. True openness and conscious control over purpose and the management of complexity in a changing environment is a growth process. It is

*Ilya Prigogine, Regents' Professor of Physics at the University of Texas, won the 1977 Nobel Prize in Chemistry for a theory which says that everything alive is surprisingly alive—and on a *twitchy, searching, self-aware, self-organizing,* upward journey. Such living systems periodically break into severe twitchiness and appear to fall apart. They do not. It is actually at such vibrating times that living systems are shaking themselves to higher ground. Prigogine states that transition to a higher order is universally accompanied by turbulence or "perturbation." He says that the disorder and disharmony in any chemical solution (or any group?) is a necessary activation of growth to a higher level. Prigogine says that the greater the turbulence and the more complex the solution (or group), the more often it will go into apparent disharmony in order to re-jiggle itself to an even higher level (*Innovation Abstracts*, November 5, 1982, Vol. IV, No. 32.) For further thought on the subject see the March 1982 Tarrytown Letter, The Tarrytown Group, East Sunnyside Lane, Tarrytown, New York 10591. In addition, see Prigogine, I. (1980), Prigogine, I. and Stengis, I. (1984), and Prigogine, I. and Nicolis, G. (1977).

progressive accomplishment on a pathway toward a goal. Systematic progress is made by stepping carefully from one milestone or objective to the next. In a changing environment, however, system goals or ideals may or may not be reached. Environmental energy surges created by environmental complexity must be monitored and managed.

The *failure to achieve goals* is not tragic. The *failure to have goals*, renew goals, clarify goals, and systematically approach them is tragic.

A group, like a person, can become unproductive. Lack of adequate functions to perform in the larger system, excessive time in a nonwork state, will lead to the removal of the group or result in an effort at complete renewal starting with vision, mission, and goals. Again, what to do must be determined in context. As with the human body, a truly diseased or distressed part needs to be either removed or healed. If truly an option, healing represents the best alternative in any human system. For example, sometimes a kidney is being poisoned by a source external to the kidney. Quick removal of the diseased kidney rather than removal of the source of the problem, may lead to the failure of the other kidney. Failure to ask the broader contextual question of "What is the problem?" can lead to an early death for the total system, group, or organization.

How Do We Achieve a More Open System?

If the reader is interested in changing the work group into a more open system, the following suggestions may be useful. The first part of the guide has to do with organization considerations; the second with kinds of growth recommended for leaders, managers, and employees to function effectively in a more open system.

A Group Leader's Guide for Identifying Conditions Conducive to a Productive Work Group Environment

1. Analyze the relationship between your work unit and its environment. Determine the forces affecting your work group that constrain or enable your efforts to convert energy input into the

unit's expected output. You can use the model in Figure 2.4—Managerial Job-Constraints Survey—as a means of visualizing a general systems approach to your work group's output. Using this model to investigate the influence of managerial job constraints, Neusch (1984) found that as constraints increase, effort (input) is increased while job satisfaction, as measured by the Job Descriptive Index, decreases.

2. Using the 7S Framework of *In Search of Excellence* (Peters and Waterman, 1982)—systems, strategy, style, skills, staff, structure, shared values—or some relevant model, study your unit's culture. Or you can utilize the open systems model of unity (purpose), internal responsiveness, and external responsiveness by completing a force-field analysis around each of these major dimensions.

3. Take time to establish or confirm vision, mission, shared values, and operating philosophy.

4. Carefully analyze existing organization structure to ensure compatibility with the vision, mission, values, philosophy, goals, and objectives of your group. Functions determine structure. Structure is not sacred.

5. Establish clearly defined goals using a process that will yield priorities. Obtain consensus from key constituents on goals, priorities, and key strategies.

6. Obtain appropriate personal commitment to the goals.

7. Help group members develop primary performance objectives from goals.

8. Ask team members to develop detailed performance objectives and to work toward a common understanding of these objectives and commitment to them by defining and negotiating individual roles.

9. Hold frequent "coaching" and problem-solving sessions to examine specific feedback on individual and group progress toward the agreed-upon objectives.

10. Establish objectives designed to "stretch" yourself and team members and invite development of the whole person.

11. Achieve a functional trust level. (See Chapter 4, on *Trust*.) Functional trust permits people to deal with their concerns

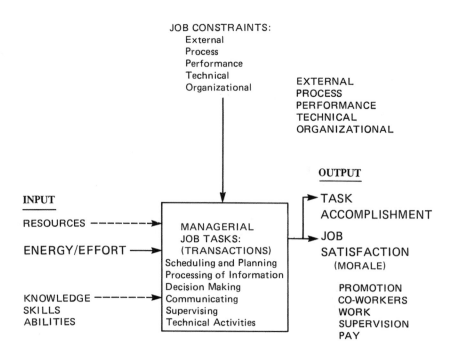

Figure 2.4. Managerial Job-Constraints Survey.

through direct confrontation, search for satisfactory solutions and means of coping, and establish working patterns that enable future satisfactory solutions of the same or similar problems.

12. Pay close attention to both process and outcomes of the work group. Maintain the team by:

12.1 seeking to establish the relationship between the unique needs of the members and the group's working objectives, connecting ability and effort with task;

12.2 asking for dedication to work and obtaining—commitment;

12.3 being willing to make suggestions for improving the support systems by reducing performance constraints;

12.4 reaching and maintaining agreements on roles through negotiation and clarification;

12.5 minimizing procedural build-up in the bureaucracy by reducing process constraints;

12.6 reducing organization constraints;

12.7 providing needed technical support;

12.8 allowing enough time to complete the project.

These items relate primarily to work group consideration. The questions below relate to personal growth. Even partial achievement of the conditions they suggest will enhance the lives of both leaders and group members. The questions are taken from Carl Rogers' chapter on "Characteristics of the Helping Relationship" (1961).

1. How authentic am I? Am I fully aware, congruent, in myself?

2. How expressive am I? Do I communicate unambiguously to others?

3. How positive am I in my respect for others?

4. Am I strong enough to respect my own needs and feelings?

5. Am I secure enough to permit others their full separateness?

6. How fully can I sense the meanings and feelings of others?

7. Can I relate so that others feel me to be in no way a threat and so that they become less fearful of external evaluation (audit) from anyone?

    8. Do I encounter others as *becoming* rather than as fixed (not by the past, to be appraised, or diagnosed)?

    9. How clearly is my own self-image one of change, development, growth, emergence?

An open group is organized around functions and purposes. Centers of power, if any, are those required to do the work. An open group provides the most growth-oriented climate for facilitating individual and group learning and success. Such a group environment is designed to respond with flexibility to a changing environment and differing employee needs. The open group appears also to be the only one that provides employees with opportunity for building self-esteem and developing autonomy. Career satisfaction is high in the open group. The challenge of continued growth exists for all members of the work group. When this challenge is met, a key aspect of a truly open group is in operation.

Developing open teams is a process directed toward getting team members to know each other better so that team goals can be achieved more effectively and members can satisfy needs for inclusion, support, power, and achievement. Teams increase information through the resources of individual members and form the kind of environment needed to work creatively. Teams set norms about how decisions are made, who will lead, and who will assume other role assignments.

Group openness depends on leaders who have a vision about the group's potential and are committed to the group's success. Managers must develop an awareness of the personal competencies that will enhance group openness. They need the ability to identify elements that hinder or help groups develop and they must be willing to work toward the personal development of themselves and others in their groups.

———

References

Applebaum, R.P. (1970). *Theories of Social Change*. Chicago: Markham Publishing Co.

Berne, E. (1964). *Games People Play.* New York: Grove Press.

Berne, E. (1972). *What Do You Say After You Say Hello?* New York: Grove Press.

Bion, W.R. (1961). *Experiences in Groups and Other Papers.* London: Tavistock Publications.

Culbert, S.A. (January-March, 1970). Accelerating Laboratory Learning Through a Phase Progress Model for Trainer Intervention. *Journal of Applied Behavioral Science, 6*(1), 24-38.

Freud, S. (1953a). The Interpretation of Dreams. In J. Strachey (Ed. and Trans.) *The Standard Edition of the Complete Psychological Works of Sigmund Freud.* London: Hogarth Press.

Freud, S. (1953b). The Psychology of Everyday Life. In J. Strachey (Ed. and Trans.) *The Standard Edition of the Complete Psychological Works of Sigmund Freud.* London: Hogarth Press.

Harvey, J. (1974). The Abilene Paradox: The Management of Agreement, *Organization Dynamics, 3,* 63-80.

Homans, G.C. (1950). *The Human Group.* New York: Harcourt, Brace, and World.

Janis, I.L. (1972). *Victims of Groupthink: A Psychological Study of Foreign Decisions and Fiascos.* Boston: Houghton Mifflin.

McClelland, D.C. (1965). Achievement Motivation Can Be Developed. *Harvard Business Review*, Nov.-Dec.

Neusch, D. (1984). Managerial Job-Constraints. *Strategies.* March-April. Austin, TX: OHRD Associates, 4 pp.

Parsons, T. (1951). *The Social System.* New York: Free Press.

Parsons, T. (1954). *Essays in Sociological Theory.* New York: Free Press.

Parsons, T. (1960). *Structure and Process in Modern Society.* New York: Free Press.

Peters, R.J., and Waterman, R.H. (1982). *In Search of Excellence.* New York: Warner Publications.

Prigogine, I. (1980). *From Being to Becoming: Time and Complexity in the Physical Sciences.* San Francisco: W.H. Freeman.

Prigogine, I., and Nicolis, G. (1977). *Self-Organization in Nonequilibrium Systems: From Dissipative Structures to Order Through Fluctuations.* New York: Wiley.

Prigogene, I. and Stengis, I. (1984). *Order Out of Chaos.* New York: Bantam.

Rogers, C. (1961). *On Becoming a Person.* Boston: Houghton Mifflin.

Seashore, C. (no date). *In Grave Danger of Growing.* Arlington, VA: National Training Laboratories.

Shonk, J.H. (1982). *Working in Teams: A Practical Manual for Improving Work Groups.* New York: AMACOM, A Division of the American Management Association.

Sorokin, P.A. (1947). *Society, Culture and Personality.* New York: Harper.

Steiner, C. (1974). *Scripts People Live.* New York: Grove Press.

Watzlawick, P., Weakland, J., and Fisch, R. (1974). *Change: Principles of Problems Formation and Problem Resolution.* New York: Norton.

3

HOW GROUPS DEVELOP

As complicated as groups may be, they are a major key to individual and organizational change. Only by becoming convinced that we can work with people effectively through increasing our skill of diagnosing particular operational situations can managers find fruitful results through use of work group teams. Increased insight into one's own sensitivity to others about the problems the group faces, and the practice of effective leadership skills, make possible the effective utilization of people in teams to achieve organizational renewal.

Gordon Lippitt, *Organizational Renewal*, 1969

A good way to begin thinking about how you can enable groups to work more productively is to ask, What do you want the group to accomplish? You will want the team to produce a product, a service, a victory, by transforming some kind of inputs into valued outputs. This focus on purpose is essential to enabling a team to produce at the highest levels.

If your team does not have a clear sense of its vision and mission, take the time to develop one. A team without a sense of purpose will wander capriciously from task to task despite the best of team-building efforts. Trying to increase teamwork for a group with a poor sense of its purpose is like trying to build a house without a foundation.

Team Needs—Balancing of Functions

How can you help your team accomplish its purposes? The answer to this question lies in the leadership process. We know some things about what a team needs in order to function at the highest levels: team members have to work together in a

35

harmonious fashion; each person must function at a high level; the team must assess its progress regularly through feedback; problems must be solved in a productive manner; and adjustments must be made along the path toward the goal. These can be thought of as *task functions*.

Often, a team has to pause in its work and take a long (and often hard) look at how it is functioning as a team. In other words, a team is periodically in need of maintenance. To use an analogy, a team is like a car. A car has a purpose to fulfill: to move people or products from point A to point B. A car that is not used in this way is an expensive toy that most people cannot afford. By the same token, a team that doesn't produce is an expensive toy that most organizations cannot afford.

To function over the long haul, a car must be properly maintained. After it is driven a number of miles, it will require a lube job, an oil change, a tune-up, and so on. Neglect the maintenance for long and the car will break down, most of the time at great cost. The group must also be maintained. The team must periodically look at how it is working as a unit. It must examine the roles its members are playing, and it must make changes from time to time in order to achieve its purposes. These are called team *maintenance functions*.

Finally, the team must provide opportunities for individual team members to meet some of their needs and wants. An effective team enables its members to meet some of their needs for friendship, for achievement, for responsibility, for security. These are *individual functions*. (See Figure 3.1.)

Effective groups maintain an appropriate balance of Task, Maintenance, and Individual functions. They are able to concentrate on tasks which help them achieve their purposes, but they are also able to shift their focus in order to maintain the group and to help individuals meet their needs through team membership.

Figure 3.1. Balancing Levels of Needs in the Team.

Effective groups attain the highest levels of excellence by developing tools to focus the team's energy on achieving its purposes and on the quality of the process of getting there. Several processes will help the team succeed at these two important objectives. Healthy individuals and teams need to be:
- internally responsive
- externally responsive
- unified.

These three factors describe ways in which individuals and teams act in and on the environment. They pose three important objectives for both people and teams:
- To acquire and use relevant information
- To influence the environment such that goals are achieved
- To establish relevant goals and objectives.

Individual Needs and Group Performance

We have focused so far on what a team or an individual needs to be able to do to attain excellence. It is equally important to understand how team effectiveness relates to individual needs.

We all need to feel that we belong to a group or a team. We need to feel *connected* to that team. Effective teams help their members meet this need for belonging or connectedness. The team which enables people to meet this need shows high levels of trust. People then feel free to devote their energies to the tasks to be accomplished instead of to protecting themselves.

People also need to feel that they are special in some manner. When a person is able to be himself and is free to grow in his own way, he develops a sense of *uniqueness*. An environment in which this need can be met strongly accepts and recognizes individuals. Such a team is described as *open*.

As people (and teams) grow in self-awareness, it is natural to want to use this new information to realize goals. To do this, it is necessary to have a sense of *vision*, or purpose, or direction. How can a team get what it wants if it doesn't know what it wants? The person (or team) who knows where he is going and how he plans to get there is said to have a sense of *models*. Effective groups provide an environment in which their members can meet these needs by providing them with goals and opportunities to succeed.

Individuals and teams will run up against obstacles in their pursuit of goals and objectives. Healthy individuals (and teams) learn how to overcome these inevitable barriers through the practice of problem solving skills. People who successfully influence the environment and overcome problems develop a sense of psychological power or *competence.* Effective teams foster the development of competence by providing members with many opportunities for reaching goals and by developing a positive view of problem solving.

People who successfully meet their needs are often described as whole. That is, they experience themselves as complete and have a sense of *wholeness.* The team can either enable the individual to develop wholeness or it can put up insurmountable barriers. Teams provide the setting or context in which each member strives to develop a sense of wholeness. We believe that in the long run, effective teams are those which enable members to develop a sense of wholeness by helping them grow. If this is true, it is vital for each of us to understand how we might help our team grow so that we can optimize individual and team potential. This is our purpose—to provide you with a useful set of tools for accomplishing the goal of optimizing your team's potential for growth and productivity.

Optimizing Individual and Group Potential

How does one facilitate the development of a positive group culture, one that optimizes both individual and group potential for productivity? A key concept for understanding the tools for optimizing group potential is that of the NORM. A norm can be thought of as a freedom or permission the group members give each other and expect in return. For example, the group can convey to its members that it is okay for them to learn and grow, or it can convey that learning and growing is not okay. The discovery processes associated with learning are favorable to the growth of the group and its members. On the other hand, the defining processes associated with not learning inhibit growth of the group and its members. The question then is: What norms (or permissions) facilitate and encourage individual and group growth and development? We believe that five key norms promote growth and development in the team; these are discussed in detail in later chapters.

Norm One: Developing Trust

Trust is the norm in a group that says that it is okay for members and the team as a whole to take reasonable risks. Trust develops in groups that reward sharing of ideas, thoughts, opinions, and feelings and that make and keep simple agreements. Such groups are characterized by a climate of cohesion, belonging, and mutual confidence.

Norm Two: Accepting and Recognizing Individual Differences

As trust develops, members develop the confidence to share more and more of themselves, especially as this pertains to the work to be done. Healthy groups develop a norm that communicates acknowledgment and respect for each person's unique point of view; they also permit members to use their special skills and talents in the process of achieving team goals and objectives.

Norm Three: Giving and Receiving Feedback

To learn, grow, and succeed, team members require feedback on how their performance compares with what is expected of them. The availability of feedback enables the individual and the team to stay on target. When the team is closed to constructively analyzing its performance against expectations, the likelihood of failure is increased immeasurably.

Norm Four: Problem Solving

Obstacles to goal attainment are inevitable. Individual team members may pose problems; technical problems may arise; political conflicts with other teams in the organization may develop; or competition from the outside may increase. Regardless of type or origin, problems arise and the successful team learns how to identify them and develop solutions. To do so, team members must feel free to admit to problems that interfere with goal achievement and to discover solutions. The alternative to problem finding and solving is binding the group's energy in fault finding and scapegoating, both of which reduce the team's effectiveness in achieving its goals.

Norm Five: Letting Go of the Past

All of us value the joy which follows accomplishing an important goal. It is what makes the effort worthwhile. Effective teams spend time celebrating their accomplishments. This process strengthens the team. It also serves another important function—it enables the team to let go of what has been done and to refocus its energy on what is to be accomplished next. Similarly, when a team experiences a setback or failure, it is important to take time to grieve together. This process frees up energy that would otherwise be tied up in resentments, regrets, and shaken confidence. Although there has been failure at the task level, the grieving process turns defeat into victory at the level of group maintenance and individual needs.

Team and Individual Development

The group must learn to focus its best energy on the task of producing something, while at the same time reserving energy to itself and help its members grow and develop.

The growth of a team is both organic and dynamic. It is *organic* in that the norms described unfold in a predictable manner. Trust is a prerequisite for the development of norms of self-acceptance and respect for individual differences; trust fosters the sharing of information; self-disclosure creates a pool of shared information, and forms the basis for achieving harmony among members' efforts.

Trust and acceptance of individual differences foster the development of the norm of giving and receiving feedback; in turn, this norm enables the group to find and solve problems (personal, interpersonal, organizational, technical). Finally, group members develop a level of cohesion and belonging that fosters the process of letting go of the past, by celebrating together the accomplishments of the team and team members and grieving together over the important setbacks.

Team development is also *dynamic* in that each of these norms is being dealt with all the time. Where the energy happens to be focused (on issues of trust, acceptance, feedback, etc.) depends on the kinds of stresses the team is facing at the time. A most important task of an effective leader is sensing the major concerns of the group and dealing with them positively. For example, a group skilled in problem solving may be stuck because it is not safe to discuss problems openly. An effective leader diagnoses this lack of trust and quickly makes positive moves to increase the level of trust in the group. The group development process is outlined in Figure 3.2.

The effective team enables its members to develop a sense of group wholeness. Teams must strive to develop this wholeness. This is because groups provide the setting or environment in which individuals either grow or not. Effective teams, therefore, possess characteristics which facilitate individual development (see Figure 3.3). The chapters that follow describe tools and concepts you can adopt to help you optimize your team's potential. As you learn to use the concepts and tools in the environment of your team, you can expect the team to become more productive. Figure 3.4 provides an overview of these concepts and tools.

Team-Building Roadmap

If you are interested in building your team, you may wonder, where do I start? How do I go about this?

As we pointed out at the start of the chapter, the place to begin is to decide where you want to go, your purpose. Where you want to go is a matter of vision and mission. The techniques in the next section of this chapter can help you with this.

Once you know where you want to go, the next step is to find out where you are. This involves assessing the team's current functioning. Analyzing Team Effectiveness is a technique to help you do this. It is a questionnaire to use with your team. Another method is to use a simulated task (see Carribean Island Survival Exercise, Chapter 7). Simulations can provide an objective measure of your group's effectiveness. They also permit you (or a skilled observer) to watch the group in action, to detect strengths and weaknesses in the processes the team uses.

Once you have a good picture of where the group stands, you can decide (a) whether the gains from team building are likely to

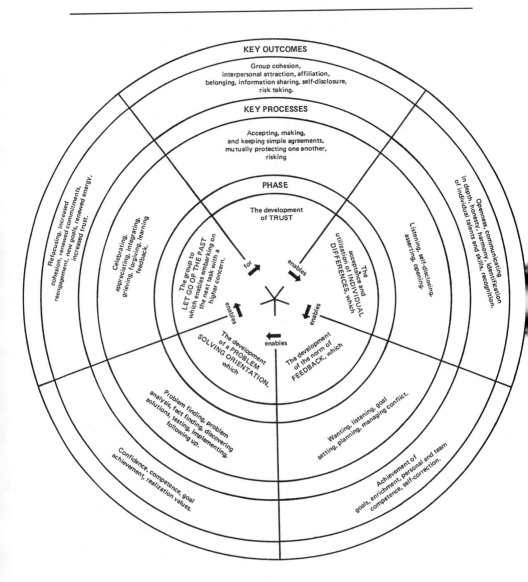

Figure 3.2. An Overview of Group Development.

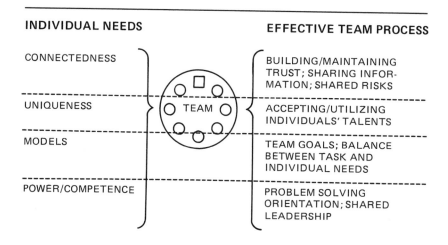

INDIVIDUAL NEEDS	EFFECTIVE TEAM PROCESS

CONNECTEDNESS — BUILDING/MAINTAINING TRUST; SHARING INFORMATION; SHARED RISKS

UNIQUENESS — ACCEPTING/UTILIZING INDIVIDUALS' TALENTS

MODELS — TEAM GOALS; BALANCE BETWEEN TASK AND INDIVIDUAL NEEDS

POWER/COMPETENCE — PROBLEM SOLVING ORIENTATION; SHARED LEADERSHIP

Figure 3.3. Team Processes and Individual Development.

justify the cost in time and resources, and (b) where it is best to start.

The five norms develop sequentially (see Figures 3.3 and 3.4). Although the degree to which the team adheres to these norms is always in flux, trust is the basic one. If your analysis of your team's effectiveness signals a low level of trust, start here. You may want to use techniques from Chapter 4. Trust building is also the appropriate place to begin with a newly formed team.

If your team analysis indicates a reasonable level of trust but poor acceptance and use of individual differences, then that is the norm to develop. The techniques in Chapter 5 are designed for this process.

Start with Chapter 6 if your team members trust each other and respect their differences but don't know how to give feedback. If your team has the first three norms in place but doesn't know how to solve problems together, start with Chapter 7.

Put simply, after you assess your team's functioning, identify which of the five key norms has not developed or is in jeopardy. Focus on trust first.

Reassess the team periodically to see if problems have changed. Monthly progress checks are recommended.

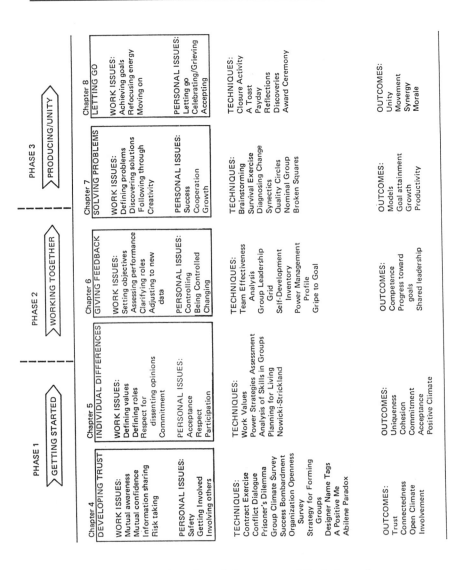

*Figure 3.4. Overview of Concepts and Techniques for
Developing the Five Key Norms: Trust, Individual Differences,
Feedback, Problem Solving, and Letting Go.*

Evaluate the effectiveness of each team-building meeting as soon as it is over. This will provide you with feedback for refining your approach. Be sure to follow up on any action plans that

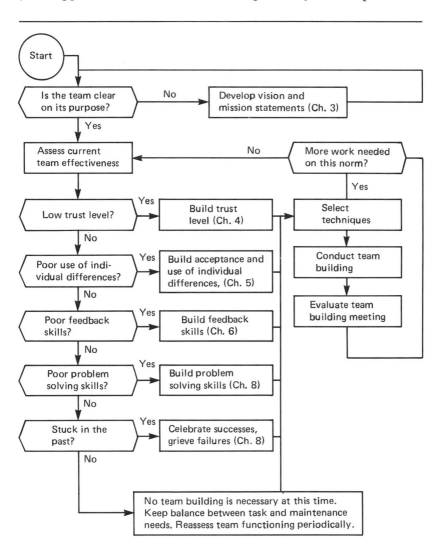

Figure 3.5. Team-Building Flow Chart.

emerge from the team building meetings. In Figure 3.5 you will find a flow chart to guide your decision-making.

VISION OF TEAM EFFECTIVENESS TECHNIQUE

Purpose

The development of a common vision is a major key to effective teamwork. A statement of team vision can aid team functioning by:

(1) clarifying team members' understanding of what the future probably holds and the impact of present decisions;

(2) permitting the team to anticipate what areas will require future decisions;

(3) increasing the speed and flow of relevant information in the group; and

(4) providing for faster and less disruptive implementation of decisions. (Warren, 1966)

This exercise is designed to help you and your team develop a vision—a common sense of the desired future you are all working toward.

Description

The Vision of Team Effectiveness Technique (Formosa, Sallustio, and Thompson, 1984) procedure is as follows:

1. Team members relax. (This lets the brain to go into an alpha-wave state conducive to creativity.) Deep breathing, silence, or quiet music (with no lyrics), muscle relaxation, closing eyes, and so forth, may be helpful.

2. Invite team members to quietly dream of what they would like the team to accomplish and become. Don't try to answer this in words, but playfully let pictures form and move in your mind, and take note of sights, sounds, and feelings. Don't restrict yourselves in any way. Allow about five minutes of silence for this.

3. After the five minutes of silence, invite team members, whenever ready, to write down their visions of the team's future.

4. Have team members choose partners they feel comfortable with, and share their visions. In discussing his vision with his partner, each member uses questions like these:
   ○ What is your understanding of my vision?
   ○ Can I clarify any of it for you?
   ○ What would you add or change?
   ○ Do you feel inspired by these statements?
   ○ How can we make them more inspiring or compelling?
   ○ Are your values reflected in this vision statement?
   ○ How will we know when the vision is realized?
   ○ Do we need a time frame for this vision?
5. Reconvene the team. Repeat Step 4 with the whole team instead of just the partnerships. Then let each member write down his or her perception of the team's consensus on the team's vision.
6. You have several different versions of the team's vision, each reflecting a measure of built-in consensus. The team may simply adopt one of these or combine the attractive elements of several statements into one.
7. Brainstorm with the team the vision target categories. These are broad categories of outcomes the team's vision aims at (such as product quality, output level, employee morale, or customer satisfaction).

This exercise provides team members the opportunity to share their "master agendas." To the extent that members are open and honest in this process, the process is as valuable as the outcome. The exercise causes a blending and linking of individual agendas.

The vision statement that emerges may well be an unreachable ideal, but functions well for purposes of navigation and direction. Even though the ideal may never be reached it is a target which team members agree to shoot for. Provide a copy of the final vision statement to every member of the team as a point of reference.

The creative, playful, dreamy nature of this exercise is at odds with the work climate in most organizations. Imagine your boss's reaction if he walked into the room during Step 1 and saw everyone sitting around with eyes closed! We have been taught to think of work and play as opposites, so that anything pleasant or relaxing seems frivolous and may cause us to feel guilty if done at work. Team members may have difficulty with the visioning exercise because of such barriers. Do your best to remove them and give team members permission to play. Play, properly channeled, is profoundly productive.

Protect the group from interruptions. An off-site meeting may be best. After lunch or coffee break, when alpha brain waves tend to occur naturally, may be the best times for this exercise.

Example

A $100 million real estate management investment firm decided to do some strategic planning in face of a downturn in the real estate industry. The "visioning" technique was employed by the consultant as a means of getting members of the executive planning team to think about where they saw the company going in three to five years. The technique of visioning was explained. The consultant asked the participants to create a mental image of where they saw the company three to five years down the road. Each person then shared his or her vision of the company. From this sharing, a corporate vision statement was evolved. It consisted of three parts: one, the group wanted to maximize the owner's return on investment by providing efficient management services; two, the group wanted to provide the best living space available to tenants; three, the group wanted the company to continue its rapid growth and increase its earnings.

After several iterations and many discussions, a corporate vision statement was created along with a related statement of corporate values and a related strategic plan. During the first year of the strategic plan the company doubled in size. It increased profitability by improving the efficiency of its management operations and by selling less profitable enterprises. It developed a more productive, committed work force. As a means of keeping an eye on where the company is and on solving problems along the way, a permanent "quality" group was established. The members learned how to apply *group values* as a means of improving the quality of all services and, at the same time, reducing costs.

Resources

Formosa, A.R., Sallustio, A., and Thompson, R.G. (1984). *Team Building Workbook.* Franklin, PA: Joy Education Center.

Kiefer, C.F., and Senge, P.M. (1984). Metanoic Organizations. In John D. Adams (Ed.) *Transforming Work.* Alexandria, VA: Miles River Press.

Mink, O., Schultz, J., and Mink, B. (1979). *Open Organizations.* Austin, TX: Learning Concepts, Inc. (Order through OHRD Associates, Austin, TX.)

Shonk, J.H. (1982). *Working in Teams.* NY: AMACOM.

Warren, E.K. (1966). *Long Range Planning: The Executive Viewpoint.* Englewood Cliffs, NJ: Prentice-Hall.

TEAM MISSION TECHNIQUE

Purpose

The Team Mission statement specifies what the team considers its major output (product or service) and to whom it provides this output. This exercise is designed to guide you and your team in developing your mission statement.

Description

The Team Mission generating exercise (Formosa, Sallustio, and Thompson, 1984) works as follows:

1. Explain a team mission to team members—a short statement of what product or service we provide and to whom we provide it. This statement must meet the following criteria:
   (a) Does it identify our main output (product or service)?
   (b) Does it identify to whom we provide this product or service?
   (c) Does it express our reason for being here as a group?
   (d) Is this what the group was created to do?
   (e) Does it specify what we must do to continue as a team?
   (f) Is it something that none of us can do alone?
   (g) Is it related to our vision statement?
   (h) Does it express a sense of nobility in our purpose?
   (i) Is it something we believe we will succeed in doing?

2. Ask each team member to write a short preliminary statement of the team's mission, concentrating on criteria (a) and (b) in Step 1. That is, for now, specify only (1) the one main output and (2) whom it is for.
3. Have each team member read his preliminary mission statement. Post each statement in full view of the group.
4. When each statement is divided into its two elements (Step 2):
   (a) Have the group discuss which preliminary mission statement best identifies the team's main product. (The team may generate a new version of what its main product is that fits better than any of the preliminary statements.)
   (b) Have the group decide which preliminary statement best identifies whom the team provides with its output.
5. Combine the two elements into a new semifinal version of the mission statement.
6. Now go through all the criteria listed in Step 1 above, one at a time. Ask, "Does the semifinal statement fit the criteria? If not, what is the simplest change we can make so that it does fit?" Add as few words as possible. Change as few words as possible. Be sure the team is unanimous on each change.

Once you have a shared vision and a unanimous statement of mission, you have agreement among team members on the two most basic issues: "What are we doing here?" and "Why?" You have established the boundaries. You have basic principles you can come back to when difficult decisions are being made. You have a framework to put the team's work in perspective.

The biggest danger in carrying out this exercise is that team members may haggle over semantics. Discourage this. Keep a sense of movement and humor. Remember, "For a difference to be a difference, it must make a difference, or what difference does it make?"

Example

American Television and Communication Corporation (ATC) is a large cable TV company with diverse holdings spread all over the county. The company has moved from an owner-founded and operated entrepreneurial business to its present structure of 23 operating divisions.

When Time, Inc. purchased ATC, it was highly centralized, run by a strong person who organized, managed, and assumed responsibility for *his enterprise*. He had a talent for selecting good subordinates. He and others in the organization took responsibility for mentoring these bright younger people to become expert in the cable business. The company excelled in the economics of its business and had the reserve talent to grow.

Spread geographically from Hawaii to New York and from Minnesota to Texas, ATC faced diverse challenges from a myriad of publics. The cable industry is very competitive and the rate of change in the technology of the industry is very rapid. Also, the controls on the industry remain the focus of municipal governments, some of which make absurd demands on their local cable franchise holders. Eventually, its size prompted ATC to become genuinely concerned about its ability to respond in a timely and knowledgeable way to its many locales.

Toward this end, the new CEO, Trygve Myhren, and other members of the Executive Committee, initiated a strategic planning agenda. A primary goal was to decentralize operations and to delegate control to the 23 resulting decentralized operating units. The question was how to do this, while maintaining and enhancing the owner's investment, paying for the cost of capital, and providing a superior service to the American viewing public. The Team Mission Technique was used as a starting point for bringing about the needed alignment of the 23 field units.

The Executive Committee began by developing a corporate vision and mission statement. They then identified corporate values and philosophy that articulated how they would act as a company to create the vision. The final result of this process is shown on the next page. In terms of the bottom line, the company is now one of the two largest Cable TV companies in the U.S. and it continues to outperform its competitors.

After seven months of sharing, discussing, and *aligning*, the executives and senior management drafted statements of vision, mission, and values and philosophy, and had identified and agreed upon seven key goals. These passages may reflect the true spirit of excellence and dedication to service in ATC.

ATC Vision
Working together to provide entertainment and information choices.

ATC Mission
We develop, market, deliver, and service in a quality and profitable manner a broad selection of electronic entertainment and information for as many customers as possible in our communities.

ATC Values and Philosophy

WE BELIEVE IN OUR:

WE WILL OPERATE OUR BUSINESS SO THAT:

HERITAGE—of high performance.

In all we do, we strive to be the best.

CUSTOMERS—the most important part of our business.

We provide our customers with quality entertainment and information choices and service at fair prices.

PEOPLE—our greatest resources.

We treat people in all positions with fairness and dignity and we give them room to grow and achieve. Our people are proud of their high standards and are rewarded equitably for high performance and contributions.

COMMUNITIES—they and we both benefit from our contributions.

Our communities benefit from our service and from our individual and company commitments and activities.

GROWTH—it provides vitality to our enterprise.	Our company grows by adding new customers, building new businesses and serving more communities.
FINANCIAL STRENGTH—from efficient and profitable operations.	We provide stable and fair returns to our shareholders, stable employment and opportunity for our people, and quality facilities and services to satisfy our customers.
ADAPTABILITY—in a competitive and changing world.	We test and try new concepts and services. We understand that one of our key strengths is the ability to identify and benefit from change.
INTEGRITY—in all our actions.	We treat our customers, people, communities and suppliers with fairness and honesty.
TEAMWORK—it enables each of us to be more effective.	We communicate openly and with trust in mutually pursuing opportunities and solving problems. Each person is important to the success of the ATC team.

Resources

Formosa, A.R., Sallustio, A., and Thompson, R.G. (1984). *Team Building Workbook.* Franklin, PA: Joy Education Center.

Kiefer, C.F., and Senge, P.M. (1984). Metanoic Organizations. In John D. Adams (Ed.) *Transforming Work.* Alexandria, VA: Miles River Press.

Mink, O., Shultz, J., and Mink, B. (1979). *Open Organizations.* Austin, TX: OHRD Associates.

Shonk, J.H. (1982). *Working in Teams.* NY: AMACOM.

PROUDS AND SORRIES TECHNIQUE

Purpose

This technique is used to help team members identify their individual and collective values so that they can design a model for organizational behavior. The process enables a team to develop a list of team values.

Description

With the team assembled around a table, ask the members to develop a list of things from their work that have made them "proud" or "sorry." An example of a "proud" might be "I am proud of the manner in which we took over two new cable operations without having lost a single customer or disrupted a day of service." An example of a "sorry" might be "I am sorry that we lost so many fine people in the process of converting the system from microwave to cable transmission."

Ask each team member to take two sheets of chart paper and make separate lists of their prouds and sorries, printing these large enough so that they might be shared with the team.

Have each member of the team share their lists (voluntarily). As the individuals share, the facilitator (and the members) listen for values implicit in the prouds and sorries. Example: When you say you are proud that we have installed a new system, it seems to imply that you value technology. When you say you are sorry that we lost so many fine people, it seems to imply that you value treating people with the highest levels of dignity and respect.

By the end of the meeting, you should have developed a tentative list of values. Have several members take the list and develop a more refined list prior to the next scheduled meeting. Ask two or more other members to take the lists and to develop a draft of a management philosophy statement prior to the next meeting.

Example

The cable TV company referred to earlier created a list of their corporate values and a statement of their corporate philosophy using the Prouds and Sorries Technique. As indicated, the process considered essential for the company was changing over from one of centralized authority to one of decentralized authority, from a dependency producing management style to one based on interdependence and cooperation. The question of vital importance was how to go about achieving this alignment of philosophy and practice among a large array of decentralized units. It was believed that values clarification was required. What has been the result? The value of quality (excellence) is more highly visible. Company performance has improved steadily over the last fiscal year, both in terms' of customer satisfaction and return on investment.

Resource
OHRD Associates
1208 Somerset Drive
Austin, Texas 78753

ANALYZING TEAM EFFECTIVENESS TECHNIQUE

Purpose
This survey is designed to take a snapshot of your team's current situation as seen through the eyes of team members. The items on the survey gauge team members' feelings and perceptions about the team's vision, mission, values, goals, objectives, trust level, use of individual talents, and so forth. The results of the survey become a springboard for discussion.

Description
The instrument consists of 24 items. Each taps a different aspect of team functioning. Team members use a nine-point scale to rate the team's functioning as they perceive it. To use this technique for team-building purposes:
1. Obtain a copy for each team member (see Resources).
2. Near the end of a meeting, distribute copies and explain the purpose of the exercise.
3. Give team members 15 minutes to read the directions and fill out the rating scales.
4. Ask members to sign or initial their surveys in the upper right-hand corner of the first page and turn them in.
5. Before the next meeting, compile the ratings. All you need is an average and the highest and lowest ratings for each scale. You may find it helpful to put the data on a grid like the one shown in Figure 3.7.

	Scale	Team Member Ratings														Low	Avg	High
Purpose	1.																	
	2.																	
	3.																	
	4.																	
Trust	5.																	
	6.																	
	7.																	
	8.																	
Individual Differences	9.																	
	10.																	
	11.																	
	12.																	
	13.																	
Feedback	14.																	
	15.																	
	16.																	
	17.																	
Problem Solving	18.																	
	19.																	
	20.																	
	21.																	
Celebration	22.																	
	23.																	
	24.																	

Figure 3.7. Team Effectiveness Instrument.

6. At the next meeting, return the surveys to team members.
7. Present the data to the team. You may want to share them all, item by item or, for each rating scale, you may want to show just: (a) average rating, (b) highest rating, (c) lowest rating, or you may want to report item clusters—purpose, trust, individual differences, feedback, problems solving, and celebration as low, medium, and high.
8. Conduct a discussion of the data, focusing on such questions as:
   • On what three scales or dimensions are scores highest?
   • What does that say about our team?

- What other strong points do we have as a team?
- What are the reasons for these ratings? Specifics?
- On what three scales or what dimension are scores lowest?
- What does this say about our team?
- What other weaknesses do we have as a team?
- What are the reasons for these ratings? Specifics?
- What can we do as a team to improve these areas?

9. Follow up on any action plans generated by this discussion. These action plans are basically agreements that the team members have made with each other. If the agreements are not carried out, serious damage to the team's trust level may result.

To the extent possible, it is best to guarantee team members that their responses will be kept anonymous and confidential. This encourages open and honest responses. Anonymity and confidentiality are good rules of thumb for any exercise that *requires* team members to disclose their thoughts and feelings on paper.

Team members should have their responses in front of them during the discussion. You may have to sacrifice a measure of confidentiality. Use your best judgment on what trade-offs to make. You know your team better than we do. In any case, team members' perceptions and feelings will come out in the group discussion. Try to give the members as many options as possible on whether and when to disclose their options to the rest of the team.

Generally, you should call attention to any scale or dimension on which the lowest rating is less than 5, and any scale or dimension on which the scores vary widely. These are clues to key teamwork issues for future team development.

Example

This instrument (see Figure 3.8) is applied periodically throughout the process of working a group through purpose (vision, mission, goals, values) and the task phases—trust, individual differences, feedback, individual and group problem solving, and celebration, as mentioned throughout the book. We have applied it in a myriad of teams at various phases in their life as a group. We tailor our interventions to move the group to the next task phase. We can thus increase the efficiency of the team development process.

A property management company decided to form an executive team for the purpose of doing strategic planning for the company. To facilitate implementation of this team, a consultant was hired to help the group learn the skills of teamwork. Following this training, the group performed well for a period of several months and then seemed to reach an impasse. Decisions were postponed, problems were tabled, and, in general, the team's level of functioning diminished. At this point the consultant suggested that the team get a feel for what its current level of effectiveness was by completing the survey. Each member of the team completed the survey. The results were tabulated and then discussed at length. As it turned out, people discovered that they were reluctant to share openly because of the powerful leadership style of the chief officer. Instead they would procrastinate or simply agree with the president. From this frank discussion the team decided to rethink its ground rules and to develop a more open method of dealing with key issues. The value of the survey is that it allows a team to focus its discussion of team functioning on key operational areas. This facilitates both an objective assessment of the team as well as a frank sharing of feelings and conflicts. In the case of this team it also led to an effort to learn how to manage agreement and to resolve differences in an equitable manner.

Resource
OHRD Associates
1208 Somerset Avenue
Austin, Texas 78753

Team Effectiveness Survey

I. PURPOSE:
   1. The team has a clear sense of purpose.
       1   2   3   4   5   6   7   8   9
       totally   uncertain   totally
       disagree   agree

Figure 3.8. Team Effectiveness Survey Instrument.

---

2. The team has well-defined values regarding performance and relationship.

1	2	3	4	5	6	7	8	9
totally disagree				uncertain				totally agree

3. I understand the team's goals and objectives.

1	2	3	4	5	6	7	8	9
totally disagree				uncertain				totally agree

4. I know what I am supposed to do in order to produce.

1	2	3	4	5	6	7	8	9
totally disagree				uncertain				totally agree

II. TRUST:

5. I can be myself in the team.

1	2	3	4	5	6	7	8	9
rarely				about half the time				always

6. I make it a point to keep my commitments to the team and its members.

1	2	3	4	5	6	7	8	9
rarely				about half the time				always

7. I share relevant information and concerns with the group.

1	2	3	4	5	6	7	8	9
rarely				about half the time				always

8. I trust the group's ability to solve problems.

1	2	3	4	5	6	7	8	9
rarely				about half the time				always

Figure 3.8 (Continued)

III.   INDIVIDUAL DIFFERENCES:

9.   I am able to use my talents and skills to help the team succeed.

1	2	3	4	5	6	7	8	9
rarely				about half the time			always	

10.   I am given the time and resources I need to succeed.

1	2	3	4	5	6	7	8	9
totally disagree				uncertain			totally agree	

11.   I am free to express my ideas and opinions deeply.

1	2	3	4	5	6	7	8	9
rarely				about half the time			always	

12.   I feel free to do things my way as long as I produce.

1	2	3	4	5	6	7	8	9
rarely				about half the time			always	

IV.   FEEDBACK:

13.   The team regularly compares its current performance against expectations.

1	2	3	4	5	6	7	8	9
rarely				about half the time			always	

14.   There is a great deal of give and take discussion about how to work together better.

1	2	3	4	5	6	7	8	9
rarely				about half the time			always	

15.   I receive relevant and understandable feedback about my performance.

1	2	3	4	5	6	7	8	9
rarely				about half the time			always	

Figure 3.8 (Continued)

16. I feel free to share my reactions to other team members' behavior.

    1   2   3   4   5   6   7   8   9
    rarely   about half   always
                        the time

V. PROBLEM SOLVING:

17. Problems and conflicts are accepted as a regular part of teamwork.

    1   2   3   4   5   6   7   8   9
    totally   uncertain   totally
    disagree   agree

18. When a problem is recognized team members seek solutions, not scapegoats.

    1   2   3   4   5   6   7   8   9
    rarely   about half   always
                        the time

19. The team seeks to identify potential problems and conflicts and to resolve them in a timely manner.

    1   2   3   4   5   6   7   8   9
    rarely   about half   always
                        the time

20. I feel confident in the team's ability to manage conflict in a productive manner.

    1   2   3   4   5   6   7   8   9
    totally   uncertain   totally
    disagree   agree

VI. CELEBRATION:

21. The team has a lot of fun together.

    1   2   3   4   5   6   7   8   9
    rarely   sometimes   frequently

22. Individual and team accomplishments are recognized and celebrated.

    1   2   3   4   5   6   7   8   9
    rarely   about half   always
                        the time

Figure 3.8 (Continued)

23. The team easily lets go of the past and keeps focused on the goals
    and the methods for reaching goals.
    1   2   3   4   5   6   7   8   9
    totally   uncertain   totally
    disagree   agree

24. The team is able to grieve over its defeats and to move toward
    accomplishment.
    1   2   3   4   5   6   7   8   9
    rarely   about half   always
                                    the time

Figure 3.8 (Continued)

4

DEVELOPING TRUST AND OPENNESS

A basic human need is to feel a sense of connectedness to other people. When one is on a team, he or she experiences connectedness mentally, emotionally, and physically. He knows that he belongs, and is valued by the group. In turn, he or she values membership in the group.

The sense of connectedness is based on development of trust in the group. Trust is a prime enabling factor in the development of productive, healthy work teams. It is the foundation of the group's climate or atmosphere, the basis for building the team's productivity. With a foundation, the team can develop into a productive unit; if the foundation is weak, the team is likely to become unproductive.

This chapter covers the concepts behind building and maintaining trust in a work team and provides a set of tools for assessing trust levels, increasing trust in the group, and maintaining trust over time.

What Is Trust?

A way to evaluate the quality of the team's atmosphere is by charting the amount and depth of sharing in the team on a continuum ranging from closed to open.

CLOSED------------------------------**OPEN**

The weight of available evidence shows that successful group functioning depends on the level of openness attained by the group. In a closed group, people are not willing to share ideas and opinions about how to work together and solve problems. In an open group, people willingly share such information. Development of openness enables the group to develop a climate of trust. A norm of trust is essential if people are to feel free to take the risks frequently involved in sharing personal reactions and ideas about team performance. Willingness to share personal information and to listen to others share such information has been called SELF-DIS-CLOSURE TRUST. When people feel free to share in the group without feeling the need to protect themselves, then it can be said that the group has a high degree of self-disclosure trust.

Another dimension of trust that operates in relationships and teams is CONTRACT TRUST, which relates to the extent that people make and carry out simple agreements. If, as leader, you agree to meet regularly with the team to discuss team concerns, and you consistently postpone the meeting, what happens? Team members begin to doubt your intentions to listen to their concerns. If, however, you regularly spend time with the team, listening to the team's concerns, then the team comes to trust that its points of view will be heard and that you will keep your word.

When a team operates within a norm of contract trust, its members come to perceive the team environment as safe, reliable, and predictable. This frees them to concentrate their energies on their goals.

Underlying the sense of trust is the belief or expectation that one can take risks in the team without fear of being taken advantage of or ridiculed or embarrassed. Trust level in a team is reflected partly by the willingness of team members to take risks in the group and partly by the level of trustworthiness of the team members.

Specific behaviors which either help or hinder the development of trust are listed in Figure 4.1. As these lists reveal, behaviors permitting members to risk openness facilitate the development of trust while those threatening self-esteem block the development of trust.

How Does Trust Develop?

The Johari Window (Luft, 1973) provides a tool for understanding the development of trust. (See Figure 4.2.) According to this model, the personality of a team or its relationships can be

Behaviors which Help Develop Trust:	Behaviors which Hinder the Development of Trust:
—Accept ideas.	—Ignore people.
—Tolerate faults.	—Embarrass someone in front of a group.
—If you disagree, criticize idea, not the person.	—Fail to keep a confidence.
—Clarify to make sure people understand each other.	—Avoid eye contact.
—Include others in your activities.	—Withhold credit when it is due.
—Offer to help.	—Interrupt when others are talking.
—Ask others for feedback.	—Withhold information important to a decision.
—Play together (ping pong, volleyball, darts, etc.)	—Break a promise.
—Work with others on a project.	
—Tell others information that checks out to be accurate.	
—Follow through on something you agree to do.	

Figure 4.1. Development of Trust.

SELF

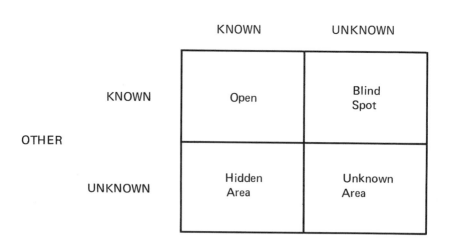

Figure 4.2. The Johari Window

compared to a window with four panes, each representing a pool of *energy* or *information*. This energy is either *available* or *unavailable* to the team for activities such as planning, decision making, problem solving, and goal setting.

The *size* of each pool of information is determined by *how much each person knows*, which in turn is related to *how willing and able each person is to share information* (self-disclosure) and *to listen to others share* (receptivity to feedback). Each pane expands or shrinks in relation to the amount of disclosure of information in the team and the amount of information heard. Each of these processes (sharing and receiving feedback) involves risk. If the risks pay off, both trust and the rate of self-disclosure and feedback grow. As more and more information is shared, the

OPEN pane or area grows, and more data are available to the group for accomplishing its goals. As the OPEN area increases, the other areas decrease.

Contents of the panes are described in Figure 4.3, which also illustrates how the size of the OPEN area expands as the level of trust in the group grows.

How Does Trust Contribute to the Group's Productivity?

As team members risk sharing what they know and feel about their goals and how to achieve them, and as team members hear this information without ridiculing, embarrassing, or rejecting the giver, more and more data enter the open area and become available for problem solving. As team members practice risk-taking in a trustworthy climate, a norm is established that risks can be taken without fear of some sort of punishment. This norm, giving people the freedom to take risks, acts to release information into the OPEN area from the BLIND and HIDDEN areas.

The way *not* to develop a trusting climate is to punish people when they risk sharing information. If team members are punished for their openness, they will seek ways to protect themselves. They will hide problems, deny them, or even repress them. More and more energy gets tied up in the BLIND or HIDDEN areas at the expense of the amount in the OPEN area. Team effectiveness is diminished as the quality of information available to accomplish tasks decreases.

Trust facilitates the release of personal and team energy—energy which can be used to help the team achieve its purposes. Lack of trust has the opposite effect—it diminishes the amount of energy available to the team for achieving its purposes. Self-disclosure and making and keeping simple contracts are the lubricants facilitating productive group functioning. Some general "truths" about development of trust in the team are listed below:

- Trust facilitates the release and development of personal and group potential for productivity.
- Trust facilitates more and higher quality sharing in the team. This sharing of information releases energy into the group which becomes available for the work of the team.

The Johari Window: Information
in the Panes

PANE 1, the OPEN area, contains information which is shared by all members of the group.

PANE 2, the BLIND area, contains information known to all members of the group except one.

PANE 3, the HIDDEN area, contains information that one member knowingly hides from the others on the team.

PANE 4, the UNKNOWN area, contains repressed information—that which is unknown to anyone.

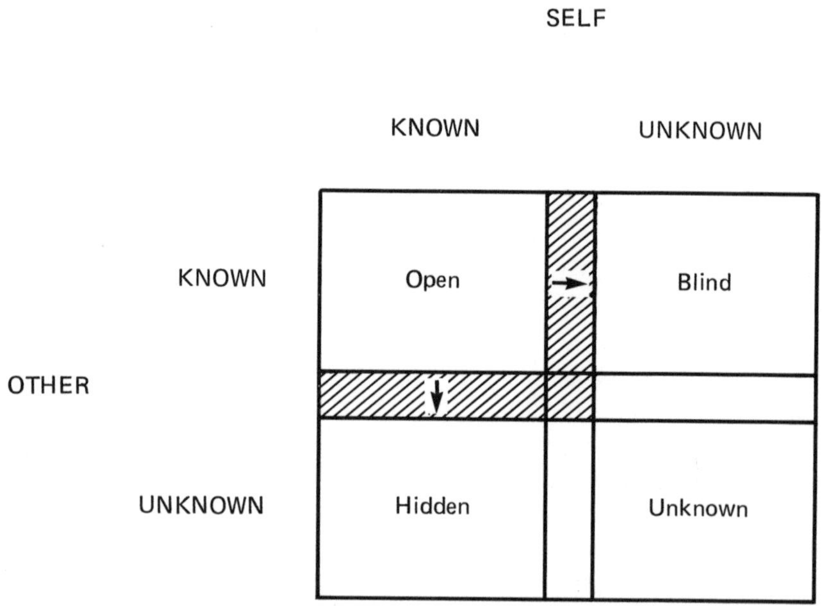

SELF

KNOWN   UNKNOWN

OTHER

KNOWN   Open   Blind

UNKNOWN   Hidden   Unknown

Figure 4.3. Growth of Group Openness (Johari Window Model).

- Trust is necessary for real learning and problem solving in the team.
- Trust facilitates development of competence in the team.
- In environments in which trust is deliberately nourished and consciously valued, the highest levels of individual and group productivity and creativity can be attained.

The model developed by Gibb (1978) illustrates the growth processes set in motion through the nurturing of trust (see Figure 4.4).

Each of the techniques in this book can be placed in one or more of the Johari quadrants. In all cases, the purpose of the techniques is to increase the size of the Open or Shared quadrant and simultaneously reduce the size of one or more of the other quadrants. You can help determine when to use a particular technique by assessing its purpose and associating it with a quadrant. A few examples are included in Figure 4.5.

What Environmental Qualities Promote the Development of Trust?

A great deal of research underlines what a manager can do to facilitate the growth of trust in the team environment. Just as an environment of safety, trust, and a sense of belonging is essential to human development in childhood and adolescents, these same qualities are essential in the environment that supports and develops productive work groups.

Figure 4.4. Gibb's Model.

Certain conditions in the environment are needed for movement to take place. First the child must feel safe, that he is connected to a human being who will not abandon him. This experience of belonging enables the child to venture forth. In the absence of this experience, the journey stops or is somehow distorted. Then development is arrested at an immature level. Fear often becomes the primary motivator in the individual's life, as he attempts to protect himself from the real or imagined dangers to be encountered.

Thus the development of the sense of connectedness can have profound effects on an individual's performance. Some people deal with the feelings of disconnectedness through inappropriate

	OPEN or SHARED	BLIND
	Contract Exercise Technique (builds contractual trust)	Self-Development Inventory for Multiple Role Effectiveness Technique (provides a clearer picture of roles, skills, and objectives)
	Abilene Paradox Technique (encourages disclosure)	Group Climate Survey Technique (assess the unknown)
	HIDDEN	UNKNOWN

Figure 4.5. Selected Methodologies for Developing Group Openness.

withdrawal or avoidance behavior (flight), while others deal with such feelings through inappropriate aggressive behavior (fight). Since some of the people who are on your team may not have developed a sense of connectedness, it will be helpful for you to understand the ways these less appropriate behaviors might reveal themselves in the team setting. (See Figure 4.6.)

Flight	Fight
When the disconnected person tries to deal with his need through avoidance, he:	When the disconnected person tries to deal with his need through aggression, he:
1. will rarely participate in team activities without prodding	1. will often disparage himself or others
2. is a loner	2. often tries to grab attention
3. will exhibit signs of anxiety and discomfort in the group	3. often tries to be the center of the team's activities
4. will often be reluctant to discuss himself or his feelings in the team setting	4. will often ridicule or devalue others' efforts to work as a team
5. is likely to be shy and find it difficult to deal with other team members	5. will often meet others' attempts to be close with hostility
6. will hide his true feelings	6. will hide his true feelings
7. will avoid seeking responsibility in the team when this involves leading others.	7. will act inappropriately independent, counterdependently or behave contrary to team goals.

Figure 4.6. Inappropriate Behavior Patterns of the "Disconnected" Person.

People who feel the sense of connectedness reveal different types of behavior in the team. Some of these patterns are listed below to clarify why some people seem to work well in the team setting. (See Figure 4.7.)

The person who has developed a sense of connectedness is able to:

1. openly share feelings and thoughts in the team

2. find it easy to cooperate appropriately to achieve team goals

3. develop relationships in the team

4. communicate nondefensively

5. hear feedback without becoming defensive

6. take responsibility in the team, even if this involves leadership roles

7. act autonomously to help the team achieve its goals and purposes

8. provide encouragement to other team members

9. take risks in the team without getting overly anxious about getting rejected

10. have fun with other team members, to share on a personal level

11. express disagreement openly

12. be helpful in settling conflicts.

Figure 4.7. Behavior Patterns of the "Connected" Person.

Four qualities in the team environment help people feel connected. Each member of the group can personally influence these norms.

1. OPENNESS OF COMMUNICATIONS. In a "connected" climate, each person feels listened to and valued as an important team member.

2. PRESENCE. A "connected" climate conveys to its members a sense of acceptance and warmth. This helps team members develop a sense of attraction to the team because they know they are a part of it.

3. SHARED PURPOSE. In a "connected" climate, every team member knows what the goals are and shares those goals. People in the team are knowledgeable about what the goals are and what kinds of output indicate attainment of those goals.

4. INVOLVEMENT. In a "connected" climate, a team is involved in producing something relevant to the environment in which it is operating. Team members receive and share regular feedback about how effectively their actions produce the expected results.

Trust, then, is the quality of the environment enabling a person to risk becoming more and more open. It is characterized by sharing, and by making and keeping agreements. In teams that are high in trust, people feel a sense of connectedness, and because they feel that they belong, team members become fully involved in achieving the purposes of the group.

What Threatens the Team's Sense of Trust?

Since trust is so important to excellent performance, it is also well to know what a manager or team member might do to inhibit the development of trust in a group. The focus of this list is on matters that most managers can control or at least influence directly. We realize that there are many things over which a manager has no direct control which might influence the trust level of the team. (See Figure 4.8.)

How Can a Sense of Trust Be Developed?

Just as team leaders can diminish trust through your actions, so,

When I see you doing these things, I tend to hide feelings, ideas, and information from team:

*Ridiculing
back stabbing
acting two-faced
ignoring
neglecting
gossiping
telling crude jokes
*Embarrassing someone in front of the
group
*Constantly correcting or nit-picking
acting as if you know it all
making me feel dumb
expecting too much
deserting me
acting inconsistently
*Neglecting
avoiding eye contact
dominating conversation
saying "yes, but" or "no, but . . ."
not listening
breaking promises
*Playing one-upmanship
*Pushing people around
*Failing to keep something confidential

*Lying
*Using information against me
*Pretending to be friendly
*Withholding credit where credit is due
*Interrupting
*Calling me or others names
*Labeling people
*Trying too hard
*Ordering people around all the time
*Controlling people excessively
*Attacking
*Fidgeting
*Blaming
*Using obscene language
*Using a tone of voice that's sarcastic,
angry, loud, superior, harsh
*Passing judgment
*Giving up
*Over-reacting when proved wrong
*Setting someone up for failure
*Not opening up to me
*Shooting down ideas
*Talking down to me
*Always getting the last word

In general, I do not trust those people who show me:

*an unwillingness to listen, an unwilling-
ness to change, an unwillingness
to compromise
*a lack of real caring
*arrogance
*a closed mind, disrespect, mistrust,
hostility, prejudice, inflexibility
*a tendency to criticize me or punish me
excessively

*a lack of real interest or concern
*that they have little time for me
*open and prolonged hostility (or who
permit this to go on in the team)
*little respect by keeping me in the dark
about important changes or other
events which affect me directly

Figure 4.8. Behaviors Which Inhibit Development of Trust.

too, can trust be increased through your actions. Specific suggestions by which you can do this are summarized in Figure 4.9.

One of the most important things you can do is make a *commitment* to build trust in your team. Your commitment to do this is as important as the skill with which you do it. Keep in mind that the suggestions need to be adapted to your team. You can sense what will work for them, what won't work, and how to go about implementing suggestions. In any event, the more flexibly you use the suggested strategies, the more effective they are likely to be.

There are ways to facilitate the development of trust in your team:

• BE PERSONAL. People find it easier to trust those whom they come to know than those who are hard to know. Use the first-person in describing your perceptions of work: "I am," "I think," "I feel," etc.

• ENCOURAGE OTHERS TO BE PERSONAL. Just as it is important for you to let yourself be known, it is also important for others to be known. You can ease this process by encouraging team members to express themselves: "What do you think about . . .?" "What is your opinion of . . .?" "How would you feel about . . .?"

• ACCEPT RESPONSIBILITY FOR YOUR FEELINGS. Learn to avoid punishing or criticizing team members when you feel bad, e.g., when you get angry when someone made a mistake. It is okay to be angry, but it is your response to that anger that will make a difference to the team's functioning. (See Chapter 6 for suggestions on how to deal with anger.) Avoid blaming or punishing people; instead move toward building team members' strength: "I am angry when you are getting to work late. Is it helping you to get to work late? Are you willing to change? . . ." "When you don't complete your work I get upset. It throws everyone off schedule. What will happen to you if you don't improve? What will you begin doing now?" The key is to accept feelings and the manner in which they are expressed. You want to let people know that you are upset, *and* you want the team member to change his behavior. So you need to help the member change negative behavior.

If you want me to open up to you with my feelings, ideas, and information, try any of these:

Smile at me

Look me in the eye

Have a good laugh with me

Listen to me

Shake my hand

Welcome me

Include me in your activities

Encourage me by:

   patting me on the back

   listening to me

   recognizing me for something

     I've done

Offer to help me

Tell me another joke

Take a little risk

Ask me for feedback

Draw me a picture

Cooperate with me

Tell me things that check out

Go an extra mile

Share with me some more

Sympathize with me

Offer me constructive criticism

Get to know me

Accept me for who I am

Spend some time small-talking with me about pleasant things

If you agree with me, say so

Confirm that you understand what I'm saying

Clarify to make sure we understand each other

Find interests we have in common

Find experiences we have in common

Tell me about a similar situation you've been in

Feel free to disagree with me, and give me the same freedom

Don't *always* disagree with me

If you disagree, then criticize my ideas, not me

Reassure me when things aren't going well

Empathize; take the time to feel how I feel

Tell me about my *behavior* that you don't like

Help me settle our conflicts

Tell me I'm valuable to the team

In general, I will open up to and trust those people who:

Are honest with me

Are sincere

Keep their word

Are genuine

Ask me a question

Tell me a good joke

Talk to me

Say hello

Ask me how it's going

Ask me another question

Share with me

Explain it to me

Spend time with me

Identify with me

Work with me on something

Play with me (ping pong, darts, etc.)

Open up to me

Offer me some more help

Forgive my mistakes

Say, "I like you"

Figure 4.9. Behaviors Which Facilitate the Development of Trust.

• ENCOURAGE OTHERS TO ACCEPT RESPONSIBILITY FOR THEIR FEELINGS. Just as the manager must learn to avoid criticism and ridicule when he is angry, so too must the team members learn to handle their feelings in a constructive manner. As a leader you can encourage others to accept responsibility for their feelings in a number of ways: *Listen actively*—"You act really angry when . . ." *Reflect feelings*—"You say you feel upset when . . ." *Confront*—"I don't know if you realize it, but it is very unhelpful when you fly off the handle like that." *Point out consequences*—"Are you aware that when you lose your temper, other members get really uncomfortable and want to avoid interacting with you? What will happen if you continue to lose your temper?" *Deliver natural consequences*—"If you continue to lose your temper like that, people will be reluctant to work with you."

• CREATE OPPORTUNITIES FOR PEOPLE TO WORK TOGETHER. Strive to design work so that people have to work cooperatively in order to achieve team goals. If people must work together to achieve common purposes, then, with guidance and training, they will learn how to work as a unit to do so. Publish team goals. Clarify each person's role in achieving team goals. Clarify how the roles fit together. Reward individual and team effort with praise. Make sure each person sees how his output contributes to the team's goal.

• SPEND TIME TOGETHER. Trust develops only when and if people spend enough time together to get to know one another. Have regular sessions as a team to discuss the progress of the work. Ask for feedback about how to make work go better. Have regularly scheduled informal get-togethers to celebrate success and to have a good time together.

• GET FREE OF ROLES. Don't hide behind your position and status as a manager. Give yourself and your people opportunities to be unique and spontaneous. Get everyone in the team involved in decision making. Give members opportunities to design their own work. Reward productive expressions of individuality. Let people take risks in the team without ridicule or embarrassment.

• DEVELOP RULES THAT PROMOTE TRUST. Communicate your expectations very clearly, both those on work output and those on how people treat each other and work together. Develop rules that encourage people to respect one another. Publish norms that in your opinion and those of the team members promote trust, e.g., honesty, openness, responsibility, no name-calling.

• FOCUS ON THE QUALITY OF RELATIONSHIPS IN THE TEAM. As manager, you should help the team monitor the quality of relationships within it and identify ways to handle problems. Regularly evaluate the team's climate. Develop with the team ways to deal with problems. Teach team members how to communicate openly.

• PAY ATTENTION TO YOUR PEOPLE. Most people like attention. Attend to each member of the team as an individual person. Talk to each team member individually. Use good listening skills to show that you have heard their concerns.

• BE SPECIFIC. Express yourself and encourage others to express themselves as concretely and specifically as possible. Stating your wants, desires, feelings, and opinions directly personalizes the environment and encourages others to do so.

• GIVE YOURSELF AND OTHERS PERMISSION TO BE IMPERFECT. Permit yourself to be imperfect, to risk exposing yourself, and make mistakes. Risk sharing ideas that are "far-out" but which seem to be innovative. Let people experiment during work time. Let people "bootleg" other people's ideas if they believe that it will improve work. Don't punish people when they make mistakes.

• USE POSITIVE REINFORCEMENT. Learn to reward even the smallest contributions to team success. Recognize contributions to team success. Provide ongoing positive feedback to each member individually.

References

Bion, W.R. (1961). *Experience in Groups.* New York: Basic Books.

Gibb, J. (1978). *Trust: A New View of Personal and Organizational Development.* Los Angeles, CA: Guild of Tutors Press.

Harvey, J. (Summer, 1974). "The Abilene Paradox." *Organization Dynamics.*

Janis, I. (1972). *Victims of Groupthink.* Boston: Houghton Mifflin.

Luft, J. (1973). *Of Human Interaction.* Palo Alto, CA: National Press Books.

MacDonald, A.P., Jr., Kessel, V.S., and Fuller, J.B. (1972). Self-disclosure and Two Kinds of Trust. *Psychological Reports, 30*, 143-148.

CONTRACT EXERCISE TECHNIQUE

Purpose

The Contract Exercise is designed to develop agreement and trust in one-to-one relationships within a team. This technique helps develop trust in an atmosphere that is less threatening than that created by exercises that call for personal disclosure in front of a whole group. Setting mutually beneficial agreements increases synergy and develops and strengthens personal relationships.

Description

1. Have each team member write a short list about himself in each of these categories: enjoyable pastimes, past work experience, outstanding personal achievements, and areas of special knowledge. These are Strengths Lists.
2. Have each member list on a second piece of paper those things he would like to learn, skills he would like to develop, and resources he would like to have at his disposal. These are Needs Lists.
3. If the team has more than seven members, divide it into small discussion groups.
4. Have groups assemble the lists. (This can be done by placing them on a table or taping them to a wall at eye level.) Instruct each member to write his name on both of the lists and place the Strengths List on top and the Needs List below it, completely visible.
5. Tell team members they will soon be making arrangements with each other on an exchange of services. Give them 15 to 20 minutes to informally discuss the data on the sheets, to get a feel for the kinds of help they might be able to get from other group members or offer to them.
6. Present these specific definitions of *contract components*:
   - mutual consent—freely given arrangement by both parties to the contract
   - valid consideration—equal worth of the goods and services exchanged, and consequences of failure to deliver
   - competency—the capability of each party to deliver the goods or services agreed upon

     • lawful object—the legality or morality of the exchange
      agreed upon.

Invite questions and discussion.

7. Present these words to be avoided in contracting: more, less,
try, attempt, might, want to, explore, work on, think about.
Contracts must involve a definite commitment to outcomes
which can be objectively measured so that both parties know
when the contract has been fulfilled. Discuss this with the
group.

8. Pair off members and have each one spend 10 minutes developing a contract with another, using the form shown in Figure 4.10.

9. Repeat Step 8 two more times. At the end of this process,
each team member will have developed contracts with three
others in his group.

10. Emphasize that contracts should be open to renegotiation if
either party discovers that the contract will not work. Contracts that cannot be carried out to the satisfaction of both
parties should be renegotiated, because a considerable amount
of trust rides on them.

The specific categories used to generate the Strengths Lists and
Needs Lists are open to change. You also may want to specify
items in one or more of the categories as work-related.

Some team members will find it hard to think of outstanding
accomplishments or areas of special knowledge. They need not
have won medals for accomplishments or be renowned experts in a
field of knowledge. An outstanding accomplishment is simply
something a person has done that he feels proud of. Areas of
special knowledge pertain to what a person knows the most about.

This exercise takes an hour-and-a-half to two hours. Much
relationship-building takes place during that time. Team members
become better acquainted with each others' strengths and goals,
establish a plan for a synergistic exchange of services, and create a
vehicle for developing and strengthening relationships.

This exercise involves a risk. It is that team members will fail to
carry out the agreements, thereby losing instead of gaining mutual
trust. Common causes of contract breaking are unrealistic or
half-hearted commitments, unspoken assumptions, and failure to

Name _____
Date _____

CONTRACT AREAS	GROUP MEMBERS			
	Name:	Name:	Name:	Name:
What I want from him or her				
What he or she wants from me				
What I want for myself in this relationship				
Observations on process				

Figure 4.10. Contract Exercise.

specify how each party will know that the contract has been fulfilled. The importance of carrying out or renegotiating contracts must be emphasized. Consequences for failure to do so should be specified and agreed upon by both parties.

Example

This exercise has been used with a state government's child welfare agency. The group was to develop interdepartmental teamwork so that hard-to-place adoptable children would be placed more quickly in homes. Members of the group were drawn from several different departments within the agency. They worked with client files on different aspects of the process. The agency's management felt that a mutual respect for each department's processing requirements and effort in placing the children was essential.

The Contract Exercise Technique served as an introduction for the personnel involved and as a humanizing activity. Managers and staff from the various departments were formed into groups with members of other departments. The Strengths Lists and Need Lists provided vehicles for the personnel to get to know each other in a positive way as fellow performers.

CONFLICT DIALOGUE TECHNIQUE

Purpose

This experience provides team members an opportunity to discover and share their attitudes toward conflict and ways of dealing with it. The exercise is structured to open the individual team member to become more aware of how he or she manages conflict and to develop more trusting relationships in the team.

Description

To use the Conflict Dialogue:
1. Form the team into pairs of dialogue partners.
2. Give each partnership (or dyad) a small booklet containing a series of open-ended statements about conflict, one statement per page; see Figure 4.11.

MANAGING CONFRONTATION: Conflict Dialogue

- -

Directions:
Read silently. Do not look ahead in the booklet.

This booklet contains a series of open-ended statements intended to help you discover and share your reactions to confrontation and conflict and your ways of dealing with it. You also will have an opportunity to learn from your partner's responses. The ground rules to be followed:

1. Take turns initiating the discussion.
   Complete each statement orally. (Please do not write in the booklet).
2. Do not look ahead in the booklet.
3. Do not skip items. Respond to each one in the order in which it appears.

When both you and your partner have finished reading, you may turn the page and begin. (Dotted lines indicate page breaks for booklets.)

- -

Conflict is . . . . 1.

- -

The time I felt best about dealing with
conflict was when . . . . 2.

- -

When someone disagrees with me about something
important, I usually . . . . 3.

- -

When someone challenges me in front of others,
I usually . . . . 4.

- -

When I get angry, I . . . . 5.

- -

When I think of negotiating, I . . . . 6.

- -

The most important outcome of conflict is . . . . 7.

- -

I usually react to negative criticism by . . . . 8.

- -

When I confront someone I care about, I . . . . 9.

- -

Figure 4.11. Open-Ended Questions.

- -

I feel most vulnerable during a conflict when . . . . 10.

- -

I resent . . . . 11.

- -

When someone avoids conflict with me, ... 12.

- -

My greatest strength in handling conflict is . . . . 13.

- -

Here is an actual situation in which I was involved in a   14.
conflict (explain).

What do you think I did? How do you think I felt?

(Tell your partner how accurate his or her prediction is.)

- -

When things are not going well I tend to . . . . 15.

- -

I imagine that you handle most conflict by . . . .

(Check out your prediction with your partner.)   16.

- -

I will sometimes avoid unpleasant situations
by (explain) . . . . 17.

- -

I am not apt to confront people in
situations such as . . . . 18.

- -

I usually hide or camouflage my feelings when . . . . 19.

- -

My greatest weakness in handling conflict is . . . . 20.

- -

When I think about confronting a potentially
unpleasant person, I . . . . 21.

- -

I sometimes avoid directly confronting
someone when . . . . 22.

- -

Figure 4.11 (Continued)

3. Instruct the members in how to carry out the activity. In particular, ask team members to be open and accepting of each other's feelings and points of view (rather than arguing), take responsibility for personal feelings by saying "I" rather than "one should" or "one might," be willing to take risks, and give here-and-now responses rather than general or hypothetical ones.
4. Each dyad partner reads the first statement silently.
5. One partner responds candidly while the other listens. Then the other partner shares his or her response while the first listens.
6. The dyad partners read the next statement silently.
7. The other partner responds first this time.
8. Dyads continue in this fashion, taking turns speaking first, until all the statements in the booklet have been dealt with. No record of the responses is kept. All responses for a page must be completed before the next page is read. Each statement is taken in the order in which it appears in the booklet.

Conflict is a fact of team life (and life itself). This exercise makes it easier to discuss conflict situations in the group by putting the focus on conflict itself, and by focusing on an exchange of views rather than on resolving specific conflicts *per se*. Team members learn how their partners react to conflict, and gain insights into how best to deal with conflict themselves. This deepening of mutual understanding usually leads to an opening of trust between the partners.

For this exercise to achieve its purpose, it is important that partners do not advise, admonish, or preach to one another, but instead speak of what they themselves do and feel, and simply listen with acceptance.

Example

The Conflict Dialogue Technique has been used with representatives of two different departments in a large bank. One unit, Information Systems, provides services to the International Banking unit. The International group requests systems/programming services from Information Systems. Typically, conflict occurs during the process when programming parameters are determined inadequate for International's needs. The subsequent delays, meetings, and duplication of effort are costly and unnecessary.

Upper management implemented strict controls over both units to avoid problems. The result was a reduction in the number of projects requested and produced. In other words, the controls encouraged the two departments to *avoid* working together, rather than risk reprisal for project difficulties.

When Conflict Dialogue was introduced, it succeeded in creating a forum for the release of frustration and subsequent understanding of each work unit's circumstances. Confusion over accountability for maintaining regular communication channels was a major issue, with no one really taking responsibility for recognizing problems and publicizing them so corrections could be made promptly. The International Banking unit agreed to identify necessary changes within three days of recognizing the need, while Information Services offered to respond to change requests within ten days of receipt.

The bank reduced waste, increased the number of projects per quarter, and decreased the completion time required per project. Overall, the improvements in "opening up" the process led to better morale and improved individual productivity.

Resource

Annual Handbook for Group Facilitators. (1979). Conflict Management: Dyadic Sharing. San Diego, CA: University Associates, pp. 54-59.

PRISONER'S DILEMMA TECHNIQUE

Purpose

Prisoner's Dilemma is a competitive exercise. It is designed to explore trust between group members and the effects of betrayal of trust. It also highlights the effects of interpersonal competition.

This exercise is very helpful when a group has been assigned or is considering a task involving a high degree of risk and a high need for trust. At the outset, it pinpoints those individuals in the group who have a need for an "I win, you lose" outcome. It also allows the group to process the concept of "I win, you win too" and heads off some of the disruptive aspects of competition within the team.

This exercise should not be used with a newly formed group. Where the team has not had time to develop the necessary cohesion, the game itself can produce a disruptive work atmosphere.

Description

Prisoner's Dilemma works as follows.

1. Divide the team into two groups of not more than eight members each. If there are more than sixteen people present, the remaining members act as observers.
2. Give each player on both teams a tally sheet on which to record the points scored by each team in the ten rounds of play.
3. The game simulates the situation of two prisoners captured by the police. The police offer immunity to the prisoners, in exchange for their testimonies. In using this technique with business groups, the original prisoner context is abandoned in favor of opportunity for financial or other tangible gain. This could be currency, sales, savings, or any other commodity. The important point is that both groups understand that winning occurs when both remain silent, i.e., maintain the combined welfare of the entire organization, instead of sacrificing one group for another. Team members engage in brief discussion of their competitive strategy and the relative merits of keeping silent *vs.* confessing. Competitiveness, risk-taking, trust, and loyalty are common themes in these discussions. On each round, the prisoners must decide whether to keep silent or testify. Points are awarded according to the following pay-off matrix:

		Player B		
		Keeps Silent	Testifies	
Player A	Keeps Silent	+10	−25	A gets
		+10	+25	B gets
	Testifies	+25	−10	A gets
		−25	−10	B gets

If both players keep silent they both win. If they both testify they both lose. However, if one keeps silent while the other "sings," the squealer wins big and the silent partner loses big.

4. Each team represents one of the prisoners. On each round the team arrives at a decision on whether to keep silent or testify. Teams sit far apart so they cannot hear each other (often in separate rooms).

5. On each round, both teams write down their decisions or signify them in some other way without the other team's knowledge.

6. Examine each team's choice, consult the matrix, and announce the payoff.

7. Prior to round 4, each team sends a delegate to the center of the room to negotiate. After the negotiations, play continues as before, except the pay-offs for round 4 are doubled.

8. Prior to round 10, each team again sends a delegate to the center of the room. Pay-offs for round 10 are multiplied by four.

9. The winning team buys lunch for the losing team. If both teams end up with less than zero, they buy lunch for the group leader. If both end up with zero, the group leader buys lunch.

10. The team reassembles as one group. Observers share their insights. The entire group discusses the experience.

Example

A large electronics firm used a variation of the Prisoner's Dilemma in the first of three training sessions of a participative management seminar. Participants were divided into groups of four and told to "Earn as many points as you can." The game was played *within the foursomes*, as individuals or partnerships (dyads) vied against each other. When all ten rounds were over and the points were counted, the winner was *not* the individual or partnership with the most points, but the *foursome* with the highest point total. This came as a surprise to participants, who thought they were competing against others in the foursome. The winning foursome, of course, was the one which most often achieved the win-win outcome. The individual or partnership with the highest point total within the foursome was actually the one who did the most *damage* to the team's cause by double-crossing the others. The exercise was effectively followed by a discussion of individual versus team thinking.

Resource

Rappaport, A., and Chammah, A. (1970). *Prisoner's Dilemma.* Ann Arbor Paperbacks, 1970.

GROUP CLIMATE SURVEY TECHNIQUE

Purpose

Groups in a basic assumption mental state (BAMs) are in a nonwork state—an inappropriate mode of functioning. This instrument is designed to help spot the basic assumption mental states in operation:

- fight/flight (avoidance-openness),
- dependency/counterdependency (dependency-autonomy), or
- fracturing (collusion or pairing for nonwork).

Characteristics of a basic assumption mental state in operation were listed in Figure 2.1. This instrument is based upon the work of Bion. (see Chapter 2, Bion, 1962). Its purpose is to diagnose the "mental state" of a team and in doing so, predict its readiness to engage in meaningful and productive work.

Description

The instrument's items can be scored on one of the three dimensions of BAMs. Participants show their level of agreement for each item, and transfer their scores to a BAMs grid. Scores show the basic assumption mental states present.

Items in the Group Climate Survey (see Figure 4.12) are shown below. Under each item in the survey, the user must respond by circling a point on a scale of 1 to 9, ranging from (1) Totally Disagree, to (9) Totally Agree. We paired our descriptors and Bion's as follows on page 91.

GROUP CLIMATE SURVEY
Karl Smith

In the survey, the following numbers relate to Fight/flight or Avoidance-openness: 2, 10, 12, 21, 22, 23; the following relate to Dependent-counter-dependent or Dependency-autonomy; 3, 4, 6, 9, 11, 13, 15, 16, 17, 18, 19, 29, 30, 31, 32, 33; and the following relate to Fracturing or Nonwork-work; 1, 5, 7, 8, 14, 20, 24, 25, 26, 27, 28, 33, 34.

1. I know each day what work needs to be accomplished.
2. I would describe the atmosphere in this office as conducive to creativity.
3. I prefer to learn by doing.
4. My best learning occurs through experiencing life and reflecting on that experience.
5. I want to set my own goals and direct my own learning.
6. I prefer being taught by others what it is that I need to learn.
7. Completed tasks are characteristic of this office.
8. I believe that we could get more work done around here.
9. A few recognizable leaders are a must in order for any office to be a success.
10. Too much anxiety exists in our office atmosphere.
11. This office has a high level of *esprit de corps*.
12. Around here we face and cope with discontent.
13. Personal development is a priority of this office.
14. My job is a satisfying experience.
15. Major decisions should be made by a supervisor.
16. I prefer that some expert tell me what I should learn.
17. I like highly structured learning.
18. It is inappropriate to ask students to set their own learning goals.
19. I hate learning experiences where no one tells me what to do.
20. It is unusual for us to actually work at tasks more than 50 percent of the time.
21. Much of the time our communications don't make sense.
22. The same problems occur over and over again.
23. We have more negative feelings around here than positive feelings.
24. We don't manage time.
25. Time manages us.
26. We do a poor job of goal setting.
27. Our rewards aren't linked to goal achievement.
28. Our productivity is low.
29. The boss is a prisoner of the job.
30. If we had control over our work, management would panic.
31. Little freedom exists here.
32. Peers don't encourage you to strive for your best.
33. We stop as many projects as we start.
34. We set people up to fail.

Figure 4.12. Group Climate Survey.

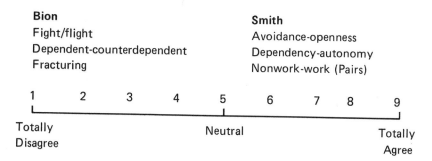

Bion
Fight/flight
Dependent-counterdependent
Fracturing

Smith
Avoidance-openness
Dependency-autonomy
Nonwork-work (Pairs)

```
  1      2      3      4      5      6      7      8      9
  |_____|_____|
Totally                   Neutral                  Totally
Disagree                                            Agree
```

Example

Groups develop a culture which is reflected in their behavior. Since one must infer culture from behavior, it is useful to have some concepts which help us to organize the behavior we observe. The Group Climate Survey helps us do this. It is based on the notion that groups operate on assumptions about how to deal with problems, how to work, and so on. These assumptions are called Basic Assumption Mental States. Groups operating in a BAMS are essentially in a non-work state. These assumptions are not conscious norms. The group members are not aware of their non-work state assumptions.

The technique is used in a manner similar to climate surveys. For example, in one company, there was a lot of obvious procrastination. We felt it would be helpful to provide team members with an objective look at their functioning, especially relative to dependency and non-work issues. The survey was administered, the results tabulated and posted. We then set about to discuss the item ratings and their significance to the team's performance. Items on the Work-Nonwork dimension, for example, will illustrate the process. Item 1 was rated (on average) at 2, which means that group members were very unclear about expectations. We asked group members to explain their rationale for rating the item so low. It was made clear that performance expectations were not widely known for members of the group. It also turned out that item 33 and 34 were also rated in the vicinity of 2. Thus, we were dealing with a characteristic of the culture; this company simply did not specify its expectations in many areas of functioning.

The leadership style of the managers made it impossible for team members to obtain feedback about whether they were doing the right thing. Thus, a two-pronged action plan was developed. We designed a leadership training seminar, and we established clear job descriptions and performance standards for each job. A follow-up survey at six months and after one year showed that the team had become much more work oriented and had made significant improvement in their productivity and in the group's climate.

By working this process through an entire assembly area in a heavy machinery plant, we were able to improve overall productivity 10 percent while rework was reduced by 85 percent. The gains added 70 percent to before-tax profits.

Resource
OHRD Associates, 1208 Somerset Avenue, Austin, Texas 78753.

SUCCESS BOMBARDMENT TECHNIQUE

Purpose
Success Bombardment is designed to focus group members' thinking on the positive side of their work lives. In most groups, successes are not mentioned as often as failures.

There are many applications of this activity. It is especially good at the beginning of an effort at developing a team. Not only does it help the group to develop trust and attraction; it also helps to build confidence and increases the energy level and enthusiasm of the group members.

Description
Success Bombardment is appropriate for use *early* in the life of a group.
1. Have each member take a sheet of paper and, considering his or her own actions, list (1) successful experience of the past year; (2) a successful experience of the past month; and (3) a successful experience of the past week.
2. If the group has more than eight members, divide it into discussion groups of eight or fewer.

3. Have discussion group members share in turn their successes. Ask each member to go into detail and try to define what he did that led to the success. Have other members of the discussion group ask probing and clarifying questions; generate an informal list of the sharing members' skills. Give each person equal time for sharing successes.
4. Have the lists of skills duplicated and distributed to the whole team for future reference if desired.

Some members may have difficulty identifying success experiences, particularly within the past week. A success is simply an accomplishment that a person feels proud of. Talking openly about personal successes may feel risky or embarrassing to some. One risk is that proud accomplishments could be sneered at by others in the group. The group should be instructed not to evaluate, but to listen, clarify, and appreciate the stories as told.

Through this exercise, team members begin to discover the resources they have in each other and in themselves. People are often blind to their own strengths. Success Bombardment confronts them with their strengths as seen through other team members' eyes.

This activity builds trust and morale by dwelling on the positive, creating opportunities for mutual encouragement, congratulations, and good will.

Example

Two brief examples illustrate the potential of this activity. A team of special education teachers was brought together in a retreat setting to do some team building. The special education programs had just undergone a budget cut. Internal dissension and competition threatened to destroy any program possibilities. There was a need to do something that would help this group come to appreciate one another and encourage their working together. The group was divided into a number of subgroups which were instructed to ask each individual to share one or more things they had accomplished in the past in special education. After listening to this individual-sharing, the remaining group members would "bombard" that individual with what they perceived as the individual's strengths. When every member was thus bombarded, the entire group reassembled to share the experience and to process what had happened. The group reported that they felt closer to one another, that they had a deeper appreciation for one another's skills, and that they had a basis for networking and sharing in the development and implementation of their programs.

The activity has also been used in a business setting. In a paper products company, we formed productivity improvement teams (PITs) throughout the plant as a means of identifying production problems and discovering ways to solve them. These teams were composed of line people, support personnel, and supervisors. Members of these new groups were to function as teams in which each person had equal input into the work of the group. Thus, it was really important that the members of the group trust one another and work well together. To begin the team building process, we used the success bombardment activity to build trust, to help the team come to understand potential contributions each team member could make, and to generate enthusiasm. The PITs kicked off a major quality program in this company which still functions. In the first quarter of the initial year of the project, the teams saved the company over one million dollars through various cost containment programs. In assessing the company's performance productivity improvement, teams were identified as the factor most responsible for these savings. Specifically, the teams generated a new level of trust and shared values, which channeled individual and team effort towards common goals.

ORGANIZATION OPENNESS SURVEY TECHNIQUE

Purpose
Use of the Organization Openness Survey helps group members examine and assess the level of openness in their larger organization. It provides a springboard for discussing the relationship between openness, trust, and effective team or organization functioning.

Description

To use the Organization Openness Survey:

1. Obtain at least two copies of the instrument for each team member. (The instrument, composed of 60 questions, is given in Figure 4.13.)
2. Ask team members to complete the survey, describing an "ideal" organization.
3. Ask them to fill out a second copy, describing their current organization.
4. Have each team member score the instruments by obtaining a simple arithmetic average of the scale value of the 60 items.
5. Have team members share the average score from their "ideal" organization. Total these on a blackboard, easel pad, or newsprint sheet so that the whole group can see it. Compute the average.
6. Repeat step 5 for the "current organization" sheets.
7. Explain that the test is designed to measure openness in the organization. What do the results say about openness and organizational quality? If needed, draw a picture of the Johari Window found in this text and explain the "open" window as the one where the degree of "openness" determines the level of problem solving and learning that can occur in the individual, group, or organization. Both problem-solving effectiveness and learning are dependent upon the degree of trust and openness that exists in the group. Raise the question, What do the results say about openness and organizational quality?
8. Divide the team into groups of four to discuss questions such as these:
   - How does this organization compare with the ideal?
   - In what ways?
   - When you described this organization, what questions would you mark above 5? What does this say about the organization's strengths?
   - What questions would you mark below 5? What weaknesses does this point out?
   - How important is trust and openness to the effectiveness of this team?
   - Why?

ORGANIZATION OPENNESS SURVEY*

Please answer the next few questions before reading the directions and completing this form.

A. How long have you been in your current position (number of months)?.....
B. How long have you been with this organization (number of months)?   .....
C. Which of the following best describe your current position (circle one):
   1. Executive or very top management of this organization.
   2. Upper-management, responsible for numerous levels of middle managers.
   3. Upper-middle management, responsible for numerous managers.
   4. Middle management.
   5. Lower-middle management.
   6. First line supervisor.
   7. Non-exempt personnel.

DIRECTIONS: The Organizational Openness Survey is designed to create an in-depth analysis of the degree of openness present in your work group or unit based on the composite data from you and others within your organization. All responses are completely confidential; data are compiled as a group rather than individually.

Since the terms "organization," "work unit" or "team" can be somewhat broadly defined, you are requested to use the following definition of organization as you complete this form: (Person who administers the survey will provide the definition.)

Once you are clear about the definition of the term "organization", respond to each of the following statements based on the following criterion:

THE DEGREE TO WHICH YOU PERSONALLY AGREE OR DISAGREE THAT THE STATEMENT IS AN ACCURATE DESCRIPTION OF YOUR ORGANIZATION (WORK UNIT).

Indicate the degree of your agreement or disagreement by circling the ONE number that is appropriate following each statement.

*Derived from 110-Item Inventory titled *Organizational Performance Profile* by Oscar G. Mink and Donna R. Neusch (OHRD Associates).

Figure 4.13. Organizational Openness Survey.

A scale similar to the following is used with each item. (Numbering should be reversed for indicated items.)

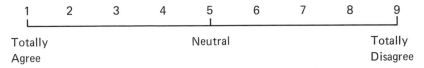

1. This organization strives to create a sense of fairness in its decision making regarding its employees.
2. There is a sense of purpose and meaning within the organization.
3. The atmosphere is grim and cheerless, very little room for any light-heartedness.
4. The organization is dynamic, always in process, rather than mechanistic or robot-like in its functioning.
5. There is allowance for dichotomies (dualities) by avoidance of black/white thinking.
6. Emphasis is on quality of work rather than allowing sloppiness and imperfection to slide by.
7. The organization appears to operate clumsily, to be straining, fatiguing, rather than moving smoothly, effortlessly.
8. My organization maintains an environment of truth, working to avoid dishonesty and covertness in INTERNAL operations.
9. The organization is comfortable with uniqueness, rather than imposing uniformity and sameness on its membership.
10. There is a sense of direction and self-sufficiency; the organization is proactive rather than reactive.
11. There is a reasonable, assured response to time pressures, rather than continual operation in a "due yesterday" mode.
12. Conflict is avoided here rather than confronted.
13. The organization provides enough time off for members to take care of personal and family needs.
14. Factors external to the organization (e.g., the economy, competition) seem to always have this organization on the defensive.
15. The organization has a real interest in the welfare of its members.
16. The difficult tasks are usually assigned to executive management.
17. Crises tend to prompt blame from the organization on factors outside of its control (e.g., the economy, competition, regulation).
18. This organization has a real interest in the welfare of its customers/clients.

Figure 4.13 (Continued)

19. Fostering good human relationships among the organizational member-
    ship is a low priority.
20. There is not enough time allocated to manage the workloads.
21. It is OK to make a mistake around here.
22. A cutthroat competition is maintained among the different work
    groups (i.e., departments, plants, divisions, task forces, etc.).
23. Feedback from organizational management is fair and objective.
24. There is an open forum for dealing with work-related frustrations.
25. Mistakes are viewed as learning opportunities rather than failures.
26. Inter-group collaboration occurs easily and is not strained.
27. Administrative policies and procedures are developed (or exist) as
    a sincere effort to help organizational members accomplish their
    jobs.
28. The organization works to reduce job-constraints for its members.
29. Feedback is straightforward, rather than indirect.
30. There are functional mechanisms in place that allow grievances to
    be addressed.
31. There is an honest commitment to group decision making.
32. Organizational goals, objectives, and values are easily identifiable.
33. This organizational structure encourages preoccupation with titles,
    status, and territory.
34. Members of this organization share goals, objectives, and values and
    put consistent energy into them.
35. Problems are clearly defined and quickly brought out into the open.
36. There is very little teamwork among organizational members in plan-
    ning and performance.
37. There exists a great deal of genuine liking and respect for others'
    judgments and opinions.
38. The organization fosters collaboration and fair competition in the
    reaching of shared goals.
39. Members have a strong sense of belonging and loyalty in this organiza-
    tion.
40. When confronted with problems, the organization solicits suggestions
    from its members.
41. The organization does not allow enough time to deal with problems.
42. It readily adjusts to the demands of a new situation.
43. This organization is sensitive to the effects of its actions on others.
44. The organization is diligent in taking corrective action to problems.
45. There are adequate resources made available for problem solving.

Figure 4.13 (Continued)

46. The organization resists changing its way of doing things.
47. There is flexibility in dealing with problems and a willingness to adjust policies and procedures to facilitate problem solving.
48. There is an unwillingness to let problems slide, steps are quickly taken when confronted with a problem.
49. The organization tends to use "problems" as a smokescreen for implementing hidden agendas.
50. Authority within the organization is based on purpose rather than position.
51. There is a reliance on the different skills of individual members rather than on the hierarchy.
52. The organization is oriented to the future, rather than to the past.
53. Management in the organization is easy to approach.
54. The emphasis here is on flexibility rather than on structure.
55. The organization is open to sharing the decision making process.
56. Organizational goals and priorities are obtained by consensus of key people.
57. The organization encourages informal communication between levels.
58. Individual skills and abilities are well utilized.
59. Organizational management relies on their higher position to influence the behavior of subordinates.
60. Decisions are made at those levels where the most adequate information is available.

Figure 4.13 (Continued)

Encourage discussion groups to get an answer from every member to each *key* or *selected* question before moving on.

9. Conduct a brief discussion with the whole group, using the following types of questions:
   - What were three points on which your whole group agreed?
   - What questions caused the most disagreement?
   - How does the relative degree of openness or closedness cause an organization or a team to be more or less effective?
   - How can *trust* and *openness* be developed in this team?

A major benefit of this instrument and exercise is that it focuses the team members' attention on trust and openness and graphically demonstrates the power of openness in life. The discussion that follows use of the instrument usually leads to a shared awareness of the desirability of openness and the will to develop it.

The instrument is easy to administer. Team members can usually work through it in approximately 25 minutes.

Example

There are many forms of climate surveys, all of which are potentially useful. This one is attractive to us because it is based on our work concerning trust and openness. We typically use this instrument as a beginning "diagnosis" of where a team or an organization is at present. This information is then used to develop a plan of action for improving the team's ability to learn and to solve problems. On one occasion, we were asked to form problem solving groups or "quality circles" in a heavy machinery manufacturing firm for the purpose of helping the company identify and resolve ongoing management problems and as a vehicle for helping the company develop a long range manufacturing plan. The people chosen to be members of the team had all had at least a year's experience with the company. In our first meeting, we discussed with the team the role of openness in influencing the productivity and quality of work life. We then had each member complete the instrument. The results we tabulated and shared with each task group. On each scale item for which there was an unfavorable response, the group discussed the whys and wherefores of the problem area and then scheduled the problem for solution.

The effect of the activity is that it allows members to share data which they may have previously hidden. It allows them to be objective about issues for which they may have some pretty strong feelings. It allows team members to share their feelings in a focused manner. In this manufacturing example, the team identified 6-10 areas in which they wanted to make improvements. For these areas, a problem solving group developed action plans. Since the original problem solving group consisted of unit managers with high level support, the action plans were implemented and closely managed. Results remain proprietary, but were described as "substantial." A second visible result was a clear improvement in the overall quality of the long-range manufacuring plan.

STRATEGY FOR FORMING GROUPS TECHNIQUE

Purpose

This exercise is flexible; it can be used for various purposes, including forming small groups out of a larger task group, spotting individual differences in personality or learning style, opening lines of communication within a team, and developing trusting relationships among group members.

Description

1. Design a personal data sheet for team members to fill out. Choose what information you will request. It can be very open-ended, calling for extensive explanation, or very simple, requiring single words or short phrases for answers. If you intend to use the data as a basis for forming groups, some of the items should tap into the criteria you will use to make these groupings. Examples of information requested may include name, address, age, interests, education, marital status, spouse's name, number of children, their names and ages, things you hate to do, skills you have outside of work, fantasies about vacations, gripes about a co-worker (who goes unnamed), the best restaurant you've discovered, the most fun you've ever had, the most terrifying experience you've ever had, the biggest fish you've ever caught, the best fish story you've ever heard, your favorite hero, etc.

2. Pass out the personal data sheets at a team meeting. Ask team members to fill them out in private before the next meeting. Tell them their responses will be as confidential as they choose. Encourage them to be spontaneous and uninhibited in their answers.

3. In preparation for a second meeting, take a large sheet of paper for each team member and draw lines on it, forming about a dozen blocks of various shapes and sizes. (See Figure 4.14.)

4. At the next meeting, give a large sheet to each team member. Ask each person to put the information from his or her personal data sheet on the large paper. The information can be laid out in any fashion the person chooses. Encourage the use of color, drawings, and other forms of creative expression. Foster a spirit of playfulness. (Note: Team members choose how much of their personal data to reveal, and how specific they wish to be. Be sure to provide plenty of colored ink pens and markers.)

5. Tape the large sheets to a wall and have team members walk around the room and view the results. Encourage informal discussion.

6. If you wish to use the data on the sheets to form small groups for further activities, you now have the information for doing so. The exercise will have already provided a get-acquainted and communication-stimulating experience.

The exercise provides a rich and flexible way to open up communications between team members and recognize individual differences. Preparation by the team leader is needed, in designing the personal data sheets and preparing the block pattern. The exercise can be done in about 30 minutes of meeting time.

Example

This exercise has been used in a very large computer manufacturing firm, as part of a lengthy orientation, indoctrination, and training program for new managers. In addition to basic information such as name, business phone number, marital and family status, and hobbies, the new hires were asked what part of the company they would be working for, their three main goals for the next five years, significant projects they would be working on, near-term objectives, outstanding personal achievement, and so forth. After the training program, this information was collected

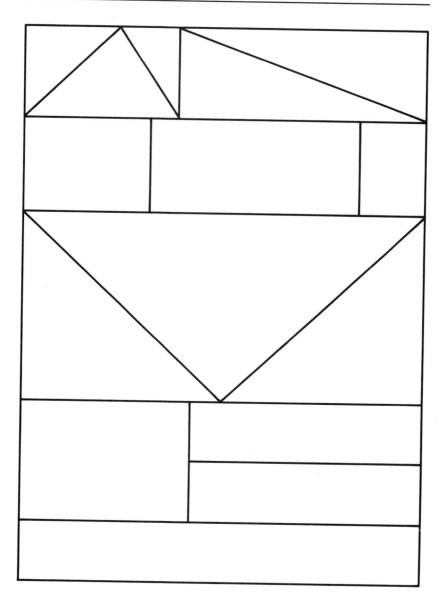

Figure 4.14. Example of Block Pattern for Personal Data Sheet Sharing.

and compiled into profiles of the individuals. The profiles were assembled into small directories (alphabetized by participants' names) and a copy was provided to each of the new managers. The directory formed the basis for a communication network which helped link managers with similar objectives, business work assignments and information resources.

DESIGNER NAME TAGS TECHNIQUE

Purpose
Designer Name Tags is an exercise in openness and is used as a get-acquainted task. It provides group members with the opportunity to find other people with similar interests, complementary skills, etc.

Description
1. Decide on four categories of information besides names that you would like strangers in the group to share. Examples are outstanding abilities, people important to you, people from history you admire, areas of expertise, hobbies, areas of interest, one thing you would do if you had a magic wand, current job, reason for joining the team, most memorable experience.
2. At the first team meeting, as members enter the room, have them write their name in the center of their name tags. Then in each of the four corners of the name tag, have each person write a word or draw a picture depicting the choices made in each of the four categories.
3. Encourage members to mingle as others are arriving and to get acquainted by explaining the words and pictures on their name tags.
4. When all team members have arrived and designed their name tags, have them pair up with someone they do not know or would like to know better and spend about five minutes sharing the data on their name tags.
5. Have pairs of patterns join into foursomes. Let each person be introduced by his or her partner. (This provides assurance that people are listening to each other and provides team members

with interesting feedback on how they are perceived by their partners.)

Designer Name Tags makes an excellent ice-breaker and promotes the formation of one-to-one relationships within a group of people. Significant insights can be gained in a short time and with minimal risk.

The categories of information for the four corners of the name tag should be chosen with care. Since this is a get-acquainted exercise, the focus should be on positive aspects of the team members' lives. Intensely personal or risky areas, such as politics, religion, and "true confessions" should be avoided. You may want to mix work-related questions with questions on personal attitudes, values, and goals. For example, categories such as "a person you admire" or "what you would do if you had a magic wand" may bring out a lot of information about the person's values. A category such as "something you've done well at work" may bring out skills and expertise that are immediately useful.

Example

Designer Name Tags has been successfully used as an opening exercise for a planning workshop in a metropolitan community. Name tags were completed during registration, prior to the first meeting. The topics for these name tags were: (1) areas of concern you have for the community, (2) areas of expertise in community planning, (3) most recent job-related accomplishment, and (4) current area of employment.

With no preliminary remarks the group leader called for pairing up and partner introductions. The name tags and the unexpected opening strategy combined to gain attention, familiarize participants with one another and required a verbal contribution from each person in attendance.

Resource

The Ungame Co.
14440 S. State College Blvd., Bldg. 2D
Anaheim, CA 92806

A POSITIVE ME TECHNIQUE

Purpose

This activity is used to enhance the feeling of trust among group members. Since work groups are often formed to perform a task, the opportunity for conversation to develop alliances is often limited. The exercise provides the opportunity for team members to learn about each other without the need for extended conversation.

Description

1. Introduce the exercise as an easy way to get acquainted.
2. Ask team members to divide a sheet of paper into three sections and label them Mind, Body, and Feelings. (Other categories can be used but should tap major dimensions of the person's identity. Other categories might be Past-Present-Future, Thoughts-Feelings-Attitudes, Skills-Attitudes-Knowledge, or Family-Career-Hobbies.)
3. Ask team members to write at least one positive statement about themselves in each category.
4. If the group has more than eight members, divide it into four- to six-member discussion groups. Have the team leader or any member of the discussion group share positive statements about himself. Then give the group two or three minutes to explore this information, asking questions, clarifying, and sharing similar experiences.
5. Repeat Step 4 until all members of the discussion group have shared their strengths with the others. A brief discussion in the entire team about major learnings, interesting things they noticed, differences in how they feel, etc., may be useful in coming to closure.

This activity is used to reinforce an atmosphere of trust and openness and to begin establishing acceptance of individual differences. It is a good activity to start a team meeting or a deeper team-building activity because it encourages discussion and communication. The positive nature of the exercise gives members a chance to feel safe, accepted, and better known by others. Mutual confidence is also enhanced.

This activity should be used no sooner than the second or third team meeting so that a nonthreatening group atmosphere can develop. Honesty and openness exhibited by the team leader may strongly influence honesty and openness among the other members. It may be a good idea, therefore, for the team leader to be the first to share strengths with the group.

Example

In a large communication corporation, a trainer used this technique to improve workshops on team problem-solving skills. After working with a group of trainers for two lackluster days, the trainer used A Positive Me to kick off the next training session. As the session began, the group took its usual reserved position. As the exercise proceeded, however, the climate changed noticeably. The air buzzed with conversation, sprinkled now and then with spontaneous laughter. Body postures and eye contact gave evidence that group members were listening attentively and were actively involved. This atmosphere carried over into the activities that followed the exercise. The exercise served to better acquaint participants with each other and to demonstrate how an atmosphere of trust contributes to the completion of a problem-solving task.

Resources

Gibb, J.R. (1979). *Trust: A New View of Personal and Organizational Development.* Los Angeles: Guild of Tutors Press.

Harvey, J.B. (Spring 1977). Organizations as Phrog Farms. *Organizational Dynamics*, 15-23.

Mink, Oscar G. *et al.* (1979). *Open Organizations.* Austin, TX: OHRD Associates.

See entire text, especially Chapter 1, on Openness; and Chapter 3, on Truth and Trust.

ABILENE PARADOX TECHNIQUE

Purpose

Many situations occur in organizations which *appear* on the surface to be disagreements but are actually *undiscovered agree-*

ments. Jerry Harvey calls this the Abilene Paradox. This technique includes three instruments designed to help you analyze the ability of your group to manage agreement and honestly disclose to one another. They will help you determine when your group is "taking a trip to Abilene" by failing to disclose information and manage agreement.

Description

Many organizational problems are perceived as conflicts but are actually not. Rather, they are situations in which existing agreement has not surfaced because people do not trust and communicate with one another. The failure to disclose and confront others with one's honest feelings often results from the fear of being dispensable. In short, people tend to feel that unless they agree with others in a group, the group will decide they are not "team players" and will take steps to get rid of them.

When people don't "level," they are forced to second-guess each other and may come to a false consensus which in reality no one wants. Harvey named this situation the Abilene Paradox after a personal experience—a failure to confront others which took him on a "trip to Abilene." Harvey's father-in-law proposed that the family drive fifty miles to Abilene, Texas, in a dust storm to eat at a "greasy spoon." Others, thinking he was serious, reinforced the idea. Finally, all decided to go, *although nobody really wanted to*. After returning home, the father-in-law revealed what he really felt. Others confessed they had not wanted to go, and a family fight ensued.

Trips to Abilene can be a way of getting nowhere in an organization. Harvey points out how critical it is for a manager or consultant to distinguish between *real and phony conflict*. The task of the group leader is to cut through surface agreement and test to see what the real agreement is before proceeding to planning or problem solution. Honest confrontation can lead to better group process, improved productivity, increased problem-solving skills, resolution of chronic ills, and improved trust in the group.

This technique includes three instruments (1) Organization Problem Analysis, (2) Diagnostic Survey, and (3) Confrontation Decision Process. See Figures 4.15, 4.16, and 4.17.

Organization Problem Analysis asks the respondent to address several open-ended questions intended to elicit a description of organizational conflict. The Diagnostic Survey is then used to determine each group member's view of his/her individual response to the conflict situation. A ten-item survey asks team members to describe their role in the conflict problem as either "characteristic" or "not characteristic." The more "Yes" answers ("characteristic"), the more likely you are on a trip to Abilene.

After tallying responses on the survey, the leader checks to see which conditions are seen as characteristic of the problem. Items 1 and 2 indicate the presence of a genuine conflict; Items 3 through 10 indicate a phony agreement, a trip to Abilene, characterized by blaming, fragmented cliques, and avoidance of disclosure at organization meetings. The Confrontation Decision Process is then used to guide the group through an analysis of "what if" items. It is designed to move the team toward resolving problems of agreement, making more effective decisions, and taking corrective action.

ORGANIZATION PROBLEM ANALYSIS

In the space below, take a few paragraphs to describe an organization conflict in which you are currently involved. Describe the situation from your point of view, including the underlying causes, your role and the role of other principals who are central to it. After you have finished, turn the page and answer the questions which make up the Diagnostic Survey.

Figure 4.15. Organization Problem Analysis.

DIAGNOSTIC SURVEY

Directions: For each of the following questions please indicate whether the conditions described *are* or *are not* characteristic of your role in the conflict or problem which you described.

Condition	Characteristic	Not Characteristic
1. You frequently feel angry, frustrated, unhappy, and impotent when trying to deal with the problem or situation.	....	....
2. You spend a lot of time and energy in trying to deal with it.	....	....
3. You frequently place blame for much of the problem on others— other individuals, other groups or the boss.	....	....
4. You tend to limit your "open" discussion of the problem to sessions involving sub-groups of trusted friends and associates during coffee, lunch, or informal "closed door sessions." During these sessions you seem to be in basic agreement with others as to the cause of the problem and the solution which would be effective in solving it.	....	....
5. Your attempts to influence the solution of the problem or to definitely solve it do not seem to work. In fact, such attempts frequently seem to compound the problem and make it worse.	....	....

Figure 4.16. Diagnostic Survey.

Condition	Characteristic	Not Characteristic
6. You frequently find you are looking for a way to "escape" from the tensions generated by the problem. For example you may avoid meetings, take sick leave and vacation, or look for jobs or more satisfying organization affiliations elsewhere.	....	....
7. You frequently feel cautious, less than candid, and/or "closed" when talking to all but your most trusted associates in your organization about the problem and your ideas for solving it.	....	....
8. You frequently carry on "fantasy" conversations with persons key to the problem and find yourself wishing you had the "nerve" to say things to them "that really need to be said."	....	....
9. You notice that other persons in the organization frequently talk about the problem one way in private and other ways in public.	....	....
10. The problem seems to be getting more complex the longer it remains unsolved.	....	....

Figure 4.16 (Continued)

CONFRONTATION DECISION PROCESS

Take the situation you have just described.

1. In an "unedited" fashion, what action would you really like to take?

2. What keeps you from taking the action you want to take?

3. If you *take* the action you want to take, what is the worst thing that could happen? Estimate its probability.

4. If you take the action you want to take, what is the best thing that could happen? Estimate its probability.

5. If you *fail* to take the action you want to take, what is the worst thing that could happen? Estimate its probability.

6. If you *fail* to take the action you want to take, what is the best thing that could happen? Estimate its probability.

7. If you take the action you want to take, what is most likely to happen? Estimate its probability. Can you "afford" the risk?

8. If you fail to take the action you want to take, what is most likely to happen? Estimate its probability. Can you "afford" the risk?

9. What help would you need from others to take the action you want to take?

10. Do you want to take action? If so, what action do you want to take and how do you plan to go about it?

Figure 4.17. Confrontation Decision Process.

Example

We have applied this three-part tool in many settings with very positive results. In one case, the process helped an executive staff realize the opportunities and benefits of strategic team development.

The company is the leader with a seven percent share in a highly fragmented market. Despite a move toward decentralization, difficulty in competing against strong, local independents led to the decision to take inventory of the work interrelationships throughout the company. The instrument exposed the organization's failure to achieve a trust level that would enable field managers to promptly reveal local market difficulties. As a result of this delayed or hidden communication, problems surfaced late and decisions were often made under crisis conditions. While the effects of the lack of trust were readily apparent to everyone, the causes surfaced only after several strategic sessions working through the Organization Problem Analysis tool.

In the course of forcing accountability to the field, the organization had not established a sufficient level of trust and openness to ensure accessibility of home office staff resources as needed.

By encouraging and, in fact, requiring field managers to communicate certain types of problem situation (i.e., landlord complaints, pending loss of key staff members) the organization has begun to open up the decision-making process and *anticipate* solutions. Improvements in decision-making were slow but visible, as are the early signs of improved financial performance.

Resource

Harvey, Jerry. (1974). The Abilene Paradox: The Management of Agreement. *Organization Dynamics, 3*, 63-80.

5

RECOGNIZING AND UTILIZING
INDIVIDUAL DIFFERENCES

Each person is unique. An individual develops a particular style that becomes his personal signature. It says: "This is me. This is who I am." This individuality of style and expression is an important element in work situations, since normally it is a dynamic source of motivational energy and drive. When tapped, it yields levels of productivity far in excess of what is typically expected in large organizations, where individuality is frequently overlooked or consumed by group direction.

Often, individual needs are in conflict with group needs. While we need to realize our uniqueness, we also need to sense connectedness to a team or group. To belong, one must harmonize with the needs of others and in so doing may need to *compromise personal desires and actions.*

In a healthy team setting, the individual is accepted and organizational norms grant opportunities for self-expression; in an unhealthy team setting, the individual is either allowed to tyrannize the group, or is suppressed and punished for asserting his or her individuality. Without rules and structure, the individual does not learn how to belong; with too many rules or with harshly administered or unfair rules, the individual learns to repress personal instincts and "fall in line" with group consensus. The challenge for the effective team leader is to build and maintain a balanced setting in which people can work toward common goals and, at the same time, express their fundamental differences.

What Is the Sense of Uniqueness?
When we work in a setting in which we are (1) treated as impor-

tant, (2) permitted to express ourselves without fear of criticism, and (3) helped to succeed at what we do, we reveal our individuality. This focus on inner self becomes an anchor or frame of reference from which we act. It provides a perspective from which we recognize our boundaries so that we can say, "This is me; this is not me." In a healthy team, each member develops unique ways of working and creating which are consistent with the team's mission and goals.

How Does the Work Group Influence the Individual's Sense of Uniqueness?

The team member's sense of uniqueness can be enhanced or threatened in a group setting. Even one who has a well-developed sense of uniqueness can be threatened in a repressive climate. On the other hand, a person with a weak sense of uniqueness can become more confident in a healthy team environment.

Yankelovich (1981) has documented a significant change in the ethics of American workers. During the 1970s many Americans pursued self-fulfillment at the expense of other forms of meaningful involvement. Most began to understand the bankruptcy of this "doing your own thing" type of self-aggrandizement. As society entered the 1980s, people began to seek more meaningful and permanent life commitments, including commitment to careers or jobs. The pursuit of self-fulfillment was discovered to be an empty pursuit and was replaced by a new set of values— values which have been integrated into mainstream American culture. Today, people believe they should be treated with respect and dignity and they expect this from their work settings.

The implication of this shift in values is paralleled by a rise in overall levels of education of American workers and a collective commitment to boost productivity. In the future, successful organizations will be those that provide the employee with a place to belong and opportunities to contribute in a unique way to the organization's goals. Two recent works, *The 100 Best Companies to Work for in America* (Levering *et al.*, 1984) and *In Search of Excellence* (Peters and Waterman, 1982), provide us with descriptions of companies which do this successfully and, not coincidentally, also produce consistent patterns of growth and profitability.

Successful organizations, groups, and teams provide a context for their members that encourages self-expression and the use of unique skills and talents to achieve collective goals. By recognizing and accepting individual differences, the team discovers how to work together, how to make the most of unique contributions to team goals, and how to help each member achieve personal and professional growth.

How Does the Acceptance and Recognition of Individual Differences Affect Team Performance?

People perform best when they are confident about their ability to achieve. Organizations that recognize this relationship stand a good chance of exposing otherwise dormant human potential. The management team of a large printing company was concerned about low productivity throughout its operation. All its efforts to improve productivity were unsuccessful. Management decided to involve the manufacturing line organization directly in finding a solution to the problem. Productivity Improvement Teams (PITs) were set up throughout Manufacturing, one for each product area. The goal was to improve productivity in each area and the teams were given the responsibility for so doing.

What happened was exciting, yet typical. Working independently, different teams began to develop similar plans. Imaginative ways to improve productivity rates were discovered and, from this creative effort, problems were identified and solutions implemented. Results included significant improvements in productivity *and* a renewed commitment to company goals. Morale improved significantly, as employees reported how much the confidence accorded them by company management motivated them to accept accountability for reaching the objectives established for the PITs.

When a person's uniqueness is valued, he is willing to share his thoughts and ideas. As more people are given permission to share their unique perspectives on a specific problem, they discover, individually and in the team context, previously unimagined ways of doing things. Recognizing and utilizing individual differences releases energy previously withheld, denied, or repressed. Everyone becomes aware of it. The result is improved team performance.

Another reason for the improvement in team performance is that in expressing their uniqueness team members reveal to one another their individual strengths and weaknesses. Team members come to appreciate what each member *can* and *cannot* do well. Most tasks place a premium on a specific set of competencies. The team that encourages individual expression stands a far better chance of delegating roles by competency level than does the team which discourages individuality. It simply has more data on which to base decisions, data which can help considerably in effectively matching individual team members with suitable roles.

People understand intuitively that they are more effective when doing what they enjoy, that is, working at tasks which express their uniqueness. People also have a sense that attainment of individual excellence is tied to attainment of team excellence. People enjoy contributing their best efforts to the team, for in doing so, they realize they are helping themselves. Selye (1974) refers to this reciprocal give-and-take as "egoistic altruism"—in helping others succeed, each of us is helping ourselves. The team whose leader helps the team recognize and utilize individual differences will outperform the team whose leader has not mastered this important learning.

How Does the Team Leader Affect
the Sense of Uniqueness of Team Members?

Who has the greatest impact on norms and rules that evolve in a group? The team leader does. He defines the group's culture. From this point of view, the leader's belief in his own sense of uniqueness significantly affects how well the team learns to value and utilize individual differences. Leaders who can *recognize and manage* their own individuality are able to tolerate and accept the individuality of others. They can then act in ways which reinforce individual differences. The leader who is not confident in his own abilities will find it hard to communicate respect for or to utilize team members' individual differences.

A leader without confidence can over-identify with the team. The team becomes an extension of himself; its members become a means to his personal success. Because of this over-identification, he sees in the team his own fears of failure. He sets into motion the development of group norms and a team culture that inhibit individual differences. Team members performing at high levels often become sources of threat to such a leader. They are likely to be ignored or pressed to produce even more. Those performing poorly or deviating from expectations are likely to become victims of excessive criticism, since performance of the team is but a reflection of the leader's sense of worth. A leader with a weak identity confuses worth and performance, and when his worth is threatened because of poor performance, he adopts a defensive posture rather than a data-seeking, problem-solving one.

What Can Leaders and Other Team Members Do to Threaten Another's Sense of Uniqueness?

While sense of uniqueness is fairly stable over time, it can be diminished by persistent threats. It is important for *everyone* on the team to develop awareness of types of behavior that can threaten and even diminish a team member's sense of individuality. Even a strong team member can come to feel inferior and weak given the wrong kind of treatment. The team leader is in a position to influence, positively or negatively, each team member, both by what he does and by what he permits others to do.

All of us at times evaluate our sense of worth in terms of our most recent performance. A person whose performance is poor can interpret feedback about it as an indication that he is a failure in general. How the leader reacts to another team member's performance is important because it almost always enhances or diminishes the individual's sense of worth. Figure 5.1 lists experiences that can result in a team leader weakening an individual team member's sense of uniqueness.

What Can You and The Team Do to Reinforce the Individual's Sense of Uniqueness?

We have seen how you may diminish a person's sense of uniqueness through your responses to self-expression. Now let's become more positive and point out some ways to enhance the individual and encourage others to do so. Keep in mind as you model these and other positive behaviors that other members of the team will

You Can Threaten Another's Sense of Uniqueness When You:

1. Evaluate the person instead of his performance.

2. Fail to acknowledge the person's contributions or in any manner discount (devalue) them.

3. Discount (devalue) the person's ideas, problems, wants, or concerns.

4. Ignore the individual (worst of all).

5. Regularly insist that the individual defer his own needs to the needs of the team or other team members.

6. Fail to provide the individual with opportunities or other resources for self-expression.

7. Lock the person into a negative role.

8. Punish self-expression.

9. Do not listen to the individual.

10. Respond inconsistently to instances of self-expression (i.e., on one occasion you reward it, on another you punish it).

11. Place the highest value on being a "team player," as opposed to focusing on the larger value of the team's purpose or vision.

12. Strictly reinforce your own values to the exclusion of others.

13. Attribute weakness to the individual for his failures.

14. Dwell on a person's weaknesses, failing to recognize strengths.

15. Insist that everyone conform to the "way things are done."

16. Expect the person to succeed at a task where he lacks skill.

17. Fail to provide norms.

18. Fail to reinforce norms.

Figure 5.1. Behaviors Which Can Threaten Sense of Uniqueness.

begin to emulate you. Expect to feel the stress of change as you introduce new behaviors and processes in the team setting. In the long run, your persistence will pay off in a more productive and healthy team. See Figure 5.2.

Develop Communication Skills to Reinforce Uniqueness

We suggest in the section on TRUST that there are two basic categories of communication skills: skills for sending messages (self-disclosure skills) and skills for receiving messages (listening skills). Sharing is a concept which is useful for understanding the use of these skills. Sharing information will help develop group norms in which individual differences are recognized and valued. Sharing is a joining process; all who are involved are engaged in mutual giving and receiving.

Three kinds of communications skills that you and team members can practice will help you in sharing and in making intelligent use of individual differences. They are acknowledging, understanding, and approving.

1. **Acknowledging**

The word "acknowledgment" means to receive with respect. When you acknowledge another person's behavior, you validate him as a person, reinforcing his sense of uniqueness and importance. There are three skills you can develop to increase your team's level of acknowledgment:

Skill 1.—Attend to the people in your team—really see and hear them.

Skill 2.—Communicate non-verbally to the other person that you have seen and heard in an accepting manner. You then demonstrate that you accept him as a person and that you understand what he is doing and saying.

Skill 3.—Reflect what you have seen and heard; paraphrase and summarize what you hear said. Put into your own words the contents of another's message and communicate it back to the sender for verification.

2. **Understanding**

You understand another when you sense the "meaning" of his behaviors and can, in an acceptable manner, convey to him this understanding. This process is "empathy." By

You and Other Team Members Can Enhance the Individual's Sense of Uniqueness When You:

1. Give all persons opportunities to express themselves; encourage them to express themselves through their work where possible; reward self-expression when it occurs.

2. Recognize each person's special skills and talents.

3. Recognize what each team member does, and provide feedback on performance; reward competent performance, and correct incompetent performance.

4. Give as much responsibility for performance as possible to each person—*make people accountable for results*, rather than for the methods they use.

5. Encourage and reward innovation.

6. Encourage and reward reasonable risk-taking.

7. Spend time with each team member.

8. Get to know each person as an individual (find out what his values are, his special interests, etc.).

9. Treat each person as an individual.

10. Encourage openness by practicing openness.

11. Use special communication skills (outlined in Chapters 5 and 6).

12. Encourage creative approaches to solving team problems.

Figure 5.2. Behaviors Which Can Enhance a Sense of Uniqueness.

communicating empathy you reveal to another that you understand his feelings and accept his experience as real and important. *Often you may not share his feelings and you may not even approve, but you at least show that you understand.*

3. **Approving**

When you communicate that you value what the other person is doing and that you believe that his behavior is worthy of praise, you are approving. Effective use of approval is not a simple matter because it is selective: of all the actions of another, you must somehow filter out those you disapprove of and reward those you approve of. Does this mean that you should ignore those of which you disapprove? Yes and no! While ignoring the behaviors that you do not value, you are in effect shaping the other person's behavior. The catch to this process is that the other person may not value your approval; it is important for an effective leader to communicate genuine negative feedback (see Chapter 6) as well as approval.

Often, you may want to confront an individual whose behavior is negative or costs you something. You can do so effectively by using acknowledgment and understanding. Acknowledge the behavior, let the person know that you understand the situation, and let him know that such behaviors will lead to specific negative consequences. Is this what he really wants? "I have noticed that you are getting to work late several times a week (acknowledgment). I know it is hard to get organized (understanding). Still, it is important to your success on this job that you get here on time (consequences)." What you are doing is pointing out that he can be late if he chooses, but that negative consequences are likely. You are concerned and want to know if he is willing to change this pattern. If he does want to change, you are in a position to help him develop a plan of action. At least the individual knows he has a choice and is responsible for making it.

**Develop a Climate Which Reinforces Recognition
and Utilization of Individual Differences**

Although the following strategies are far from exhaustive, they are generally recognized as effective in establishing a group context for accenting individual differences.

Establish Team Policies that Encourage Uniqueness. A powerful way to encourage acceptance and recognition of individual differences is to develop practices and policies that reinforce and communicate respect for individuals. Ways to accomplish this include the following:

- Let team members know what results are expected of them, then give them flexibility in choosing methods to achieve goals.
- Seek input from each person on how to improve work in the team; then use the suggestions that are valid.
- Regularly recognize individual contributions to team goals.
- Let the team know that you expect members to treat each other with respect at all times.

Balance Team and Individual Needs. While needs of the team sometimes conflict with needs of individual members, a climate can be created in which both team and individual can win. For example, when conflicts between individual and team needs arise, find a way to give the individual a "small win." ("You can do this, but will you do that?") The important thing is to remember that winning is not an "either/or" thing. Both sides in a conflict can win.

Encourage Creativity. Give people freedom to do things differently. Always reward ideas, even bad ones, for a bad idea may lead to a good one. Most great ideas come from individuals and are enhanced by good groups.

The Vision

The vision structures the group to perform and determines the kinds of roles to be filled. For the team to achieve the vision, individual roles have to be created and filled with persons who are competent to meet the expectations associated with each role.

Each role is expected to produce *specific results*, which collectively will achieve the group's purposes. There are many ways to achieve results; building a sense of personal uniqueness to enhance group performance requires that individual team members have flexibility as they design the ways they will obtain the expected results and as they envision and create the roles they will fill.

Structuring for Individuality

Every group has a structure. Structure refers to the individual roles and functions in the group and the way these are organized for the team to achieve its objectives. Within structure, there must be potential for individual members to personalize their roles as team members.

Energy

Accepting and using individual differences are the processes involved in affirming team members' worth and the value of their work. These processes free people from the tendency to feel inadequate, releasing into the team's environment a motivational energy that can be used to help the team discover new ways to work together and achieve goals. A climate evolves in which there are high levels of participation, mutual give and take, accomplishment, mutual positive regard, positive identification with the group, and team cohesiveness.

Groups which purposefully involve each team member release energy that can be channeled into productive behavior; those that suppress individual differences use up a lot of their energy in protecting themselves. The latter tend to accomplish little, for they lack adequate energy and data to pursue team goals successfully. Important differences between groups that rank high in developing individual differences and those that rank low are outlined in Figure 5.3.

———

References

Levering, R., Moskowitz, M., and Katz, M. (1984). *The 100 Best Companies to Work for in America.* Reading, MA: Addison-Wesley.

Peters, R.J., and Waterman, R.H. (1982). *In Search of Excellence.* New York: Warner Publications.

Selye, H. (1974). *Stress Without Distress.* New York: Lippincott.

Yankelovich, D. (1981). *New Rules: Searching for Self-Fulfillment in a World Turned Upside Down.* New York: Random House.

Groups That Are Low	Groups That Are High
1. Show little ability to innovate.	1. Tend to be innovative.
2. Overemphasize rules to the detriment of performance.	2. Are flexible and organize to produce results.
3. Are overly dependent on the leader.	3. Show high levels of individual initiative.
4. Reinforce conformity even at the expense of productivity.	4. Utilize individual talents to increase productivity.
5. Are uncommunicative.	5. Are open in communication.
6. React to problems inappropriately (e.g., avoidance, panic).	6. Deal with problems by sharing and problem solving.
7. Demonstrate low energy.	7. Demonstrate a high level of energy.
8. Evolve manipulative relationships.	8. Develop open, honest relationships.
9. Are uncomfortable with changes and generally avoid them.	9. Accept changes and strive to deal with them productively.

Figure 5.3. Performance Differences in Teams
High/Low in Developing Individual Differences.

WORK VALUES TECHNIQUE

Purpose

Career choices, motivation, commitment to goals, job satisfaction, and other important variables are strongly influenced by what we value in a job. The Work Values instrument provides a vehicle enabling individuals and groups to examine what is most important to them in choosing and carrying out work.

Description

The instrument has 33 statements (see Figure 5.4). Each describes a potentially enjoyable aspect of a job, and is followed by a nine-point scale. The team member indicates on the scale the importance of that job quality, then chooses from those rated highest the five most essential to him or her personally.

1. Secure a copy of the instrument for each team member and distribute them. (Directions are self-explanatory.)
2. Allow about ten minutes working time.
3. As team members fill out the survey, post a list of the items from the survey (use newsprint, chalkboard, or some large display medium).
4. As team members finish the survey, ask each to come to the posted list and place a check mark by each of the top five values they have selected.
5. Have each member of the group share his or her rankings with a partner, explaining the whys and wherefores of his choice, especially for the top five. Allow the partner to respond, clarify, and probe, with the emphasis on understanding and accepting the sharer's values, *not* persuading him or her to a change of heart (although this can happen).
6. Conduct a five-to-ten-minute discussion with the whole group using questions such as these to focus discussion.
   - What items received the most check marks? Which values does the group choose most often as important?
   - What does this say about what it will be like to work with this group of people?
   - What does this say about the kinds of conflict that might evolve?

7. Emphasize that it is not important, nor even desirable, for everyone to agree on values. An effective team accepts and respects each other's values and each other's right to decide upon their values for themselves.

8. Combine parts into groups of four, and have each person share what he/she will need from the other team members in order to work comfortably with the group. Let each partner respond on his willingness to make such adjustments and to negotiate if necessary.

The key to success here is acceptance. The exercise provides an opportunity for team members to share information about themselves and to understand each other at fairly deep levels. Rejection or ridicule at such levels can be very damaging to the group's trust level. Acceptance and respect, on the other hand, will increase trust and reduce the need for team members to justify, explain, or defend themselves. This in turn frees up energy for problem solving and goal seeking.

The instrument does not provide an exhaustive list of important considerations people use in choosing their work. For example, there is no item to gauge the respondent's need for "Work that challenges me to perform to the limit of my abilities," and no item tapping status or prestige needs such as "Have a roomy private office and an expense account." The instrument is not strictly based on any particular theory of career choice or job satisfaction, but it functions well in preparing group members to confront a potential clash of values.

Example

The Work Value Technique was used in a telecommunications company to address a problem related to community service. The organization had a task force for planning and organizing a program of volunteer service to the community. After its first year, however, the group still had not come up with a plan because some members were not interested enough to participate in the meetings of the group and because those who did attend had difficulty reaching a consensus on what community problems were appropriate for the company to become involved with.

WORK VALUES INVENTORY

Please respond to the following thirty-three work value statements by indicating the degree of importance which you associate with that value using the nine-point scale:

1	2	3	4	5	6	7	8	9

Of No Importance　　　　　　　　　　　　　　　　　　Of Great Importance

1. HELP SOCIETY: Do domething to contribute to the betterment of the world I live in.
2. HELP OTHERS: Be involved in helping other people in a direct way, either individually or in small groups.
3. PUBLIC CONTACT: Have a lot of day-to-day contact with people.
4. WORK WITH OTHERS: Have close working relationships with a group; work as a team toward common goals.
5. AFFILIATION: Be recognized as a member of a particular organization.
6. FRIENDSHIPS: Develop close personal relationships with people as a result of my work activities.
7. COMPETITION: Engage in activities which pit my abilities against others where there are clear win-and-lose outcomes.
8. MAKE DECISIONS: Have the power to decide courses of action, policies, etc.
9. WORK UNDER PRESSURE: Work in situations where time pressure is prevalent and/or the quality of my work is judged critically by supervisors, customers, etc.
10. POWER AND AUTHORITY: Control the work activities or (partially) the destinies of other people.
11. INFLUENCE PEOPLE: Be in a position to change attitudes or opinions of other people.
12. WORK ALONE: Do projects by myself, without any significant amount of contact with others.
13. KNOWLEDGE: Engage myself in the pursuit of knowledge, truth, and understanding.
14. INTELLECTUAL STATUS: Be regarded as a person of high intellectual prowess or as one who is an acknowledged 'expert' in a given field.
15. ARTISTIC CREATIVITY: Engage in creative work in any of several art forms.

Figure 5.4. Work Values Inventory.

16. CREATIVITY (general): Create new ideas, programs, organizational structures, or anything else not following a format previously developed by others.
17. AESTHETICS: Be involved in studying or appreciating the beauty of things, ideas, etc.
18. SUPERVISION: Have a job in which I am directly responsible for the work done by others.
19. CHANGE AND VARIETY: Have work responsibilities which frequently change in their content and setting.
20. PRECISION WORK: Work in situations where there is very little tolerance for error.
21. STABILITY: Have a work routine and job duties that are largely predictable and not likely to change over a long period of time.
22. SECURITY: Be assured of keeping my job and receiving a reasonable financial reward.
23. FAST PACE: Work in circumstances where work must be done rapidly.
24. RECOGNITION: Be recognized for the quality of my work in some visible or public way.
25. EXCITEMENT: Experience a high degree of (or frequent) excitement in the course of my work.
26. ADVENTURE: Have work duties which involve frequent risk taking.
27. PROFIT: Have a strong likelihood of accumulating large amounts of money of other material gain.
28. INDEPENDENCE: Be able to determine the nature of my work without significant direction from others; not have to do what others tell me to.
29. MORAL FULFILLMENT: Feel that my work is contributing significantly to a set of moral standards which I feel are very important.
30. LOCATION: Find a place to live (town, geographical area) which is conducive to my life style and affords me the opportunity to do the things I enjoy most.
31. COMMUNITY: Live in a town or city where I can get involved in community affairs.
32. PHYSICAL CHALLENGE: Have a job that makes physical demands which I would find rewarding.
33. TIME FREEDOM: Have work responsibilities which I can work at according to my own time schedule; no specific working hours required.

Figure 5.4 (Continued)

After the first year, when it became time to appoint new task force members, the public relations department invited all those employees interested in serving on the committee to a workshop where the Work Values instrument was used. New members for the task force were selected among participants who gave high "importance" ratings to work values such as Help Society, Help Others, Work with Others, Creativity, and Community.

This process resulted in the selection of members who formed a much more active task force. The members, sharing common work values directly related to the task of the group, developed and began implementing a community volunteer service program within just four months.

Resources

The Work Values instrument, developed by Barbara Mink and Oscar Mink, is available from:

OHRD Associates

1208 Somerset Avenue

Austin, Texas 78753

A microcomputer based version of the Work Values Inventory is available from Paradise Software, Inc. of Austin, Texas. As part of the Organizational Performance Excellence Network (OPEN), this software version of the Work Values Inventory allows you to run a survey, quickly compile the results, and store the data for current or later use. Survey results may be reported by individual items with bar graph and statistical detail, or in list form by the five highest/lowest values or by rank order of all 33 work values. Group or individual data are easily combined to develop organizational norms.

POWER STRATEGIES ASSESSMENT TECHNIQUE

Purpose

The purpose of this technique is to help each team member examine uses of power. Each of the following questions is considered: What types of power do you use? How effective is each type of power? How do others respond when you use power strategies? How do you feel when others use them?

Description

The instrument is divided into three parts: Identifying Your Power Strategies (Figure 5.5), Assessing the Effects of Your Power Strategies (Figure 5.6), and Exploring Your Use of Power (Figure 5.7).

The first section lists 27 sources of power. Team members are instructed to note whether they use these sources of power for resolving differences in their personal and professional lives. Examples of power sources are wealth, rank, title, sex, age, physical force, and controlling information.

In Assessing the Effects of Your Power Strategies, the team member chooses five power sources used most often, then rates how extensively and how effectively he uses each, and reflects on how he feels when others use it on him.

Finally, Exploring Your Use of Power poses five questions for team members to consider and answer, preferably discussing their reactions with a partner or with the team as a whole. The questions concern self-limitations, effectiveness, and realism about self in the use of power; personal reactions to certain power models; and differences between personal and professional uses of power. Total working time for the form and the discussions that accompany it comes to about an hour and a half.

Participants may find it hard to respond to the first part of the instrument for two reasons. First, the subject of power is an uncomfortable one for many people, especially when it comes to examining the ploys they themselves use. People are blind to many things they do for power over others, and so are frequently unaware of their own power strategies. They are also often unwilling to admit some of the tactics that they are aware of using.

Second, some of the power sources listed are items not usually thought of as power sources, such as humor, eye contact, and furniture arrangement. It may take some deep thinking to determine whether one uses some power strategies. On the other hand, this is the main strength of the instrument. *People must think about power in new ways.* The instrument is especially effective in getting people who feel powerless to recognize how many different levers are available and to start using some of them.

IDENTIFYING YOUR POWER STRATEGIES

Directions: Write a short description of how you use the following power
strategies for resolving differences in your personal and professional life. If you don't use a particular power model leave that
cell blank.

Power Model   How I use the Power Model in:

	My professional life	My personal life
1. **Physical force** Body (i.e., pushing, restraining) Use of body (i.e., person hyper- ventilating) Mechanical extension of body (i.e., paddle, stick, gun, auto)		
2. **Wealth** Money and other real assets Control of Resources (i.e., bud- get officer) Contributions (i.e., largest con- tributor to an organization)		
3. **Rank** Hierarchical status (i.e., President, Supervisor, Dean, General)		
4. **Title** Earned or honorary title (i.e., Doc- tor, Reverend, Your Honor; e.g., "Dr. Smith is calling for a reservation" instead of "John Smith is calling")		
5. **Position** Temporary or permanent posi- tions (i.e., treasurer, secretary, committee chairperson)		

Figure 5.5. Identifying Your Power Strategies.

	Professional Life	Personal Life
6. **Status** Elite. Majority. Minority. (e.g., turning to the only woman on a committee to get the "women's opinion")		
7. **Reputation** Credibility (i.e., usually no title but person is respected) Visibility (i.e., using references to celebrities)		
8. **Sex** Masculinity/Feminity (i.e., using your sex as power; e.g., a woman gets a management position under the banner of "women's rights") As a trade-off (e.g., man gets access to information through secretary and then builds sexual encounter)		
9. **Seduction** Words (i.e., flattering or guilt-inducing statements) Behaviors (i.e., slap on the back, arm around the shoulder)		
10. **Physical Appearance** Physique/Build/Size (e.g., a 6'4" man has power) Appearance/Attractiveness (e.g., a very attractive male or female has power)		
11. **Speaking Ability** Voice loudness/softness Voice quality/delivery Mastery of vocabulary		

Figure 5.5 (Continued)

	Professional Life	Personal Life
12. Data Having exclusive possession of Selectively imparting		
13. Age Older persons Youth		
14. Experience Longevity with an environment (i.e., "When you have been around this place as long as I have, you will understand it") Experience in a unique environ- ment (i.e., "You don't know what it is like to work in a bank until you've done it")		
15. Withholding Response Verbally (i.e., silence) Affectively (i.e., "I don't care" or show no response) Activity (i.e., boycotting)		
16. Doing Something for Another Developing a feeling of obligation		
17. Name Dropping Calling on the name of a super- visor or well-known person to support a position or get something done)		
18. Race Similar to status (i.e., majority/ minority)		
19. Skill—Performance Not sharing your skill or knowl- edge		
20. Time Control of work or vacation schedules		

Figure 5.5 (Continued)

	Professional Life	Personal Life
Structuring meetings to have your items brought up right before scheduled adjournment		
21. **Disability** Using a real or supposed disability to get others to do something for you (i.e., "weak heart," "fragile female," "I've never been good at math")		
22. **Filibustering** Loud and boisterous voice Monopolizing conversation		
23. **Humor** Keeping people laughing while getting what you want accomplished		
24. **Mysterious** Being vague (i.e., "There are several people around here who . . .") Mystical		
25. **Eyes** Steady contact or no contact		
26. **Organization Culture** Using ghost rules or norms of organization to get something accomplished		
27. **Furniture/Space** Structuring arrangement of space and furniture to influence how people relate to each other		

Figure 5.5 (Continued)

ASSESSING THE EFFECTS OF YOUR POWER STRATEGIES

Directions: From the above list select five power models that you most frequently use
and evaluate them according to the following scales.

Power Model 1: _____

I use this power
    model . . .   minimally __:__:__:__:__:__:__:__:__: extensively
                                          1 2 3 4 5 6 7 8 9

When I use this
power model, I   very   very
see myself being . . .   ineffective __:__:__:__:__:__:__:__:__: effective
                                         1 2 3 4 5 6 7 8 9

When .... sees me
use this power model,
he/she sees me as   very   very
being . . .   ineffective __:__:__:__:__:__:__:__:__: effective
                                         1 2 3 4 5 6 7 8 9

When others use this
power model on me
I feel   _____ .

Power Model 2: _____

I use this power
    model . . .   minimally __:__:__:__:__:__:__:__:__: extensively
                                            1 2 3 4 5 6 7 8 9

When I use this
power model, I   very   very
see myself being . . .   ineffective __:__:__:__:__:__:__:__:__: effective
                                         1 2 3 4 5 6 7 8 9

When ...... sees me
use this power model,
he/she sees me as   very   very
being . . .   ineffective __:__:__:__:__:__:__:__:__: effective
                                         1 2 3 4 5 6 7 8 9

When others use this
power model on me
I feel   _____ .

Figure 5.6. Assessing the Effects of Your Power Strategies.

Power Model 3: _____

I use this power
   model . . .   minimally __:__:__:__:__:__:__:__:__: extensively
                           1 2 3 4 5 6 7 8 9

When I use this
power model, I   very   very
see myself being . . .   ineffective __:__:__:__:__:__:__:__:__: effective
                           1 2 3 4 5 6 7 8 9

When .... sees me
use this power model,
he/she sees me as   very   very
being . . .   ineffective __:__:__:__:__:__:__:__:__: effective
                           1 2 3 4 5 6 7 8 9

When .... sees me
use this power model,
he/she sees me as   very   very
being . . .   ineffective __:__:__:__:__:__:__:__:__: effective
                           1 2 3 4 5 6 7 8 9

When others use this
power model on me
I feel   _____ ,

Power Model 4: _____

I use this power
   model . . .   minimally __:__:__:__:__:__:__:__:__: extensively
                            1 2 3 4 5 6 7 8 9

When I use this
power model, I   very   very
see myself being . . .   ineffective __:__:__:__:__:__:__:__:__: effective.
                           1 2 3 4 5 6 7 8 9

When .... sees me
use this power model,
he/she sees me as   very   very
being . . .   ineffective __:__:__:__:__:__:__:__:__: effective
                           1 2 3 4 5 6 7 8 9

When others use this
power model on me
I feel   _____ .

Figure 5.6 (Continued)

Power Model 5: _____

I use this power
model . . .   minimally __:__:__:__:__:__:__:__:__: extensively
                                  1   2   3   4   5   6   7   8   9

When I use this
power model, I   very   very
see myself being . . . ineffective __:__:__:__:__:__:__:__:__: effective
                                    1   2   3   4   5   6   7   8   9

When .... sees me
use this power model,
he/she sees me as   very   very
being . . .   ineffective __:__:__:__:__:__:__:__:__: effective
                                    1   2   3   4   5   6   7   8   9

When others use this
power model on me
I feel   _____ .

Figure 5.6 (Continued)

EXPLORING YOUR USE OF POWER

Directions: 1. Discuss with another person or with your team your personal
use of power.

(a) Are you limiting the number of power strategies that you use?

(b) Are the ones that you do use effective for you?

(c) Is there a discrepancy between how effective you perceive your use of
power to be and how effective others see you as being?

(d) What did you discover when you thought about how you feel when a
particular power model is used on you?

(e) Is there a difference in the types of power models you use in your
personal life from the ones you use in your professional life?

2. Obtain participant support for your efforts to:

(a) Eliminate non-productive power strategies, or

(b) Try new power strategies.

Figure 5.7. Exploring Your Use of Power.

Example

The Power Strategies Assessment Technique has been used with a group of 30 volunteer services coordinators in a state government agency. The people in this group felt powerless to influence their volunteer staff since they had no authority or monetary incentives for motivating them. Use of the instrument helped them become aware of the power modes available and choose the ones that fit. They soon discovered that they could effectively influence their staff in several ways they had not thought of before, including (1) referencing authorities to preface suggestions, (2) recruiting someone with strong persuasive ability or leverage to present data and ideas, (3) trading on their experience within the organization to influence staff in deciding what to do, and (4) being selective in what information to share with staff and what to withhold.

Resource

The Power Strategies Assessment instrument is available from:
OHRD Associates
1208 Somerset Avenue
Austin, Texas 78753

ANALYSIS OF SKILLS IN GROUPS TECHNIQUE

Purpose

The Analysis of Skills in Groups Technique provides a simple vehicle for team members to examine their own strengths and weaknesses in contributing to the group's functioning. It can also serve as a mechanism for recognizing the different roles each member plays in the group's success.

Description

The instrument consists of 16 items (see Figure 5.8). Each item describes a *process skill* important in making a group successful.

ANALYSIS OF SKILLS IN GROUPS

Directions

This form is designed to help you think about your attitudes and behavior in groups (staff meetings, committees). First, read over the scales, and on each one place a checkmark at the point that describes you when you are a member of a group. Label this mark "P" for "present." Do the same for the point that describes where you would like to be as an effective member of a group. Mark this check "F" for "future." After marking all the scales, pick out the three or four that are your strongest skills and one that you would most like to change.

1.   Clarity in expressing my thoughts

1	2	3	4	5	6	7	8	9
Quite vague				Partly cloudy			Exceptionally clear	

2.   Ability to listen in an alert and understanding way

1	2	3	4	5	6	7	8	9
Very low				Typical				Very high

3.   Ability to present ideas forcefully and persuasively

1	2	3	4	5	6	7	8	9
Very low				Typical				Very high

4.   Ability to "stay with" the topic being discussed

1	2	3	4	5	6	7	8	9
Very low				Average			Excellent	

Developed by Gordon L. Lippitt. Reprinted by permission from *Eleven Instruments for Diagnosing and Planning Individual, Group, and Organization Development*, 1968. This instrument is a copyrighted publication of Organization Renewal, Inc. of 5605 Lamar Road, Washington, D.C. 20016, and is not to be reproduced without permission. Adopted to a 9 point scale by O. Mink.

Figure 5.8. Analysis of Skills in Groups.

5. Tendency to trust others

1	2	3	4	5	6	7	8	9
Quite suspicious				Typical			Extremely trusting	

6. Willingness to tell others what I feel (express emotions)

1	2	3	4	5	6	7	8	9
Conceal everything				About Average			Reveal everything	

7. Readiness to accept direction from others

1	2	3	4	5	6	7	8	9
Very reluctant				Can if necessary			Like to very much	

8. Tendency to "take charge" of the group

1	2	3	4	5	6	7	8	9
Don't try				Occasionally			Try very hard	

9. Usual behavior toward others

1	2	3	4	5	6	7	8	9
Cold				Moderate			Warm	

10. Reactions to comments about or evaluation of my behavior

1	2	3	4	5	6	7	8	9
Ignore them				Consider the source			Take them very seriously	

11. Understanding the feeling of others (empathy)

1	2	3	4	5	6	7	8	9
Don't know what they feel				Moderate Understanding			Really understand	

Figure 5.8 (Continued)

12.   Understanding why I do what I do (insight)

       1   2   3   4   5   6   7   8   9
       Don't   Typical   Really
       know   understand

13.   Tolerance for conflict and antagonism in the group

       1   2   3   4   5   6   7   8   9
       Can't   Typical   Like it
       stand it   very much

14.   Tolerance for expressions of affection and warmth

       1   2   3   4   5   6   7   8   9
       Can't   Typical   Like them
       stand them   very much

15.   Thinking creatively in groups

       1   2   3   4   5   6   7   8   9
       Seldom   Moderate   High
       contribute   output   idea
       ideas   production

16.   Tolerance of opposing opinions

       1   2   3   4   5   6   7   8   9
       Low   Typical   High

Figure 5.8 (Continued)

Examples are, "ability to listen in an alert and understanding way," "willingness to tell others what I feel," and "tendency to take charge of the group." Each item is followed by a nine-point scale on which team members indicate their opinions of their own abilities and tendencies, as well as the levels they would like to achieve.

To use the form for surfacing individual differences:

1. Allow team members ten minutes to fill out the form, assessing themselves and identifying the three areas where they would most like to improve (change).
2. Have team members choose partners who know them pretty well. Have pairs of partners join to form foursomes.
3. Have each team member silently go over the form and identify three strengths and one weakness for each of the other members of the foursome. This can be done in about five minutes.
4. Have each team member spend five minutes with each of the others in the foursome, sharing opinions of each others' strengths and weaknesses.
5. Have each team member get together with the partner originally chosen and discuss these questions:
   - How do others' views of my strengths and weaknesses compare with my self-perception?
   - What unique role do I seem to play in this group?
     What are my chief strengths or contributions?
   - In what *one* area would I most like to improve?
     How can I go about doing this?

The exercise provides for primarily positive and some negative feedback, increasing opportunities for clear, problem-solving confrontations between members. As a natural byproduct, it builds appreciation for individual differences, as team members pause to reflect on each other's skills, as well as their own.

Example

This process was adapted for use as a follow-up to a survival simulation on the first day of a three-day team-building workshop. The participants were a group of about 25 middle managers at a computer manufacturing company.

A group of eight of these managers participated in the simulation, while the rest observed. Each manager involved in the simulation had two observers assigned to watch him or her. The action was videotaped and played back to the group, while the trainer commented on strengths and weaknesses in the group's process.

Each manager in the simulation then joined with the two people who had been observing. This triad used the Analysis of Skills in Groups Technique to rate the group process skills of all three persons. This instrument was chosen because it taps key dimensions of group behavior, and it is short and nonthreatening.

After identifying one or two of each person's strengths and weaknesses, each member of the triad identified one group skill to improve. This led to the formation of simple helping agreements, such as, "I would like to express my objectives more clearly; the next time I express an objective, would you tell me what you understood me to say?"

One or two of the managers felt their skills were so weak that they wanted to improve in a number of areas. (This is a potential risk of this technique.) These people were being too hard on themselves, of course, and their triad partners felt they could not support so many change efforts. The trainer worked with these triads to focus on one or two of the most critical areas for change. The networks of mutual support built in this way encouraged the managers to feel safe in trying out new group skills, such as dominating less, tolerating warmth and affection, being more patient with conflict, and feeling confident about decision making.

After identifying their own individual strengths and weaknesses, the managers were in a much better position to identify others in the organization whose abilities complement their own. As a part of the networks of mutual support which developed, some of the managers formed partnerships with individuals with complementary strengths and weaknesses, enabling them to learn new skills in areas where they wanted to improve. These partnerships, referred to as "consulting pairs," increased each partner's capacity to perform new and unfamiliar tasks under actual work conditions and gave each an opportunity to develop new skills and to become more effective in group situations.

Resource
The Analysis of Skills in Groups instrument is available from:
> OHRD Associates
> 1208 Somerset Avenue
> Austin, Texas 78753

PLANNING FOR LIVING TECHNIQUE

Purpose
Self-awareness is basic to effective interactions with others. Planning for Living provides a unique set of tools for exploring, "Who am I?" "Where am I going?" and "Where am I now?"

Description
Planning for Living includes five exercises: "Life Line," "Who Am I?," "Eulogy," "Fantasy Day," and "Life Inventory." See Figure 5.9.

1. **Life Line.** Each team member draws a line representing his or her life as he or she has experienced it, and indicates its general direction for the foreseeable future. Team members then share and discuss their life lines in pairs or small groups.

2. **Who Am I?** Each team member writes down ten *different* answers to the question, "Who am I?" These can be major roles, traits, feelings, loyalties, etc., as long as they are important to the team member's sense of self. Team members then choose from their ten answers, rank-ordering them for which would be the easiest to give up and which the hardest. Team members then discuss results of this exercise in pairs or small groups.

3. **Eulogy.** Each team member writes what he would like said about him at his funeral. This is a way of expressing long-term goals. Team members then share their eulogies in pairs or small groups.

4. **Fantasy Day.** Each team member describes a day he would like to experience at some time in the future. This description can

take any form the person chooses to use in articulating "the dream." This exercise takes long-term goals, gives them a more detailed shape, and identifies behavioral objectives. Team members discuss their fantasy days in pairs or small groups.

5. **Life Inventory.** Each team member responds to seven questions by quickly and spontaneously writing down as many answers as come to mind. The questions deal with skills the person has, experiences that bring him to life, areas for learning, dreams to revive, and resources to develop. Then the person has someone who knows him well answer the same seven questions about him. He works with a third person, someone he trusts, who examines each question in depth, probing and clarifying to generate still more answers.

Each of the exercises in Planning for Living provides opportunities for deep and rich sharing and mutual understanding between team members. Some of the data can be personal and high-risk; the trust level of the group will be enhanced where the leader uses the following keys for this sequence of exercises.

First, let participants choose partners with whom to share their data. People tend to gravitate toward partners they trust. Pairs are the best structure for sharing in these exercises. Each additional group member raises the risk of rejection and tends to cause a close-down of communication. If the group as a whole is warm and close, discussion groups of as many as four may work. Otherwise, too large a group may expose individuals to too much risk and even cause team members to rebel against the exercise with disruptive, facetious, or withdrawn behavior.

Second, team members must be free to explain or not explain parts of what comes to light in discussion; promote a spirit of mutual tolerance, understanding, and respect.

Third, team members need to have the option of not participating in exercises that are too uncomfortable for them. This may cause inconvenience, especially for the partner, but trust building is best served by this safeguard. It is up to the group leader to resolve these problems so that team members feel safe and partners have opportunities to take part in the exercise.

The exercises can be used separately or together. The first four can be carried out in about 20 minutes each. They may serve as

PLANNING FOR LIVING

Introduction. America is not a traditionalist or fatalist society, yet most of us as individuals often act as though we think the future is something that happens to us, rather than as something we create every day. The emphasis of psychology on how childhood experience determines later adult behavior, coupled with the fact that most of us accumulate obligations as we go through life, leads many people to explain their current activities in terms of where they have been rather than in terms of where they are going. Because it is over, the past is unmanageable. Because it has not happened, the future is manageable. The following exercises are designed to help you think about where you are, where you want to go and what resources you have for getting there.

1. **Life line.** Using the lower half of this sheet of paper, draw a line to represent your life line, and put a check mark on it to show where you are on it right now. The line can be straight, slanted, curved, convoluted, jagged, etc.; it can be "psychological" or "chronological." It's a subjective thing— it represents something about how *you* think about *your* life. After you've drawn it, share what it means to you with others in your group.

2. **Who Am I?** This exercise is to explore the check mark on your life line. Write ten different answers to the question "Who am I?" in the space provided below. You may choose to answer in terms of the roles and responsibilities you have in life, in terms of groups you belong to and beliefs you hold, in terms of certain qualities or traits you have as a person, in terms of behavior patterns, needs or feelings that are characteristic of you, etc. List those things which are really important to your sense of yourself: Things that, if you lost them, would make a radical difference to your identity and the meaning of life for you.

Adapted by O. Mink from concepts introduced by Herb Shepard, at a Workshop for Interns of the National Training Laboratory (NTL), Bethel, Maine, Summer, 1969.

Figure 5.9. Planning for Living.

(1)	
(2)	
(3)	
(4)	
(5)	
(6)	
(7)	
(8)	
(9)	
(10)	

Silent, individual reflection is necessary while doing the above. Before sharing with others in the group, follow the instructions given on the next page.

3. **Identity Review.** Consider each item in your list of "Who -am-I's" separately. Imagine, or feel, how it would be if that item were no longer true of you. (For example, if "husband" or "wife" is one of the items, what would the loss of your spouse mean to you? How would you feel? What would you do? What would your life be like?) After reviewing each item

Figure 5.9 (Continued)

in this way, rank-order the items in the list by putting a number in the box to the right of each item. Put "1" beside the item which is most essential to your sense of yourself, whose loss would require the greatest struggle to adjust to. Put "10" beside the item which is least essential to your sense of yourself. Rank-order all items in this way, without any items in your list tying for first place, second place, third place, etc. If some items in your list are aspects of you that you dislike and would like to be rid of, they don't *necessarily* fall in the lower end of the rank order. The question for rank-ordering is how big would the adjustment struggle be if you lost that item? Some aspect of yourself that you dislike might be very hard to give up!

4. **Sharing.** Share the experience you've had privately with the Who-am-I and Identity Review exercises with the rest of your group. No one should be forced to share their list, and no one can be forced to share all the thoughts and feelings that occurred, but be as open as you can. If you're willing to share your list, take the initiative and share it with the others, invite their comments and questions, invite comparison with theirs.

5. **Eulogy.** Through the above exercises, you've explored the check mark on your life line. This exercise is to explore the future end of the life line. The task is to write the eulogy that you wish it would be possible and realistic to have delivered about you at your funeral. Don't write the eulogy that could realistically be delivered if you died tomorrow, unless that represents all you want to be in the future. So give yourself time, hope and even allow yourself some fantasy and wishful thinking, in composing a eulogy to your life. As in the Who-am-I exercise, this exercise requires reflection, silence, being alone with yourself. Don't share with others until you've written all you can.

Use the rest of this sheet to write your eulogy.

6. **Fantasy Day.** Having explored the check mark and the future end of the life line, now sample the space in between. To do this, construct a fantasy day sometime in the future. The day can be a "special day" that you would really love to experience. Or it can be the kind of "typical day" that you really wish would characterize your life. (Or you can create a week instead of a day, etc.) The important thing is to create an experience you really want some time in the future.

Figure 5.9 (Continued)

You may find it helpful to make notes about your fantasy day. If so, use the space below for that purpose. Or you may find it works better to just close your eyes and let your imagination roam.

When you're finished, share your fantasy with the rest of the group.

7. **Life Inventory.** In this experience you generate as many answers as you can to a list of seven questions (A through G) about your values and the resources you have for realizing those values.

A good procedure for constructing your Life Inventory is as follows. First, take a few minutes alone to write down as many answers to the seven questions as come to mind quickly and without thinking too deeply. In fact, the more spontaneous you can let yourself be, the better. Second, compare the answers generated by you and the other members of the group. This may suggest additional answers, to be added to your list. Third, use the other group members as consultants to take a more search-ing look at your life inventory, to help you discover still more answers.

A. When do I feel alive? When do I feel that life is really worth living, that it's great to be me and to be alive? (You can list things, events, activities, etc.)

B. What do I do well? What have I to contribute to the life of others; of what skills do I have mastery; what do I do well for my own growth and well-being?

C. Given my current situation and given my aspirations, what do I want to learn to do?

D. What wishes do I want to be turning into plans? Any dreams I've discarded as "unrealistic" that I want to start dreaming again?

Figure 5.9 (Continued)

E. What under-developed or misused resources do I have? (Resources might be material things or talents or friends, etc.)

F. What do I want to start doing *now?*

G. What do I want to stop doing *now?*

Figure 5.9 (Continued)

warm-ups at the beginning of meetings or to resume working after a break. Used together, the entire sequence of five exercises should take about two and one-half hours.

Example

The Planning for Living Technique sequence was used with a group of about 40 senior managers at an equipment manufacturing company, as a framework for a career-development seminar. The exercises helped the participants think of their career decisions in the larger context of life planning and personal values.

The Planning for Living Technique was used in three sessions of the seminar. The "Life Line" exercise was used early in the first session to help put participants in a thoughtful frame of mind and to build trust in pairs and small groups. In later sessions, "Eulogy" helped managers to identify their long-term goals; "Fantasy Day" helped them to identify what type of role they wished to play in what type of organization; and "Life Inventory" was used by each manager to build a professional development plan.

In evaluating the seminar, one participant made the following comments: "The Planning for Living sessions helped me to decide to accept a new position in the company which I had been offered. In the Eulogy and Fantasy Day exercises, I realized that I really wanted to take on the new challenge of the position, but I was holding myself back because I wasn't sure if I would be successful at it. In the Life Inventory exercise I made a plan to obtain the support from my co-workers and my spouse that I needed to feel confident about the new position."

Resources

The Planning for Living sequence is available from:
OHRD Associates
1208 Somerset Avenue
Austin, Texas 78753

ANSIE TECHNIQUE (Adult Nowicki-Strickland Internal-External Scale)

Purpose

Psychologists have found that the degree to which we think we are responsible for our rewards and punishments plays a dramatic role in shaping our personalities, relationships, and life outcomes, including success at work. The Adult Nowicki-Strickland Internal-External (ANSIE) Scale measures how much control team members believe they have over their own lives.

Description

The Nowicki-Strickland Scale (see Figure 5.10) consists of 40 yes-no questions, such as, "Do you think people can get their way if they keep trying?" "Do you believe that most people are just born good at sports?" Each question tests whether the team member believes life outcomes are mostly a matter of uncontrollable factors or are caused by individual efforts. With a key provided after the instrument is completed, the team member scores the test. The higher the score, the more often the team member believes his life is controlled by factors outside himself.

The Nowicki-Strickland Scale is simple, nonthreatening, and easy to use. The test is written at about an eighth-grade reading level. It takes about 10 to 15 minutes plus half that time for scoring.

....
Name

OPINION SURVEY

....
Code Number

INSTRUCTIONS:

Below are a number of questions about various topics. They have been collected from different groups of people and represent a variety of opinions.
There are no right or wrong answers to this questionnaire, we are only interested in your opinions on these questions. Please circle "yes" or "no" for
each question below.

1. Do you believe that most problems will solve themselves
   if you just don't fool with them?   YES   NO

2. Do you believe that you can stop yourself from catching
   a cold?   YES   NO

3. Are some people just born lucky?   YES   NO

4. Most of the time do you feel that getting good grades
   meant a great deal to you?   YES   NO

5. Are you often blamed for things that just aren't your
   fault?   YES   NO

6. Do you believe that if somebody studies hard enough he
   or she can pass any subject?   YES   NO

7. Do you feel that most of the time it doesn't pay to try
   hard because things never turn out right anyway?   YES   NO

8. Do you feel that if things start out well in the morning
   that it's going to be a good day no matter what you do?   YES   NO

Figure 5.10. Adult Nowicki-Strickland Internal-External Scale.

9. Do you feel that most of the time parents listen to what their children have to say?   YES   <u>NO</u>

10. Do you believe that wishing can make good things happen?   <u>YES</u>   NO

11. When you get punished does it usually seem it's for no good reason at all?   <u>YES</u>   NO

12. Most of the time do you find it hard to change a friend's (mind) opinion?   <u>YES</u>   NO

13. Do you think that cheering more than luck helps a team to win?   YES   <u>NO</u>

14. Did you feel that it was nearly impossible to change your parent's mind about anything?   <u>YES</u>   NO

15. Do you believe that parents should allow children to make most of their own decisions?   YES   <u>NO</u>

16. Do you feel that when you do something wrong there's very little you can do to make it right?   <u>YES</u>   NO

17. Do you believe that most people are just born good at sports?   <u>YES</u>   NO

18. Are most of the other people your age stronger than you are?   <u>YES</u>   NO

19. Do you feel that one of the best ways to handle most problems is just not to think about them?   <u>YES</u>   NO

20. Do you feel that you have a lot of choice in deciding who your friends are?   YES   <u>NO</u>

21. If you find a four leaf clover, do you believe that it might bring you good luck?   <u>YES</u>   NO

Figure 5.10 (Continued)

22. Did you often feel that whether or not you did your homework had much to do with what kind of grades you got?   YES   <u>NO</u>

23. Do you feel that when a person your age is angry at you, there's little you can do to stop him or her?   <u>YES</u>   NO

24. Have you ever had a good luck charm?   <u>YES</u>   NO

25. Do you believe that whether or not people like you depends on how you act?   YES   <u>NO</u>

26. Did your parents usually help you if you asked them to?   YES   <u>NO</u>

27. Have you felt that when people were angry with you it was usually for no reason at all?   <u>YES</u>   NO

28. Most of the time, do you feel that you can change what might happen tomorrow by what you do today?   YES   <u>NO</u>

29. Do you believe that when bad things are going to happen they just are going to happen no matter what you try to do to stop them?   <u>YES</u>   NO

30; Do you think that people can get their own way if they just keep trying?   YES   <u>NO</u>

31. Most of the time do you find it useless to try to get your own way at home?   <u>YES</u>   NO

32. Do you feel that when good things happen they happen because of hard work?   YES   <u>NO</u>

33. Do you feel that when somebody your age wants to be your enemy there's little you can do to change matters?   <u>YES</u>   NO

34. Do you feel that it's easy to get friends to do what you want them to do?   YES   <u>NO</u>

Figure 5.10 (Continued)

35. Do you usually feel that you have little to say about what you get to eat at home?   YES   NO

36. Do you feel that when someone doesn't like you there's little you can do about it?   YES   NO

37. Did you usually feel that it was almost useless to try in school because most other children were just plain smart-er than you are?   YES   NO

38. Are you the kind of person who believes that planning ahead makes things turn out better?   YES   NO

39. Most of the time, do you feel that you have little to say about what your family decides to do?   YES   NO

40. Do you think it's better to be smart than to be lucky?   YES   NO

Scoring: Responses which indicate external locus of control (those which are underlined) are counted, as "1," other responses as "0." Add up the total of responses to obtain the score. (Don't share the key with participants until *after* they have completed the questionnaire.)

Figure 5.10 (Continued)

A low score shows that the team member feels he is almost always in control of his own outcomes, good or bad. A moderate score signals that the person feels out of control in some situations, but in control of others. This may be realistic or it may suggest that the person tends to panic under some circumstances. A high score profiles a person who feels helpless much of the time. Such a person is very susceptible to anxiety, depression, low self-esteem, and poor physical and mental health.

The Nowicki-Strickland Scale can help the team leader identify team members with weak self-images and strong feelings of helplessness. Such members need to be given small, bite-sized tasks they can feel confident with. They may need more coaching and encouragement than others or special attention of the team leader since they are likely to express many negative feelings and hopelessness, and this can infect the entire team.

Example

The Nowicki-Strickland Scale was used in a career development workshop with a group of 45 middle managers in a large international bank's operational services department. These bankers had all been with the company for five years or more. They were deciding between careers in management or in technical specialties.

The scale was used as a check on the seriousness with which the managers were likely to pursue the goals they were setting. After taking and scoring the test, managers wrote their scores on a chalkboard. Names were not shown. The session leader explained the meaning of the scores and asked whether the people with high scores were really serious about designing their lives. He did not identify them personally. A discussion ensued on the wording of the test items, the situations managers could control versus those they could not, and alternative ways of responding to each situation.

As an example, one participant responded "Yes" to three items, each of which placed him in control of situations involving his immediate subordinates. However, on other items, he answered "Yes" to questions that suggested a near hopeless sense of submission to external control from powerful outside authority figures. The session leader saw potential conflict in these response sets and suggested that a manager with these responses might be reluctant to independently promote or encourage the career growth of powerful, highly motivated subordinates. The discussion encouraged the respondent voluntarily to identify himself and focus on his motivations in subordinate/peer relationships and the effects of these dynamics on the organization's productivity.

Resource

The Nowicki-Strickland Internal-External Scale is copyrighted by Stephen Nowicki, Ph.D., and can be obtained by writing to him at the Psychology Department, Emory University, Atlanta, Georgia.

6

KEEPING ON TARGET:
GIVING AND RECEIVING FEEDBACK

In a trusting environment where respect for the individual is evident, people have a natural tendency to move toward important goals and objectives. In order to grow, most people need to have goals, a plan of action to achieve them, and a method of feedback for comparing actual results against expected results. The system for monitoring actual versus expected results requires feedback. This chapter describes the role of feedback in improving group performance, and provides suggestions for giving and receiving it, including suggestions for dealing with the anger which commonly accompanies negative feedback.

Feedback and Achievement

Focusing on the prerequisites for individual success helps clarify the relationships between feedback and team development. Two sets of conditions are needed for individual achievement, one relating to things inside the individual, the other to environmental factors. To achieve success, the individual must have a *vision* of what he wants to accomplish and the *skills* necessary to achieve his or her goal. Without a vision, manifesting the individual's goals and values, efforts will lack purpose and direction, and little will be accomplished. Most tasks also require specific skills; without the requisite skills, the individual will lack the equipment necessary to perform the task.

In addition to purpose and skills, the individual must have the *belief that he or she can succeed* in achieving the vision. The expectation of success helps keep efforts "on track" toward the ultimate goals and provides incentive to perform the necessary tasks. Without this expectation of success, vision becomes a pipe dream and skills become wasted potential.

Successful achievement of vision also requires *data* to keep efforts on track. As illustrated in Figure 6.1, goals are often reached less directly than is at first expected. Periodic comparison of actual progress to expected performance provides data which enable the individual to effectively progress toward achieving the vision. Team members receive the data they need in a variety of ways, but the feedback and information they receive through incentives, training and education, strokes, and evaluation are especially important to individual and group success.

The other side of individual success is the team environment. While success is largely an individual matter, we often forget the powerful effects that the environment has on individual performance. In a high-performance climate, the team provides *incentives*, or payoffs, that reinforce the individual's personal goals and values and reward goal-oriented performance in achieving team

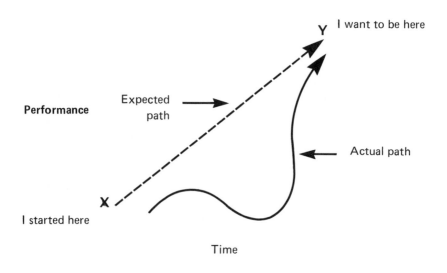

Figure 6.1. Feedback and Actual and Expected Performance.

objectives. The incentives provided by the team environment thus help motivate team members to strive toward excellence while keeping on track in achieving group goals.

The effective team environment also provides *training and education*, through which the individual can develop competencies needed for success. As team members develop new skills and competencies, they develop professionally, are likely to have enhanced self-esteem and confidence, and they have more to offer to the work of the group.

High performance teams have been found also to provide their members with feedback in the form of *strokes*, encouragement, and recognition. This type of feedback affirms the individual's sense of uniqueness and validates his sense of worth as a member of the group.

Finally, the high performance team provides *evaluative feedback* to its members about their actual performance in relation to expected achievements. Whether this information is negative (reflecting poor performance) or positive (recognizing performance at or above expected levels), evaluative feedback enables team members to accurately assess their performance and to stay "on track" in contributing to team goals.

Individual and team success are interdependent; one is unavoidably intertwined with the other in a homeostatic system. Neither individual nor team goals will be achieved unless success is realized in both areas. Characteristics of effective and ineffective teams in giving and receiving performance feedback are outlined in Figure 6.2.

The team that learns how to give and receive effective feedback is much more likely to succeed in today's fluctuating business environment. Feedback is the team's method for keeping on track through providing team members with up-to-date information about performance relative to expectations and about the quality of the relationships in the team.

Feedback and the Basics of Interpersonal Communication

Feedback needs to be an ongoing process. It provides data to the team so as to keep it and its members on track in pursuit of team vision. Feedback can be a powerful tool in promoting the

Groups That Are Ineffective	Groups That Are Effective
1. do not regularly monitor individual or team performance	1. regularly monitor individual and team performance
2. have no measures for performance that are related to excellence of performance	2. have measures for performance that are related to excellence of performance
3. tend to have poorly stated expectations for individuals and the team	3. tend to state expectations in a clear, understandable manner
4. tend to provide feedback that is inconsistent, overly critical, and punitive	4. tend to develop feedback that is consistent, based on behavior, and positive
5. develop norms for concealling poor performance	5. develop norms that allow for an open examination of performance
6. maintain and support unproductive practices	6. frequently assess practices and make changes when needed
7. are closed to change	7. are open to change
8. produce poor quality goods and services	8. produce excellent goods and services
9. suppress conflict	9. deal with conflict openly
10. do not reach goals	10. regularly reach goals
11. are unproductive	11. are productive

Figure 6.2. Performance Differences Between Groups That Are Effective Versus Ineffective in Giving and Receiving Feedback.

growth of the team, or it can reduce the effectiveness of the team and its members, depending on how it is supplied.

Work teams need two types of feedback, performance feedback (on individual productivity) and interpersonal feedback (on how an individual's actions affect other members of the team). One may also provide work-related personal feedback ("You are important to our team") or purely personal feedback ("I really like you!"). A person both gives feedback and receives it. Soliciting or receiving feedback involves getting another's perceptions and feelings about your own behavior.

Because feedback is always taking place in a team, it is useful to develop awareness of current feedback processes among the team members. The effective team will be attentive to its feedback processes and will strive to develop increasingly effective methods and processes of giving and receiving feedback. Some training techniques for increasing group awareness and skills in giving and receiving feedback are described in this chapter.

To understand the value of feedback techniques, let's explore how information is exchanged between people. When Person A decides to act, he chooses behaviors which reflect his intentions. Person B, not being privy to A's intentions, must interpret A's intentions, and then respond based on his own intentions. Person A in turn perceives and responds to B's behavior, either confirming or correcting Person B's response. If B's response corresponds with A's original intention, A and B are communicating. If B's response does not correspond with A's intentions, communication is distorted and feedback is required. *Feedback is the process of exchange through which people communicate their intentions and make their intentions and behavior congruent.* By achieving congruence between intentions and behavior, people are able to meet their own needs (intrapersonal) and to help others meet their needs (interpersonal). Figure 6.3 illustrates this process.

Who Is Responsible for Feedback?

It is the responsibility of the team leader to model effective feedback behaviors and to provide norms of open communication. In a team setting, however, each person's behavior affects all the other team members, directly or indirectly. The issue of each team

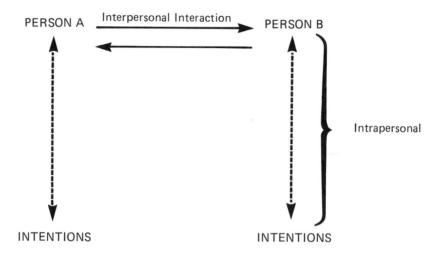

Figure 6.3. Information Exchange.

member's responsibility for feedback is therefore important. How much responsibility do the giver and receiver of feedback have? If A's behavior has a negative effect on B, to what extent is each responsible for his part of the exchange? Some people want to be responsible for taking care of everyone, while others want to deny any responsibility for the effects of their actions. Both types of extremes in taking responsibility for the exchange are likely to increase the level of conflict in the team.

A way to decide on the issue of responsibility is by considering the purpose of communication in the context of individual and group needs and goals. Communication should permit an individual to have his needs met while simultaneously allowing other team members to meet their needs. If your actions prevent me from getting my needs met, I am responsible for giving you feedback. It is your responsibility to give my feedback an honest appraisal, or to accept the consequences of rejecting it. Similarly, when you have been of help to me, it is my responsibility to give you positive feedback.

I am responsible for giving feedback if:
*   your actions pose a threat to my needs (negative feedback)
*   your actions help me meet my needs (positive feedback)
*   your actions make it hard for the team to meet its goals (negative feedback)
*   your actions make it easier for the team to reach its goals (positive feedback)

I am responsible for listening to feedback if:
*   we must work together to meet group needs
*   you care about how I feel
*   I want to remain in good standing on the team
*   I intend to meet personal performance objectives

Figure 6.4. Responsibility for Feedback.

When someone's actions make it difficult for the team to work as a unit and the other team members fail to give him feedback, everyone loses. If the members choose to provide feedback, everyone has at least a chance of meeting shared needs and moving toward shared goals (see Figure 6.2).

By establishing group norms of giving and receiving feedback, the leader helps your team members grow through achieving shared goals. In terms of the Johari Window (see Chapter 4), when we give and receive constructive feedback we are increasing the size of the open area. More energy is thus available to the group for achieving its goals. See Figure 6.4.

How Do You Give Effective Feedback?

Feedback may be used to reinforce desirable behaviors, to change problem behavior, or to elicit new behaviors from group members. Feedback is often given under stress conditions, and the feedback itself may elicit stress. People under stress are less able to listen clearly. It is possible to learn communication skills which reduce the stress of feedback and help the recipient to hear the message, to understand, and to respond appropriately. The stress that accompanies confrontation, conflict, or negative feedback can be minimized when the communication has the following characteristics. These skills will also help the leader or team member to give feedback which will have the desired effect on people's behavior.

Effective Feedback
1. *Directly expresses feelings*
   EXAMPLE: I don't like your tardiness,
                 —as opposed to—
                 Why can't you be here on time?

2. *Describes behavior and not intentions*
   EXAMPLE: When you are late, I am annoyed,
                 —as opposed to—
                 You really are not trying to contribute, because you are late so often

3. *Is nonevaluative*
   EXAMPLE: You have been late twice this week,
                 —as opposed to—
                 Don't you have enough discipline to get here on time!

4. *Focuses on behavior that can be changed*
   EXAMPLE: You have been late so often that I have been wondering if there is something I can do to help you get here in time.
                 —as opposed to—
                 Is this the way you learned to get back at people, making them wait on you?

5. *Is specific to the behavior which elicited the feedback*
   EXAMPLE: John, you did a great job closing that sale,
                 —as opposed to—
                 You are a great salesman!

6. *Focuses on alternatives as opposed to solutions*
   EXAMPLE: Some options I see for you to arrive to work on

time are: car pool, bus, getting your car fixed,
—as opposed to—
You had better get your car fixed, if you want to
get here on time.

EXCEPTION—Persistent negative or other nonproductive behaviors which a team member refuses to correct can create
severe problems for the team. While only the individual can
choose to change negative behavior, there are consequences to
persistently disruptive behavior. It is the team's responsibility
to allow natural consequences (e.g., dismissal for tardiness) to
flow from persistently negative behavior. Still, you are giving
the recipient a choice: change this behavior to remain a team
member.

7. *Is immediate or given as soon as possible after the initiating
event*
EXAMPLE: I am concerned about your lowered production for
the last two days,
—as opposed to—
Your production was down on two consecutive
days last month.
Let's get after it!
EXCEPTION: Some feedback sessions, such as formal periodic
performance reviews, are held at regular intervals, and feedback
may be delayed. Timely feedback, however, provided as soon as
possible after the initiating event, is more likely to have the desired impact on a person's behavior.

8. *Is focused on a change in behavior that will help the recipient
perform better*
EXAMPLE: If you redo these two charts in the report, it will
be clearer.
—as opposed to—
You really loused up this report! Do it over!

The Problem of Anger
People often respond to negative feedback with anger and hurt.

You may respond to a team member's negative feedback with your own version of defensive and unoptimistic behavior. These guidelines are helpful in handling the anger which commonly accomplished negative feedback.

Dealing with Your Own Anger

Understand how your anger develops, and accept the fact that, when your expectations differ greatly from those held by a team member, anger and hurt are almost always involved and may be predicted. At whom or what do you allow yourself to get angry? If you list some anger-provoking events you have experienced, you will see that they usually violate your expectations and are perceived as a threat to your well-being. When an event is contrary to expectation, it creates fear that we will be unable to handle this event or the repercussions it is likely to cause. Often this fear will turn into anger, as illustrated in Figure 6.5.

To develop more control over your anger, ask yourself, "What can I do to increase my level of control in those situations that I let anger me?" List all the alternatives you can and decide on the most effective course of action. This is a way to "vaccinate" yourself against anger.

Accept your anger as anger, and choose to deal with it in a positive manner. That is, admit that you *choose* to get angry as a way to gain control over certain situations. It is okay to be angry; what counts is what you do in response to your anger. We sometimes respond, however, in ways out of proportion to how much anger we feel.

You may learn to choose to respond to negative feedback in terms of the *degree* to which you are angry. Degree of anger is related to both the level of threat presented by another's behavior and its potential cost to you. Once you have assessed the threat and potential costs, you may choose the most appropriate response, as shown in Figure 6.6. This is just a theoretical framework but it may help you think through your responses to threats *before* you fly off the handle.

Express your feedback (e.g., "I am angry with you because . . .") and then listen to the other person's story without interruption. If a problem does exist, try to deal with it in a positive, problem-solving manner.

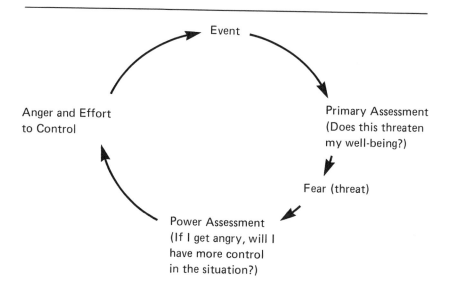

Figure 6.5. Assessing and Responding to Anger.

IF THE DEGREE OF THREAT OR POTENTIAL COST IS	THEN, CHOOSE TO EXPRESS
LOW	ANNOYANCE
MODERATELY LOW	IRRITATION
MODERATELY HIGH	FRUSTRATION
HIGH	ANGER

Figure 6.6. Assessing Level of Anger.

Learn to forgive (yourself and others) and to let go of anger. If you can't do this, repeat the process we have just described; perhaps you haven't fully defined what threatens or scares you. In most situations you may ask yourself if it is worth it to express anger at all. The most effective business managers know when to get angry and when not to. *Learn to practice the art of expressing your anger effectively—to get results—and of retreating when to do so might help you reach your goals in the long run.* Expressing our anger is often not to help the other person but to satisfy a need to get even. At such times retreat may be the best choice.

Dealing with Another's Anger

Little is accomplished when anger prevails in a group. One way to reduce such conflict is for you to choose not to respond to another's anger by getting angry yourself. Instead, ask yourself:

- What is the problem?
- Is it mine or is it his?
- If it is mine, will I gain anything by solving it?
- If it is his, can I benefit by allowing it to become mine?

Don't attempt to force the other to be logical during anger. Instead, choose to accept the feelings and actively listen to the other's anger. You can choose to ignore abuse while responding to reasonable statements. As soon as possible, find out what the other person wants and let him know what you want.

It is helpful to make it a rule that others (and you) can renege on things said in the heat of anger. You may say things you wish you hadn't, and so might others. Forgive others and allow yourself to ask for forgiveness. Understandings like this can help you to deal with difficult situations without undermining the level of trust in the group.

Choose not to do anything that would escalate conflict in the situation. If efforts to remain calm fail, you may choose to leave the scene, at least temporarily. When appropriate, however, use confrontation: let the other person know what the natural consequences are if inappropriate behavior continues.

Be clear about your bottom line. Understand your limits and be prepared to ler the other know what those are. Try to always make sure that the other person knows what you mean, asking for feedback if necessary. Similarly, always make sure you know what he means. You may ask questions such as "What do you understand me to be saying? or reflecting what you understand him to be saying or thinking, and asking "Is this what you mean? . . ."

Learning to accept and deal with anger in a direct, honest manner is an important lesson for the successful team leader. Anger is a natural consequence of many of the processes involved in achieving important goals and objectives. Accepting it and learning to deal with it in a responsible manner frees the team to keep focused on the important issues it confronts.

In summary, feedback is the principal means by which team leaders can nurture a sense of competence in team members; competent team members make a strong team. Goals should be established for the expected performance of the team and its members, and processes should be developed for the team to regularly review progress and share feedback about individual and team performance. Effective and constructive feedback practices which focus on behavior change and on reduction of counter-productive stress can be developed in the team to enhance its overall performance. Feedback information is used by the effective leader to determine what kinds of changes, if any, are needed. Even if changes are not needed, it will be helpful to reward excellence and correct ineffectiveness as soon as possible.

TEAM EFFECTIVENESS ANALYSIS TECHNIQUE

Purpose

The Team Effectiveness Analysis Technique is a useful, informal "health check-up" exercise for groups at work. It is a vehicle that team members use to assess and discuss how they feel about clarity of team goals, level of trust and empathy, leadership, and use of group resources. The discussions that take place in Parts 3 and 4 provide an opportunity for valuable feedback within the team.

Description

Team members rate how well the group is doing on each of eight teamwork items on a five-point scale. Teamwork factors include goal clarity, leadership, trust, etc. The instrument also contains a guide to informal analysis and discussion of the ratings.

1. Secure a copy of the form for each team member (See Resources at the end of this section). See Figure 6.1.
2. Introduce the instrument as an informal way of checking up on how well individuals are functioning as a team. Get agreement from team members to proceed.
3. Allow about 10 minutes for completion of Parts 1 and 2.
4. Ask members to share the ratings given for each teamwork factor. Chart these in full view of the group.
5. Conduct a discussion of the ratings, using the discussion questions on the back of the instrument (Part 3).
6. Allow five minutes for team members to jot down ideas for improving teamwork. These are things to be done by each individual, by the team leader, and by the team as a whole (Part 4).
7. Arrange an agreed-upon way to collect members' suggestions on what you as leaders can do.
8. At an appropriate time, either right after conducting the exercise or at a future meeting, ask members to share their suggestions on actions the whole group could take. Add these to the group's ongoing agenda items for follow-up.

Any group that meets on an ongoing basis can profitably use this instrument. Group maintenance problems often develop unseen, not becoming apparent until there is a crisis. By that time, it may be too late. For this reason, the technique is very much like a preventive health check-up; it can help bring issues to the surface while they are still small and manageable. If the group is working well together, the instrument will make this fact visible, which will boost morale and increase team confidence.

The main advantages of the instrument are speed, informality, and simplicity. Some of the terminology, however, is group dynamics jargon (for example, "Balance between task and maintenance needs"). Team members unacquainted with these terms may have difficulty rating some of the items.

TEAM EFFECTIVENESS ANALYSIS FORM

Introduction

As expressed in the book ORGANIZATION RENEWAL*

"In organizations, the face-to-face work group is the place where the individual potentially can satisfy his needs, influence the organization, and attempt the integration of his goals with those of the group and the organization of which the group is a part. The 'psychological contract' that takes place between the individual and the organization helps us to see the importance of the work group.

"Another reason for the importance of the face-to-face group, according to recent research, is that these overlapping work groups enable leaders to be a "link" between the various levels of organizational functioning.

"An organization leader is a *member* of one group in the organization with his superiors, and a *leader* of his own work group, and serves thereby as a 'linking pin' between the two groups. A manager, therefore, belongs to one group with his superior, to another group as the leader, and is usually a member of a horizontal or peer group working on a task or project.

"Generally speaking, the task assigned to or chosen by a group deals in some manner with a situation or a problem, and the resolution or solution usually involves effective *teamwork*. Herein lies one of the essential reasons why many leaders and managers decline to try to take advantage of group action when confronting organizational situations. The frustrations he anticipates in securing teamwork—perhaps not without reason—are simply more than he cares to suffer. Insofar as organization renewal is concerned, however, these frustrations should and can be overcome."

*Lippitt, Gordon, L. (1969). *Organization Renewal.* Appleton-Century-Crofts, New York, Chapter VI.

Figure 6.7. Team Effectiveness Analysis Form.

PART 1

Note

Research and experience have indicated that eight key teamwork factors are essential to the relationships of a group. Prior to turning to Pages 2 and 3, please list some basic information about the group you will be analyzing. Resource and group will determine guidelines for selection of group(s) to be analyzed.

---

1. Group you will analyze: . . . .
. . . .
2. Size of Group: . . . .
3. How long has the group been in existence? . . . .
4. How long have you been a *member* of the group? . . . .
5. Are you the group leader? . . . . 6. If so, how long? . . . .
7. How would you rate the present level of teamwork in the group?

| _____ | _____ | _____ | _____ |
| Excellent | Very Good | Fair | Poor |

8. How important is it to you to see teamwork improve in this group?

| _____ | _____ | _____ | _____ |
| A great deal of importance | Important to me | Some Importance | Of little Consequence |

PART 2
A YARD STICK FOR MEASURING THE GROWTH OF A TEAM

As a group begins its life and at several points during its growth, the leader and members might reflect on the following group characteristics and spend some time sharing the data that is collected. Through rating each character-

Figure 6.7 (Continued)

istic it is possible to get a general picture of the perceptions which various members have about the team and how it is developing. It is also possible to identify areas in which there may be some difficulties which are blocking progress. Each person please rate the group chosen to be evaluated.

A. Goal Clarity

1.	2.	3.	4.	5.
No apparent goals	Goal confusion	Average goal	Goals mostly clear	Goals very clear

B. Trust and openness

1.	2.	3.	4.	5.
No trust and no openness	Little trust and openness	Average trust and openness	Considerable trust and openness	Remarkable trust and openness

C. Empathy among members

1.	2.	3.	4.	5.
No empathy	Little empathy	Average empathy	Considerable empathy	Remarkable empathy

D. Balance between group task and maintenance needs

1.	2.	3.	4.	5.
No balance	Little balance	Average balance	A good balance	Excellent balance

E. Leadership needs

1.	2.	3.	4.	5.
Leadership needs not met	Some leadership needs met	Average meeting of leadership needs	Good meeting of leadership needs	Excellent meeting of leadership needs

F. Decision making

1.	2.	3.	4.	5.
Unable to reach decisions	Inadequate decision making	Average decision making	Good decision making	Full concensus

G. Utilization of Group Resources

1.	2.	3.	4.	5.
Group resources not utilized	Group resources poorly utilized	Average use of group resources	Team resources well used	Team resources fully and effectively used

H. Sense of belonging

1.	2.	3.	4.	5.
No sense of belonging	Some sense of belonging	Average sense of belonging	Good sense of belonging	Strong sense of belonging

Figure 6.7 (Continued)

EXAMINING YOUR RATINGS

1. On what three items on Page 2 did you rate your group the highest?
        Item Ranked #1 . . . .
        Item Ranked #2 . . . .
        Item Ranked #3 . . . .
  What evidence can you cite to justify these three ratings?
        Item #1 . . . .
        Item #2 . . . .
        Item #3 . . . .
2. On what three items on Page 2 did you rate your group the lowest?
        Item Ranked #1 . . . .
        Item Ranked #2 . . . .
        Item Ranked #3 . . . .
  What evidence can you site to justify your ratings?
        Item #1 . . . .
        Item #2 . . . .
        Item #3 . . . .
3. How do you predict that your ratings will compare with others in the group? Why?

. . . .
. . . .
. . . .
. . . .
. . . .

Tabulation Directions

In your group, share the ratings of each member of the group and put these individual ratings on a chart in front of the group for discussion purposes. When this is done please turn to Page 4 of this TEAM EFFEC-TIVENESS ANALYSIS FORM.

Figure 6.7 (Continued)

PART 3
FACTORS AFFECTING THE ACHIEVEMENT OF
TEAMWORK IN YOUR GROUP

Now that you have reviewed both your own rating of the group and those of other members of the group, please work with the group in planning the discussion and analysis of the results:

Possible Discussion Questions

1. What are the causes underlying those ratings receiving the **lowest** scores amongst the members of the group?
2. What are the causes underlying those ratings receiving the **highest** scores among the members of the group?
3. Why was there such a wide difference of opinion on certain items?

PART 4
STEPS IN IMPROVING GROUP TEAMWORK

1. Some of the action steps that I as a **member** of the group can take to improve teamwork in our group:

....

....

....

2. Some of the action steps that the **total group** might take to improve our teamwork:

....

....

....

3. Some of the action steps that the **group leader** might take to improve our teamwork:

....

....

....

The effect and/or reality of these action steps can be reviewed either now or at a later time to be determined by a group as a continuing process of its team-building activities.

Figure 6.7 (Continued)

In such groups it will be helpful to discuss these principles of group dynamics before using the instrument.

Example

A group of research and development project managers which held regular meetings found that the group typically worked well together for a few months, then "fell apart." After a period of idleness, the group would form again and start over. After the third such failure, a member of the group introduced the Team Effectiveness Analysis Form. The team used this form after every second meeting for a year. This allowed them to pay attention to team maintenance needs in a legitimate fashion. Concerns came to light about members being voted down and disregarded, group decisions being arrived at improperly, too much emphasis on task, too much time spent in activities that were unimportant, and so forth. By using this exercise to periodically take stock of progress the team survived an entire year without another breakdown in the process, developing an effective and realistic set of norms and procedures governing the group's life.

Resources

Lippitt, G.L. (1969). *Organization Renewal.* New York: Appleton-Century-Crofts.

The Team Effectiveness Analysis Form is available from:
Development Publications
5606 Lamar Road
Bethesda, Maryland 20816

USED BY PERMISSION: This instrument is commercially available and may not be reproduced or duplicated in any form without the permission of the author, whose address is provided above.

GROUP LEADERSHIP GRID TECHNIQUE

Purpose

The Group Leadership Grid Technique provides positive feedback to a team on the amount and type of leadership exerted by each member. The instrument focuses on quantifying and measuring the contributions of individual group members.

Description

The column down the left side of the grid lists 12 kinds of behavior that contribute to the successful operation of a group. Across the top are blank spaces to be filled with the names of group members (see Figure 6.8). Definitions of leadership functions (Lippitt and Seashore) appear in Figure 6.9.

1. Enlist the services of an observer who is not a member of the group.
2. Before the observer attends a meeting, give him or her time to study and become familiar with the grid and the definitions of leadership functions.
3. At the next team meeting, introduce the observer as someone who will later give the team some feedback on how they interact. Get the team members to consent to this plan.
4. Have the observer sit apart from the group and intrude as little as possible in the meeting.
5. As the observer watches and listens, have him or her make a tally mark each time he observes a team member performing one of the leadership functions. The tally mark goes in the column under the team member's name, in the row for that leadership function.
6. Before the next meeting, count up the tally marks in each box of the grid. Also add up the rows and columns. This will give a profile of the team members and their individual styles of leadership, and will provide a profile of the team as a whole, showing areas of strength and identifying where more leadership would help.
7. Present the results to the team at the next meeting, using photocopies of the checklist. Discuss your interpretation of the numbers, and invite the team's questions and comments.

This way of providing feedback is a simple and inexpensive confidence builder. Team members learn to think of themselves as leaders and to see simple ways to increase and share leadership in the group.

Instructions: For each member, place check marks in the column corresponding to the roles he/she has played most often in the group. Include yourself.

MEMBERS

ROLES										
Task Roles										
1. Initiator										
2. Information or Opinion-Seeker										
3. Information or Opinion-Giver										
4. Clarifier or Collaborator										
5. Summarizer										
6. Consensus-Tester										
Maintenance Roles										
1. Encourager										
2. Expresser of Group Feeling										
3. Harmonizer										
4. Compromiser										
5. Gatekeeper										
6. Standard-Setter										
Anti-Group Roles										
1. Blocker										
2. Recognition-Seeker										
3. Dominator										
4. Avoider										

Adapted by Barbara Mink after Leland P. Bradford (1976).

Figure 6.8. Group Leadership Grid.

1. **Task Functions:** These leadership functions are to facilitate and coordinate group effort in the selection and definition of a common problem and in the solution of that problem.
   - *Initiating:* Proposing tasks or goals: defining a group problem; suggesting a procedure or ideas for solving a problem
   - *Information or opinion seeking:* Requesting facts: seeking relevant information about a group concern; asking for suggestions or ideas
   - *Clarifying or elaborating:* Interpreting or reflecting ideas and suggestions clearing up confusion; indicating alternatives and issues before the group; giving examples
   - *Summarizing:* Pulling together related ideas; restating suggestions after the group has discussed them; offering a decision or conclusion for the group to accept or reject
   - *Consensus testing:* Sending up "trial balloons" to see if the group is nearing a conclusion; checking with the group to see how much agreement has been reached
2. **Maintenance Functions:** Functions in this category describe leadership activity necessary to alter or maintain the way in which members of the group work together developing loyalty to one another and to the group as a whole.
   - *Encouraging:* Being friendly, warm and responsive to others and to their contributions; showing regard for others by giving them an opportunity for recognition
   - *Expressing group feelings:* Sensing feelings, moods, relationships within the group; sharing feelings with other members
   - *Harmonizing:* Attempting to reconcile disagreements; reducing tension by "pouring oil on troubled waters"; getting people to explore their differences
   - *Compromising:* When one's own idea or status is involved in a conflict, offering to compromise one's own position; admitting error; disciplining oneself to maintain group cohesion
   - *Gatekeeping:* Attempting to keep communication channels open; facilitating the participation of others; suggesting procedures for sharing the discussion of group problems
   - *Setting standards:* Expressing standards for the group to achieve; applying standards in evaluating group functioning and production

Figure 6.9. Group Leadership Functions and Their Definitions.
(See Lippitt and Seashore, Resources.)

3. **Blocking (Anti-Group) Functions:** _____

_____
_____
_____
_____
_____

- Blocker: _____

_____
_____
_____
_____
_____

- Recognition-Seeker: _____

_____
_____
_____
_____
_____

- Dominator: _____

_____
_____
_____
_____
_____

- Avoider: _____

_____
_____
_____
_____
_____

Figure 6.9 (Continued)

The skills of the observer can strongly affect the quality of the feedback. Ideally, the observer should be someone skilled and experienced in watching, recording, and judging ongoing processes; try to select someone with a background in organizational dynamics, behavioral science, industrial engineering, or sports officiating.

No observer can capture on the grid everything that happens in a meeting. First, the team consists of people acting simultaneously. Second, many of the maintenance functions (encouraging, harmonizing, expressing feelings, etc.) are subtle and nonverbal. Little things like nodding, smiling, and listening with eye contact fall into these categories. There will always be some team members whose faces the observer cannot see. Still, use of the grid can provide valuable information on the group's patterns of interaction. If more rigor and precision are needed, videotape cameras or a team of trained observers can be used. Such measures are more expensive, however, and cameras or a team of observers may distort team members' behavior by making them more self-conscious.

Example

A computer manufacturing firm began experimenting with participative management. The changes introduced put new emphasis on decision-making by small groups of production workers. These people were not accustomed to group work, so a trainer worked with them to teach them the basics of group effectiveness. One of the qualities of an effective group in action is that leadership is shared broadly, rather than concentrated in one or two members. To bring this concept home, the trainer observed the group using the Group Leadership Grid Technique, and provided feedback on the results. His observations validated the contributions of group members, made them aware of contributions by quiet leaders as well as talkative ones, and showed that leadership is a lot of little things rather than one big thing. For example, one group member's leadership style was to listen consistently, engage in eye contact, respond to humor, and volunteer to take responsibility. Another tended to raise good questions and move the group logically from point to point. Another frequently threw bits of valuable information into the conversation. Under ordinary circumstances, these kinds of contributions tend to be taken for granted, and even when they are noticed by other group members, verbal recognition may not follow. The exercise provided recognition to individual contributions to the team's work, raised the level of awareness of feedback processes in the group, and gave the members some new concepts to use in assessing future team processes and performance.

Resources

Bradford, L.P. (1976). *Making Meetings Work.* San Diego, CA: University Associates.

Jones, P.E. (May, 1984). *Developing a Training Program for Effective Group Problem Solving.* Unpublished master's thesis, University of Texas at Austin, Department of Curriculum and Instruction.

Lippitt, G., and Seashore, E. (1980). *Group Effectiveness.* Fairfax, VA: Leadership Resources Inc.

Shaw, M. (1971). *Group Dynamics.* New York: McGraw-Hill.

SELF-DEVELOPMENT INVENTORY FOR MULTIPLE-ROLE EFFECTIVENESS TECHNIQUE

Purpose

The Self-Development Inventory for Multiple-Role Effectiveness Technique is designed to aid team members in assessing themselves and giving each other feedback on their effectiveness as individuals, team members, and organization members. It provides an opportunity for deepening and strengthening interpersonal bonds between team members, for clarifying mutual expectations, and for increasing open communications.

Description

The instrument consists of 36 ten-point scales. There are scales concerning the team member's role as an individual, as a team member, and as an organization member. On each scale the team member makes two self-ratings: one for where he sees himself now, and one for where he would like to be in the future. Each team member selects another member of the team to mark the scales to indicate where he feels his teammate now stands.

Examples of scale items follow the discussion of this technique.

1. Secure a copy of the instrument for each team member (see Resources).

2. Allow team members about 10 minutes to go over the directions for using the instrument and another 20 minutes to fill out the instrument describing themselves.

3. Allow 15 minutes for members to swap booklets with someone they trust and rate each other. (Total working time is about 45 minutes.)

4. Decide how you wish to structure the group discussion. It frequently works well in groups of three; one person discusses one or more of his growth goals with a listener, and the third person watches the interaction for signs of supportiveness and defensiveness. Growth goals often reflect areas in which the individual feels inadequate. To discuss these with another person involves risk and may lead to defensive behavior. Groups of four are less awkward to form, and handle the task as well. The two people who earlier swapped forms and rated each other form a natural partnership. Have pairs of partners join to form groups of four. If there are people left over, form them into groups of two or three. Avoid groups of five or more.

5. Once the groups have formed, allow one hour for the discussions. Divide the hour so that each member of the group has equal time to talk about himself. Allow about five minutes in each round for observer comments.

The Self-Development Inventory for Multiple-Role Effectiveness (see Figure 6.10) is an informal tool. It can evoke strong feelings and assist team members in sharing information about themselves at significant levels.

Because of the personal and probing nature of many of the items, there is potential for high-risk personal disclosure to take place. This instrument, therefore, should only be used with groups of persons who know and trust each other reasonably well. For the small-group discussion, each member of the team needs to have at least one other person in the group (usually the

A. As An Individual

Ability to understand my motivation—why I do what I do

(SELF ESTIMATE)

0   1   2   3   4   5   6   7   8   9   10
Very Low   Very High

(ESTIMATE OR OTHER PERSON)

0   1   2   3   4   5   6   7   8   9   10
Very Low   Very High

Extent to which I tend to hide or cover up my true feelings and emotions

(SELF ESTIMATE)

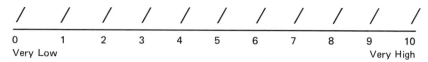

0   1   2   3   4   5   6   7   8   9   10
Very Low   Very High

(ESTIMATE OR OTHER PERSON)

0   1   2   3   4   5   6   7   8   9   10
Very Low   Very High

B. As A Group Member

Ability to be open with others and to accept feedback from others

(SELF ESTIMATE)

0   1   2   3   4   5   6   7   8   9   10
Very Low   Very High

Figure 6.10. Sample Items from Inventory.

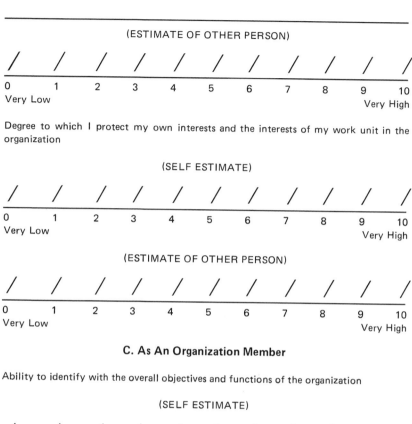

(ESTIMATE OF OTHER PERSON)

0   1   2   3   4   5   6   7   8   9   10
Very Low   Very High

Degree to which I protect my own interests and the interests of my work unit in the organization

(SELF ESTIMATE)

0   1   2   3   4   5   6   7   8   9   10
Very Low   Very High

(ESTIMATE OF OTHER PERSON)

0   1   2   3   4   5   6   7   8   9   10
Very Low   Very High

C. As An Organization Member

Ability to identify with the overall objectives and functions of the organization

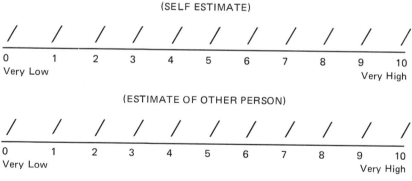

(SELF ESTIMATE)

0   1   2   3   4   5   6   7   8   9   10
Very Low   Very High

(ESTIMATE OF OTHER PERSON)

0   1   2   3   4   5   6   7   8   9   10
Very Low   Very High

Degree to which I accept my personal role and responsibility as a renewal agent in my organization

Figure 6.10 (Continued)

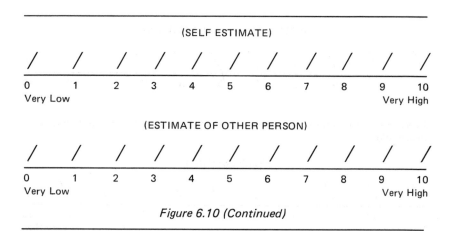

Figure 6.10 (Continued)

partner) whom he trusts. The presence of even one person in the small group whom another member of the group actively distrusts will cause communications between those two to be very risky. They may respond by clamming up or, less likely, by attacking each other. Either situation defeats the purpose of the exercise.

The guidance given for conducting the group discussion is sketchy and tentative. Coupled with the potentially risky nature of the issues tapped, this instrument requires that a person skilled in human relations lead the exercise.

The total time needed to fill out and discuss the instrument is about two hours. This exercise is more appropriate for an off-site staff development retreat than for a normal meeting of a group at work.

In the third section of the instrument, the language occasionally becomes jargony (e.g., "renewal agent"). Some items may need to be explained for team members who are less knowledgeable of group development jargon. The instrument is most appropriate for midmanagers.

Example

A mid-level manager in a manufacturing firm with a strong interest in effective teamwork called on a member of the organization development staff for resources. The manager had been working with his immediate staff of line supervisors for over a year.

They worked together competently and got along well, but most of the group tended to work very independently; frequently there were problems caused by lack of communication between groups of staff members working on different projects. The manager perceived that the group lacked a sense of common purpose, frequently resulting in poor coordination between projects, duplication of effort, and inefficient expenditure of resources. The manager had noticed that, as this situation further developed, production had declined.

The manager and the organization development specialist considered the Self-Development Inventory for Multiple-Role Effectiveness Technique, and decided the group could handle the risks involved. They held an all-day off-site staff meeting, with the second half of the morning spent filling out and discussing the instrument. The organization developer led the exercise and the manager participated.

The opportunity to know each other on a more personal level opened up the group's communication channels considerably. As the participants worked through the exercise, a number of staff members were surprised to learn that many of their behaviors were viewed as counter-productive to the goals of the team and the organization as a whole.

Discussion in the afternoon session centered around individual group members' needs and expectations, the goals and expectations of the organization, and ways in which these expectations could more effectively be met by opening lines of communication. Many issues about the team and the organization came to light, providing an opportunity for the staff members to gain a stronger consensus about organizational goals and about how the organization could more effectively support their career development. Concern over career mobility within the company was a strong incentive for supervisors to re-evaluate the impact they were having on group and organizational performance.

In the following weeks this group of supervisors began communicating more frequently with each other about individual and organizational objectives. Building on the new level of trust that had been developed during the workshop, they worked together more effectively, resulting in fewer occasions for conflict between individuals and in significant gains in productivity.

Resources

Haney, W. (1967). *Communication and Organizational Behavior.* Homewood, IL: Richard D. Irwin, Inc.

Lippitt, G. (1966). *Quest for Dialogue.* Washington, D.C.: Development Publications.

Lovin, B., and Cassterens, E. (1971). *Coaching, Learning, and Action.* New York: American Management Association.

Luft, J. (1969). *Of Human Interaction.* Palo Alto, CA: National Press Books.

This, L. (1966). *Leader Looks at Personal Communication.* Washington, D.C.: Leadership Resources, Inc.

The Self-Development Inventory for Multiple-Role Effectiveness is available from:

Development Publications
5606 Lamar Road
Bethesda, Maryland 20816

POWER MANAGEMENT PROFILE TECHNIQUE

Purpose

The Power Management Profile Technique is designed to assess a leader's motives and behavioral style in exercising power. It provides group members with a structured mechanism for providing feedback on the group leader's use of power and control.

Description

The Power Management Profile has three sections, reflecting power motives, power style, and morale. Sample items for each section appear in Figure 6.11. The first section has 60 items, each item consisting of a sentence stem, followed by two choices for

Part 1

1. **In setting goals and identifying objectives for us, my manager's major concern is:**

    C. That our individual needs and capabilities are well met and utilized.

    OR

    A. That the goals and objectives we aspire to are high enough to stretch and challenge all of us.

    C A

2. **In delegating authority to us, my manager is most mindful that:**

    A. Authority should be commensurate with responsibility such that people can discharge their duties and be held accountable in a fair manner.

    OR

    C. The delegation of authority is a delicate matter which must be done in such a way that no one feels they are simply being asked to do more work.

    A C

3. **When I go to my manager with problems, he or she prefers to:**

    B. Act more as a consultant or coach and let me struggle with the problem until, perhaps with my manager's help, I can begin to see my various alternatives more clearly.

    OR

    C. Let me know that someone cares and is willing to do whatever possible to help me through my dilemma.

    B C

4. **When it is necessary to discipline someone, my manager:**

    B. Tries to make sure that the disciplinary action taken is fair.

    OR

    A. Tries to make sure that the disciplinary action taken serves as an example to the rest of us.

    B A

5. **In making work assignments for us, my manager is most comfortable:**

    A. When he or she controls the process and makes assignments which yield the best "fit" of job requirements with available talent.

    OR

    C. When people are allowed to volunteer for the jobs they would like to do.

    A C

Figure 6.11. Sample Items from Profile.

Part 2

1. In making work assignments for me, typically:

    My manager   We   I
       decides   decide   decide
   completely   jointly   completely

: ____ : ____ : ____ : ____ : ____ : ____ : ____ : ____ : ____ : ____ : ____ :

2. In setting goals and identifying the scope of my individual job, typically:

    My manager   We   I
       decides   decide   decide
   completely   jointly   completely

: ____ : ____ : ____ : ____ : ____ : ____ : ____ : ____ : ____ : ____ : ____ :

3. In determining my training needs, typically:

    My manager   We   I
       decides   decide   decide
   completely   jointly   completely

: ____ : ____ : ____ : ____ : ____ : ____ : ____ : ____ : ____ : ____ : ____ :

4. In setting my break-times, meal-times, etc., typically:

    My manager   We   I
       decides   decide   decide
   completely   jointly   completely

: ____ : ____ : ____ : ____ : ____ : ____ : ____ : ____ : ____ : ____ : ____ :

5. In establishing production schedules and work deadlines for me, typically:

    My manager   We   I
       decides   decide   decide
   completely   jointly   completely

: ____ : ____ : ____ : ____ : ____ : ____ : ____ : ____ : ____ : ____ : ____ :

Figure 6.11 (Continued)

Part 3

In general, **who provides the leadership** in discussions between you and your manager?

In general:

9 My manager leads completely
8 My manager leads quite a lot
7 My manager leads a little more than moderately
6 My manager leads moderately
5 My manager and I lead about equally
4 I lead moderately
3 I lead a little more than moderately
2 I lead quite a lot
1 I lead completely

While each of us may be held accountable for how well we put work-related decisions into effect, we may or may not have a feeling of personal responsibility for their success. In general, **how responsible do you feel** for making such decisions really work?

I typically feel:

9 Completely responsible
8 Quite responsible
7 Moderately responsible
6 A little more responsible than not responsible
5 Neither very responsible nor very irresponsible
4 A little more irresponsible than responsible
3 Moderately irresponsible
2 Quite irresponsible
1 Completely irresponsible

Reactions to the decisions which govern one's work may range from total approval to various degrees of frustration. In general, **how frustrated do you feel** with trying to work within the decision framework governing your work?

Figure 6.11 (Continued)

In general, I feel:

9 Completely frustrated
8 Quite frustrated
7 Moderately frustrated
6 A little more frustrated than approving
5 Neither very frustrated nor very approving
4 A little more approving than frustrated
3 Moderately approving
2 Quite approving
1 Completely approving

Figure 6.11 (Continued)

completing the sentence. The team member chooses the sentence ending which best describes the team leader's tendencies. Based on these responses, three power motive scores are compiled: Personalized, Socialized, and Affiliative.

The second section consists of ten items. Each item focuses on how decision making is shared between the leader and the individual team member. Items are rated on an 11-point scale, yielding a power style score.

The third section consists of six questions concerning personal satisfaction and confidence. Team members indicate their answers on a nine-point scale. Based on these responses, an index of morale is computed.

1. Allow each team member about two hours to fill out and score the instrument, describing their perceptions of the leader's power tendencies. Care should be taken to preserve team members' anonymity. The team leader fills out a companion survey describing his own use of power.
2. The team leader scores his own responses and studies the interpretive materials until he understands the significance of his own scores.
3. The leader charts and summarizes the team members' scores on the Power Management Profile, which provides a composite view of team members' perceptions.
4. Study and interpret the group's perceptions as reflected in the scores. The instrument yields scores for each of three power motives: Personalized, Socialized, and Affiliative. It also pro-

provides a behavioral power style measure and a measure of individual morale. Comparison of group leader perceptions with those of the team members can reveal a great deal about how use of power affects the team.

5. The leader decides whether or not to discuss the results with the team. Usually, it is best to discuss the results with the team, but there are exceptions. The discussion should not be used to identify and punish critics, for example. If the results are too embarrassing or painful, group discussion might not be in the team's best interest.

6. If results are discussed with the group, the group leader should:
   (a) briefly present the results, and his understanding of what they mean;
   (b) invite group members to add their interpretations;
   (c) ask any key questions he would like the team to address; and
   (d) invite questions from the team members.

The discussion should be aimed at reaching mutual understanding and agreement, or at least acceptance of differing points of view, regarding the use of power in the team. The eight characteristics of effective feedback presented earlier in this chapter could act as a useful set of ground rules for this discussion.

Many leaders are uncomfortable using power. Frequently, inappropriate or misdirected use of power prompts anger, hostility, and reduced productivity from subordinates. The instrument is intended to generate open discussion on the group leader's management skills and use of power. The aim is to encourage a better understanding and acceptance of the way the leader uses and shares power.

The instrument is research-based and extensively normed. Although it is primarily designed for use by a manager and his immediate staff, it is suitable for use in other team settings as well. Simply substitute the term "chairperson" or "leader" for the word "manager."

The Power Management Profile Technique is value-laden. An ideal profile is identified. The results can therefore put the leader on the defensive. For this reason, it is important that:
   (1) the leader have an opportunity to view the results in private first;

(2)   team members' responses to the survey are anonymous; and

(3)   the leader has full freedom to choose whether or not to discuss the results with the team.

Example

During executive development, OHRD Associates uses the Power Management Profile Technique with a McGraw-Hill/CRM film on motivation. The film describes two dimensions of power—socialized and personal self-aggrandizement—and the need for affiliation and achievement.

Joy Machinery's Coal Group used the Power Management Profile to help its executives manage a newly decentralized organization. Each participating manager was asked to bring completed instruments to the session. By having peers and subordinates complete the profile in advance, managers were prepared with actual feedback from their groups, ready to assess their use of power in a nonthreatening context away from the workplace. Anxiety over co-worker perceptions was reduced, and participants were more willing to acknowledge their own abuses and underutilization of power. Using the completed profiles as a basis for discussion, managers saw the exercise as a vehicle for becoming aware of their everyday uses of power—both constructive and destructive. The use of feedback from subordinates strengthened the executives' capacity to effectively use the new organizational structure.

Resources

Jones, P.E. (1984). *Developing a Training Program for Effective Group Problem Solving.* Unpublished master's thesis. University of Texas at Austin, Department of Curriculum and Instruction.

McClelland, D.C. (1975). *Power: The Inner Experience.* New York: Irvington Publishers.

Mink, O., and Owen, K. (1983). *Connecting to Others Through Straight Talk.* Unpublished training packet. Austin, TX: 1208 Somerset Avenue.

Murray, M.F. (1979). *Meeting Effectiveness Training.* Unpublished training packet. Arlington, TX: 1018 Arlena Drive.

The Power Management Profile and Inventory used with permission of:
Teleometrics International
1755 Woodstead Court
The Woodlands, Texas 77380

FROM GRIPE TO GOAL IN SEVEN MINUTES TECHNIQUE

Purpose

This exercise permits team members to share concerns and frustrations regarding the team's work, and helps turn them into constructive goals while eliciting help from teammates to resolve them. Positive results rarely result from gripe sessions. This is an organized alternative for group members to share feedback while recognizing complaints and focusing on solutions.

Description

From Gripe to Goal in Seven Minutes is a one-page, six-item form. Each item is an unfinished sentence. Team members complete each sentence in order. By the time the fourth item is completed, the team member has established a goal in place of the gripe. If the goal seems particularly difficult, team members complete the fifth and sixth items to gain insight into the obstacles and the learning needed (see Figures 6.12 and 6.13).

1. Distribute a copy of the form to each team member.
2. Allow team members seven minutes to complete the form. Encourage them to pick something that is really bothering them, especially if it concerns things happening with the team or its members.
3. Have team members pair up with partners they trust or feel comfortable with.
4. In each partnership, one person becomes the griper, and the other person the helper. The griper begins by stating his gripe, just the way he has written it down. The helper listens and responds with a statement of the Helper Form (Figure 6.12),

---

FROM GRIPE TO GOAL IN SEVEN MINUTES

1. My gripe is . . .

2. My real concern is . . .

3. What I am really wishing for is . . .

4. Therefore, my goal is to . . .

If you do not know how to reach the goal, complete items 5 and 6.

5. What makes achievement of this goal especially difficult is . . .

6. Therefore, in order to reach this goal, I need to learn . . .

Figure 6.12. Getting a Problem Statement.

FROM GRIPE TO GOAL IN SEVEN MINUTES

1. What is your gripe? I won't tell anyone else without your permission.

2. It sounds like you're feeling . . . ., because
    . . . .

    Right?

3. It seems that what you're really concerned about is
    . . . .

    Is that it?

4. So what you're really wishing for is
    . . . .

    Is that it?

5. So your goal is . . . . Right?

6. (Brainstorm with the griper on ways he or she can accomplish the goal.
    Come up with as many different ideas as you can, including funny ones.
    For right now, don't worry about what will work and what won't.)

7. Do you think this will be difficult for you?

    (If the answer is no, this is the end of the exercise.
    Congratulations!)

    (If the answer is yes, proceed to Steps 8, 9, and 10.)

8. Why? What are the main obstacles?

9. Sounds like you will need to learn
    . . . .

    in order to deal with this.

10. Is it worth it to you to do all these things in order to reach this goal?

Figure 6.13. Helper Form.

"It sounds like you're feeling .... because
.... (It will be helpful to write this and
other formats on a chalkboard, easel pad, or other large display that the whole group can see, or to use the Helper Form
shown in Figure 6.13). The griper tells the helper whether
this is accurate or not, and clarifies.

5. The helper then completes the sentence, "It seems that what
   you're really concerned about is ...."
   The griper tells the helper whether this is accurate or not, and
   clarifies.

6. Helper says, "So what you're really wishing for is ....
   ...." The griper provides feedback and clarifies.

7. Helper says, "So your goal is ...."
   The griper provides feedback and clarifies.

8. Griper and helper brainstorm for five minutes on alternative
   ways the griper can accomplish the goal.

9. If the goal seems difficult or perplexing to the griper, the two
   spend another five minutes identifying the main obstacles
   and what the griper must learn to solve the problem.

10. Helper asks, "Is it worth it to you to do all these things to
    reach this goal?" Griper responds.

11. Partners swap roles and repeat Steps 4 through 10. Allow
    about 15 minutes for this cycle.

12. Invite team members to comment on the exercise, their cur-
    rent feelings, etc. Ask if anyone has a goal to propose for the
    whole group to work on. Treat these goals as action items for
    the team.

Often a team will seem to lose momentum and energy in the
course of its work together. This can be a signal of frustrations
and concerns that are going unaddressed. This exercise gives team
members permission to air their gripes and get support from a
sympathetic listener. These gripes are then reframed as problems,
and the griper is encouraged to take responsibility for working
something out. It is simple and inexpensive.

The outcome depends on the types of gripes and the team
members' skills in handling conflict. It is important for the helper
to keep the gripe confidential, allowing the griper to choose whom
to tell, when, and how.

Example

A midmanager in a manufacturing firm and his staff of line supervisors worked reasonably well together for a period of several months. At one of the regularly scheduled staff meetings, however, the manager noticed that the team seemed restless and uncomfortable.

The next meeting seemed unproductive, too. The manager sensed that there were problems going unspoken, and tried without much success to get them out in the open. He realized he needed more feedback from the group. He decided to devote the next meeting to a gripe session, if he could find a way to handle it constructively. He consulted the director of management training, who suggested the Gripe-to-Goal format.

The team worked through the exercise in about 45 minutes. Several problems were identified by members of the team. One problem related to production scheduling was mentioned by several supervisors and was selected for action planning by the group.

Some of the line supervisors felt that they had inadequate input to the production schedule, and wanted the manager to make changes in the timing between delivery of supplies and completion of their units' work on the product.

These adjustments were made, and this seemed to improve morale slightly. The manager decided to include in regular meetings of the team a time period at each meeting for members to share feedback about problems and outline action plans to resolve them.

During the following month two supervisors had a frank confrontation. The supervisors dealt with this conflict openly at the following staff meeting, using the gripe-to-goal technique in the discussion.

Though the group experienced awkwardness at first, the supervisors resolved their conflict, then began to work together better than ever before. As other problems in the group became viewed as opportunities for sharing feedback for constructive action planning, the morale and productivity of the group improved considerably.

Resource
OHRD Associates
1208 Somerset Avenue
Austin, Texas 78753
(From material originally presented by Michael Murray, Arlington,
Texas)

7

PROBLEM SOLVING:
RELEASING ENERGY FOR GROWTH

In the previous chapters we developed a framework for problem solving. First, we focused on the concept of *trust*. Trust is essential for successful problem solving. Without a shared contract that specifies openness, keeping agreements, and personal safety as rules of conduct, it is virtually impossible to identify, define, and solve problems.

Second, we focused on the *unique qualities* each individual member brings to the group. An acceptance of individual differences is required to solve problems, for each person is a repository of personal creative power. If there is an atmosphere of fear, if uniqueness is punished, then people will be unwilling to share *all they know* about a problem. In the context of individuality, we focused on two kinds of skills, self-awareness and communications skills. The *process* of problem solving relies on these skills in eliciting all available relevant information.

Our third focus was on feedback about *goal oriented behavior*. When you and other group members know the goal(s), then feedback about progress is useful. Feedback is a way that teams stay on course, moving consistently toward a desired goal. Feedback is also a way that people identify problems to manage self and the processes that connect individuals in a group.

Now we are ready to focus attention on the problem-solving process and describe some techniques which help to solve problems.

What Behavior Patterns Are Essential
to Problem Solving in the Team?

When a team is busy finding and defining problems, it behaves differently than when it is busily implementing a plan of action. These two types of behaviors require distinct attitudes and roles. Type A, made up of concentrated, controlling methods for solving a problem, and Type B, consisting of open, noncritical methods for discovering problems, are both required to solve problems successfully. Figure 7.1 lists the differences between these two behavior patterns.

Every problem situation has its own rhythm; there is a time for being relaxed and open, for seeing with soft eyes, for letting everything in without prejudice, and a time for being closed and concentrated, for seeing critically, and for filtering out what is irrelevant to the problem at hand. Type B behavior is appropriate in generating and exploring alternatives for defining the problem, coming up with possible alternatives and decision criteria, and selling the solution. Type A behavior is appropriate for clarifying the problem, fact-finding, evaluating choices, testing, deciding, and monitoring progress.

What Behaviors Block Group Problem Solving?

Either the team leader or individual team members can block problem solving. To describe many problem solving blocks, we use the concept of "discounts." To discount* means to deny something its full value.

Discounting the Person with the Problem or Discounting Oneself. To solve problems, the group and its members need an agenda. This agenda is actually a form of permission based on the acceptance of others or self. A person in the group who does not accept himself ties his own hands. A person who does not accept others undermines their sense of competence, and thus their ability to succeed.

Discounting the Existence of the Problem. The employee may say, "Boss, what are we going to do about the low morale around here?" The supervisor responds, "The morale couldn't be better!"

*The concept of discounting is taken from Transactional Analysis.

TYPE A behavior is:	TYPE B behavior is:
goal directed	unfocused
striving	laid back
hard	soft
controlling	democratic
concentrated	unconcentrated
hurried	relaxed
closed	open
logical, left-brained	creative, right-brained
critical, judgmental	accepting, nonjudgmental
thinking and sensing	intuitive and feeling
convergent	divergent

Figure 7.1. Type A Versus Type B Behavior.

If the team or its members refuse to recognize that problems exist, then, of course, it is not possible to solve them.

Discounting the Possibility of Defining or Doing Something About a Problem. If the team or its members believe a problem's complexity puts it beyond solution, it will not be solved. This is a common way to maintain the status quo, especially in multi-layered organizations where approval cycles and "red tape" are convenient excuses for not tackling problems.

Discounting the Context of the Problem. Often a problem is related to its environment. A problem-solving team can become ineffective and inefficient if it ignores situational factors that surround the problem being solved. Situational factors that contribute to a problem should be identified, and organizational resources which may be used in overcoming the problem should be considered.

Other ways a team can block problem solving include:

- avoiding defining the problem clearly, or confusing the problem with its solutions
- prejudging ideas and facts about the problem
- procrastinating
- competing for whose solution is accepted
- being undecided about the criteria for success

- being uncommitted to a shared vision of success
- having unclear values.

Figure 7.2 outlines some of the varieties of such inhibiting behaviors.

What Is Problem Solving?

Problem solving is a set of methods for analyzing the gap between what *is* and what is *needed*, between what *is* and what *should* or *could* be. The methods may be formal or informal; rational, intuitive, or both; structured or unstructured.

Whatever the method, each has key elements:

P: Project

to decide there is a problem; identify and define the problem situation and *project a vision* of how it should or could be different

O: Observe

to analyze the discrepancy or gap between what is and should be

W: Work Out a Plan and Implement It

to evaluate alternatives, choose those that are appropriate, create and implement an action plan

E: Evaluate

to monitor progress and achievement

R: Revise

to make changes in plans as needed.

The acronym POWER reflects the psychological experience of the group that learns how to solve problems. It gains a sense of potency or a confidence in its ability to change or cause change when change is necessary.

What Is the Structure of a Problem?

All problems share a similar structure despite the many techniques for solving them. In all cases, a team has a goal it wants to achieve. The "problem" is a state of creative tension or a gap between the current situation (WHAT IS or the REAL) and the desired situation (WHAT SHOULD/COULD BE or the IDEAL). When a group observes that there is such a gap they have taken the first step in problem solving: they have determined that there

Problem-Solving Step	Critical Roles	Inhibiting Behavior
Defining the problem	Exploring Clarifying Testing Summarizing	Overgeneralizing Overpoliteness Splitting hairs Grandstanding
Gathering Data	Fact-finding Surveying Testing Orienting	Jumping to conclusions Opinions without facts Lethargy Pursuing tangential questions not related to the problem
Identifying and Listing	Risking ideas Encouraging Recording Expediting	Overanalyzing Alternatives Lobbying Attaching ideas to persons Arguing and debating
Testing Alternatives and Forecasting Results	Reality testing Clarifying Harmonizing Standard setting	"Not invented here" withdrawal "Playboy cynicism" Straw voting Avoiding well defined goals and objectives
Selecting the Best Plan	Summarizing	Failure to reach closure
Implementing	Testing for consensus Clarifying Assigning Energizing	Voting (When consensus is really necessary) Generating ambiguity Failing to pin down responsibility Lack of involvement

*Figure 7.2. Steps, Critical Roles, and Inhibiting Behaviors
in Team Problem-Solving Process.*

is a problem. The challenge is to define the problem while examining the discrepancy between real and the ideal, as illustrated in Figure 7.3.

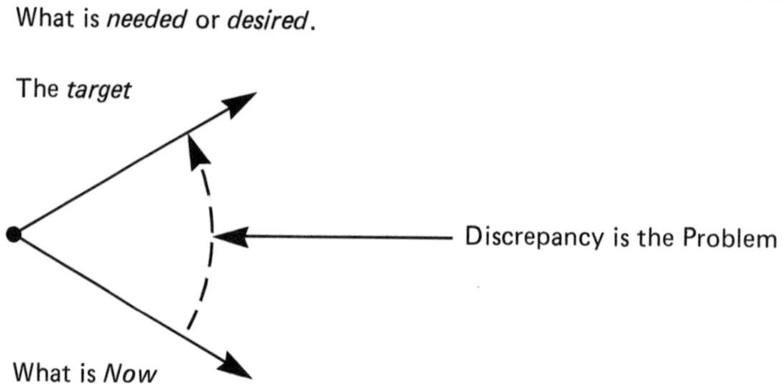

What is *needed* or *desired*.

Figure 7.3. Structure of a Problem.

In this framework, a problem is defined as the gap between what is observed and what is desired. Teams are likely to observe many problems which deserve attention, however, and frequently need guidance in deciding what problems to work on. A team needing some criteria for prioritizing problems may ask these questions:

Duration—How long has this situation persisted?
Frequency—How often does this situation occur?
Intensity—How severe is this problem?
Price—What does this problem cost?
Consequence—What will happen if this problem is ignored?
Manageability—Is the problem controllable?
Feasibility—Is it feasible to manage this problem?
Timing—Is time a high priority?

The variance or discrepancy between what is and what is needed becomes a problem when you and the group are CONCERNED enough to do something about it. The concern is *experienced* because the variance obviously is not manageable. Uncontrollable variance, frequently eliciting feelings of frustration or helplessness, causes stress. Stress tends to initiate coping behaviors, many of which are likely to be dysfunctional to the work of the group. It is important to remember that, at any point, there are probably many problems. The problem chosen for solution is the one of greatest concern *and* easiest to manage at the specific time.

The Problem Solving Process

Phase 1: Projecting. The main goals for this phase are to define the problem and project a vision for solving it.

1. Identify the current situation that needs to be changed and imagine how it could be improved.
2. State the problems selected for solving in terms of the discrepancy between the real and the ideal.
3. Project the desired results.

A problem that is accurately identified and clearly defined is more likely to be solved than one which is poorly conceived; an accurate and clear statement of the problem will help keep group efforts on track as possible solutions are developed and implemented. A widely used method for defining a problem and projecting desired results is first to produce a three-part problem statement, as illustrated in Figure 7.4.

Once the problem is stated adequately, it is time to observe the situation and dissect the problem.

Phase 2: Observing. The second phase of problem solving is collecting data which will help gain a deeper understanding of the problem and clarify your definition of the problem and its component parts; when this is done, you know that the problem is precisely the one you intend to be solving.

The goals of the observing phase are:

1. Gathering data about the problem.
2. Identifying and analyze the facets and components of the problem.
3. Clarify and refine your definition of the problem, in the light of new data and new insights which have been gained.

An excellent method for analyzing the problem is to define its boundaries, i.e., what is included and what is excluded from the problem. The causes of the problem then begin to move from general to specific.

CURRENT RESULTS	SOURCES OF VARIANCE	DESIRED RESULTS
Describes what is	Hunches about what contributed to the current situation	Describes what needs to be
Current market share has declined to 40%	Three new competitors	Increase market share to 50%

Figure 7.4. Three-Part Problem Statement.

First, list possible sources of the problem, including people, places, things, and points in time. Then seek data which support the notion that a particular place, person, material, or time is part of the problem's causes, and ask, "If this source is included in the problem, what effect does it have on the problem situation? If this dimension were changed would it affect the problem?" This analysis can become extensive, requiring categorization and prioritization of problem sources.

Phase 3: Working Out a Plan of Action. When the problem is analyzed and its most likely causes identified, it is time to develop solutions and work out a plan of action. The goals of Phase 3 are to:

1. Generate potential actions that will solve the problem.
2. Evaluate these ideas and select those which are most feasible for implementation.
3. Develop and implement an action plan for solving the problem which includes criteria for determining what progress has been made at various stages of the process.

1. *Generating Potential Solutions.*

A *solution* is an *action step* or a set of steps (a strategy) which, when implemented, will lead to the accomplishment of goals. Some techniques for generating possible alternative solutions in team settings are described later in this chapter. As potential solutions are discussed, a measurable result and ways to achieve it need to be listed for those ideas which the group will further consider. A method for outlining proposed solutions, expected results, and ways to measure results is illustrated in Figure 7.5.

PROPOSED SOLUTION	MEASURABLE RESULTS	MEASUREMENT PROCEDURES
Describe strategy or steps in reducing discrepancy between what is and what is desired	State objectives or desired outcomes which can be measured	Detail how progress toward attainment of results will be measured
Establish Productivity Improvement Teams (PITs) to increase productivity and market share	1. Implement PIT plan by end of second quarter. 2. Increase productivity by 16 tons per week. 3. Increase market share by 10%	1. Were PITs established? 2. Did they function effectively? 3. Assess change in productivity. 4. Assess increase in market share.

Figure 7.5. Generating Potential Solutions.

2. Evaluating and Selecting Proposed Solutions

After a problem has been selected and defined and a number of alternate solutions have been proposed, it is time for the team to specify which solution(s) will be pursued. To select the best solution, a team needs to achieve two objectives: (1) choose the one that will solve the problem, and (2) obtain support for its implementation. How the group makes the decision to act is critical to the process and to the success of the effort. The process used should insure that each person has adequate input and that each solution gets a thorough evaluation. Here are five criteria against which each alternative may be evaluated:

- Effect on the problem—will the proposed solution actually solve the problem? Is the effect measurable?
- Practicality—can the solution be implemented? Are the resources needed available or can they be obtained? Are

others to be involved in the solution? How can their support be gained?

- Costs—what will it cost to implement the solution? How do the costs compare to the gains?
- Acceptance—will the solution be acceptable to management and other people affected by it?
- Time—can the solution be implemented within a reasonable time?

3. *Developing and Implementing an Action Plan*

An action plan details how an objective will be accomplished, by whom, when, at what cost, and so forth. It is a schedule of events, times, people, and their interrelationships. It is a management plan which enables you to monitor the effectiveness of your problem solving. A good plan has the following characteristics:

- It is a DO plan, specifying action objectives at each step of the process.
- It is progressive, moving step by step toward a goal.
- It specifies what is to be done, by whom, and when.
- It is results-based.
- It is measurable.
- It requires commitment on the part of individuals and the group.

The central objective of action planning is to clarify each person's role. It starts with identifying steps needed to implement a given solution strategy, then arranging the steps in the most effective sequence, and assisting time limits to each step. Finally, agreement is reached on who will be responsible for implementing each step. As the plan is implemented, progress in achieving successful completion of each step should be monitored at key intervals.

Phase 4: Evaluating the Plan. *Problem solving is useful only if it yields results.* Evaluation is the process for judging whether or not the problem-solving effort succeeds. Evaluation should be performed at intervals during the plan's implementation, to keep efforts on track, and after the plan is completed, to determine to what extent the ultimate goals were achieved. Steps in the evaluation process are to:

1. Select a method for evaluating progress in resolving the problem.
2. Collect data.
3. Evaluate the data to determine what progress has been made.
4. Decide whether to continue with the plan, to quit, or to recycle the problem-solving process.

Evaluation begins with the criteria for success established in the process of selecting solutions. Under most conditions, when a solution has been defined and a problem solving action plan is established, the measurements for determining whether that objective is attained will be defined. The evaluation process then consists of looking at the outcomes and comparing them with expected results. If the results of this monitoring process are favorable, you continue with the plan as it has been developed; however, if a significant variance between obtained and expected results still exists, then you have to decide if the variance is significant or if it is due to chance.

Where there is a significant discrepancy between planned outcomes and actual achievement, it is necessary to decide whether to develop a new plan or to stick with the original. Criteria are needed for making this decision; while no set of criteria will apply to every problem situation, the ones listed below will prove helpful in many situations:

1. Is the plan failing because of concurrent events outside your team's immediate control? If yes, are the events temporary or chronic? If temporary, modify the original plan; if chronic, develop a new plan taking into account these events.
2. Is the plan feasible for the kinds of results you aim to achieve? If no, develop a new plan taking into account current realities.
3. Are the steps of the plan under the *direct control* of your team members? If not, develop a plan that is based on actions over which the team has direct control.

Phase 5: Revising and Recycling. Healthy teams are productive; they set goals, plan, act, and solve problems. The goals for the Revising and Recycling phase are:

1. Decide if continuing problem solving will be effective (based on the evaluation outcomes in Phase 4).
2. Recycle through the problem solving process when a new or revised plan is needed, developing and implementing new plans as appropriate.
3. Continue to adapt and grow according to current realities, looking at new opportunities and visions.

The team that actively solves problems is a team that knows where it is going and develops and uses problem solving processes that keep it on track for both the task and the human relationships required to achieve exemplary performance. Such teams, focusing on goals and on methods of achieving them, differ in many ways from teams that do not use models. These differences are outlined in Figure 7.6.

References

Gordon, W.J.J. (1961). *Synectics: The Development of Creative Capacity*. New York: Harper & Row.

Hanson, P.G. (1972). What to Look for in Groups in Pfeiffer, J.W., and Jones, J.E. (Eds.) *The 1972 Annual Handbook for Group Facilitators*. San Diego, CA: University Associates.

Harriman, R. (1984). Creativity: Moving Beyond Linear Logic, *The Futurist*, August (XVIII, 4, 17-20).

Kepner, C.H., and Tregoe, B.B. (1981). *The New Rational Manager*. Princeton, NJ: Princeton Research Press.

Koberg, D., and Bagnall, J. (1976). *The Universal Traveler: A Soft Systems Guide to Creativity, Problem Solving, and the Process of Reaching Goals*. Los Altos, CA: Kaufman.

Mellor, K., and Schiff, E. (July, 1985). Discounting. *Transactional Analysis Journal, V, 3*.

Osborn, A.F. (1953). *Applied Imagination*. New York: Charles Scribner and Sons.

Parnes, S.J. (1981). *The Magic of Your Mind*. Buffalo, NY: Creative Education Foundation.

Prince, G.M. (1970). *The Practice of Creativity*. New York: Macmillan.

Prince, G.M. (1980). Learning as Skills, not Talents. *The Philips Exeter Bulletin*, June-July and September-October.

Rawlinson, J.G. (1981). *Creative Thinking and Brainstorming*. New York: John Wiley and Sons.

Simpson, D.T. (1985). *Creating Creativity*. Santa Barbara, CA: The Fielding Institute.

GROUPS THAT ARE LOW	GROUPS THAT ARE HIGH
1. are low in productivity	1. are high in productivity
2. do not regularly monitor individual or team performance and do not provide feedback	2. regularly assess where individuals and teams are, relative to goals, and provide performance feedback
3. do not have clearly stated expectations on performance or human relationships	3. have clearly stated expectations about performance and human relationships
4. develop unproductive norms	4. develop productive norms
5. foster efforts to conceal actual performance	5. create the conditions for an open examination of performance
6. persist in maintaining unproductive practices	6. frequently assess methods and change those which are unproductive
7. waste time	7. use time according to desired results
8. have difficulty in prioritizing what is to be done	8. work according to priority
9. have unclear values	9. have clear values
10. suppress conflict	10. have methods for dealing with conflicts
11. have poorly defined visions and missions.	11. have clearly defined visions and missions.

*Figure 7.6. Performance Differences in Teams
High/Low in Utilizing Problem Solving Models.*

Vroom, V.H. (1976). Can Readers Learn to Lead? *Organizational Dynamics*, Winter, 17-20.

BRAINSTORMING TECHNIQUE

Purpose
Brainstorming is used to enhance the number and quality of ideas or alternatives weighed by the team as it reaches a decision. Team members are freed from the risk of negative comments and the need to justify or explain suggestions. In problem solving this process can be especially useful when the group is generating alternative solutions for a problem which has been defined.

Description
The rules for brainstorming are simple.
1. A problem is stated and a desire expressed for as many possible solutions as the group can imagine.
2. Team members are invited to voice any idea that comes to mind. All ideas are accepted at face value and written down so that the whole group can see them.
3. No suggestion is evaluated when it is made. All critical evaluation of ideas is postponed. *Quantity* of ideas is the goal.
4. Fanciful, humorous, even wild ideas are sought.
5. Combining ideas and extending other team members' ideas are encouraged.

Left to their own devices, one or two persons in a team habitually evaluate ideas the moment they are expressed. Such criticism discourages other group members from offering ideas. Usually, the more alternatives a team allows itself to choose from, the better the quality of the eventual decision. Brainstorming stimulates the quantity of ideas by reserving critical remarks for a later stage and stimulates creativity by encouraging a playful atmosphere.

On the downside, brainstorming does not ensure the full participation of all members. While some group members may get "turned on" and enthusiastically offer several ideas, others may remain silent, perhaps unable to get a word in edgewise. (Some structured problem solving techniques for groups, such as the

Synectics Technique and the Nominal Group Technique, described later in this chapter, build in mechanisms which ensure that everyone participates in the brainstorming phase). Brainstorming relies on a fairly well developed level of disclosure trust, so that members feel safe and supported in speaking freely.

Brainstorming can be useful at many points in the process of problem solving. Examples include:

- selecting a problem to work on
- identifying key issues to address in fact finding
- identifying resources needed
- identifying resources available
- identifying criteria for decision making
- suggesting possible solutions
- creating alternative action plans for implementing solutions.

Example

A group of educational researchers was considering how to provide recognition for outstanding performance. In generating alternatives, they were chronically undisciplined; each suggestion was critiqued in depth as it was entertained. After three suggestions were considered—commendation forms, employee-of-the-month dinners, and merit raises—no more were forthcoming. The group found each of the three suggestions lacking and, in frustration, tabled the issue.

Two months later, the issue came up again. The chairperson, realizing that a larger number of alternatives needed to be considered, suggested that they generate ideas using the brainstorming approach, with the sole purpose of coming up with as many ideas as possible, saving all criticisms for later. This time the group produced no less than a dozen ideas—singing telegrams, office pins, gag gifts, personal thank-you notes. They combined the attractive elements of several ideas into a group once-a-month luncheon format that became an institution.

Resource

Osborn, A.F. (1963). *Applied Imagination: Principles and Procedures of Creative Problem Solving.* New York: Charles Scribner and Sons.

CARIBBEAN ISLAND SURVIVAL TECHNIQUE

Purpose

The Caribbean Island Survival Technique is one of several simulations available from various sources designed to examine and improve a group's ability to reach adaptive consensus decisions. These simulations are rich learning experiences which (1) bring out group leadership and creative problem-solving abilities of individual group members, (2) teach team members to trust the group's decisions, and (3) provide an objective and realistic measure of the group's effectiveness.

Description

This exercise simulates the plight of a group of people shipwrecked on a small, uninhabited Caribbean island. The task is to survive. The exercise takes about two hours and should be completed at one sitting. This is an overview of the steps required:

1. Obtain copies of the instrument, as listed in *Resources*, and find someone to conduct the simulation. This person's job is to brief the participants, give directions, enforce rules, keep time, debrief participants, and conduct a group discussion.
2. The Conductor studies the simulation and prepares for the actual group exercise.
3. Recruit one or two observers to watch the team in action and provide feedback on how the group members work together.
4. The team convenes for the exercise. The Conductor briefs the team on the situation they face and answers all questions.
5. Team members, working alone, rank nine action steps in the order they think these should be carried out. They also rank thirteen salvaged items in order of their importance to the group's survival. (It is helpful to have such materials on hand for inspection.) The Conductor keeps a strict time limit on this phase.
6. The team works together to reach consensus decisions on the ranking of each action step and salvageable item. The Conductor keeps a strict time limit on this phase, and observers watch and take notes on the group process.
7. The Conductor debriefs the team by providing the "correct" rankings as determined by navigational, Park Service, and Coast

Guard survival experts. Team members compare their individual answers to the experts' and derive their own scores. The team compares its group decision to the experts' opinion to derive a team score.

8. The team discusses the results and implications with help from statistical information provided in the Conductor's Manual. Observers comment on the interesting things they saw and heard.

The key to success or failure of any simulation as a learning exercise lies in the skills of the Conductor, and to a lesser extent the observers. In recruiting a Conductor for your simulation you need someone with strong skills in three areas: supervision, human relations, and discussion leadership. Your best bet is someone trained in conducting simulations. Your next best bet is a training and development professional (especially a group facilitator) or a manager with strong oral communication and discussion leadership skills. If you cannot find a willing Conductor from one of these walks of life, look for someone with a background in teaching, coaching, sports officiating, military command, chairing committees, or similar "group shepherding" experience. If need be, you can have the Conductor lead the group through Steps 4 through 7, and a second person (perhaps an observer) lead the discussion.

Observers need to be skilled in observing and recording complex human interactions, and in providing factual (and sometimes confrontive) feedback. Training and development professionals, managers and supervisors, coaches, and industrial engineers are good examples.

Example

A property division of a large electronics firm is responsible for orchestrating office moves. It often found itself at odds over details with other divisions (as well as individuals) whom they were moving to new office space. Typically, the preferences of different internal units for "special consideration" conflicted with the master plan for moving an entire division in an efficient and effective manner. In addition, various members of the property group were "playing favorites" at the expense of other internal clients.

Various persons in the property group were in competition with each other, and their internal clients were discovering that external vendors could move them cheaper than their own in-house group. The property group's existence was threatened.

The Caribbean Island Survival Exercise was used by the firm's organizational development specialist, in conjunction with an external consultant, to allow the property group to experience in a new context the importance of focusing on the overall goal and total team considerations before jumping into specific problem solving strategy decisions. Three groups (each with three observers) went through the exercise, compared their results with the expert rankings, and discussed with their observer the problem solving process. General discussion focused on these questions:

- Did the team clarify and agree upon the goal and action alternatives before the specific salvageable items were ranked? *Answer*: Actually no! Do we treat our clients this way! Yes! Now they had a problem to be solved.
- What effect did this goal clarity (or lack of goal clarity) have upon the ease to which the order ranking of the salvageable items was agreed upon? *Answer*: An extensive effect. Are we confusing ourselves and clients? Yes. What can we do?

The discussion then turned to strategies for working together and for obtaining consensus with the clients (the persons/divisions) on the overall purpose and goals of a move, as well as best methods to achieve client satisfaction at costs lower than external vendors. New strategies developed by the property team centered around including clients in the problem solving process. The team began to plan meetings with the leadership of units to be moved *prior* to developing moving plans. In these meetings the property team discussed with the "client" group (a) overall organizational goals of the firm (to establish a basis for consensual planning), (b) the goals of the "client" unit as related to those goals, and (c) special needs of the unit which the property division might need to be aware of during the moving process.

The friction and conflicts which had typically accompanied each move were reduced considerably, in part because the units had established a sense of common purpose while engaging in cooperative problem solving and planning and in part because the "client" groups gained a sense that their particular goals and needs were being considered by the organization. The performance improvement achieved in the next 12-month period resulted in an overall savings to the corporation of $550,000 under the total cost of private vendors. Client satisfaction was very high.

Resources
The following is a brief list of some group problem solving simulations and information on how to obtain them.

Caribbean Island Survival Exercise
> Designs for Organizational Effectiveness
> P.O. Box 13232
> Richmond, Virginia 23225

Desert Survival Situation and Project Planning Situation
> Human Synergistics
> 39819 Plymouth Road
> Plymouth, Michigan 48170

NASA Moon Survival Task
> Teleometrics International
> 1755 Woodstead Court
> The Woodlands, Texas 77380

Bridge Game
> Didactic Systems
> P.O. Box 457
> Cranford, New Jersey 07106

Note: The "Bridge Game" differs from the survival exercises in the following ways. The group's task is to estimate how long it will take them to build a toy bridge from a blueprint. Groups submit competitive bids, then build the bridge to see how long it actually takes them. It is designed to examine the supervision process, but serves most of the same purposes as the survival simulation.

DIAGNOSING THE CHANGE PROCESS TECHNIQUE

Purpose
This form provides a framework for planning a change effort. It focuses the user's attention on defining and analyzing the problem, on action planning, and key questions to answer if the change effort is to be successful.

Description
The instrument is an eight-page booklet, divided into three parts. Part I, Change Situation Identification, helps the user examine the situation to be changed, the change strategy contemplated, and his or her own motives and risks in undertaking it. It challenges the user to describe what state of affairs would exist after the change, what the costs of achieving the projected results would be, and whether it seems to be worth the price.

Part II uses Force Field Analysis to examine the state of the system to be changed. The system is assumed to be in a state of equilibrium between forces working for the change and forces working against it. The analysis form helps the user identify and weigh these forces and provides guidance on how best to alter the balance of forces.

Part III is Action Planning Steps. It guides the user in probing several key issues to be addressed in carrying out the change plan. It challenges the user to identify his or her proper role, anticipate new restraining forces that will arise with the change effort, clarify who is to do what, and specify how he or she will know when the change is complete.

The Analysis Form for Diagnosing the Change Process does not provide an exhaustive step-by-step road map for change. Instead, it raises key issues for the user to address. Some show the need for data gathering; others probe the goals, motives, and opinions of the user. The identification of driving and restraining forces in Part II is largely a matter of the user's intuition. Although Part I will help in deciding whether to go forward with a change effort, the form overall is intended primarily to aid in carrying out the change.

Example

A large international manufacturing company's executive officers used this technique while planning strategies for dealing with an economic downturn threatening their company's existence. Officers filled out Part I individually, then shared their views of the problem in group discussion. The group then brainstormed forces working in favor of the company's solvency and those working against it.

Part II of the form was used to help identify restraining forces and potential pay-offs of various possible change strategies. The officers then grouped into task forces, with each task force working on one of the restraining forces targeted for action. Each group developed and implemented action plans.

After the task forces implemented their action plans, the officers met again as a large group. The form was again used, this time to evaluate the problem solving efforts and to assess the new equilibrium resulting from the task force interventions and the passage of time. New driving and restraining forces emerged, with a new mix of weights. The restraining force chosen for change this time was the company's organizational structure. The officers decided to decentralize the company into regional offices, each with increased responsibility for its own functions in marketing, design, human relations, and so forth. As the group discussed the officers' new roles (using Part III of the form), the need for cross-training quickly became apparent. Each officer designed a training program in his field of specialty, and served as trainer for those wishing to advance their expertise in his field. Within five years the company saved over two million dollars in training alone, and it established itself as a leading producer because of customer service, engineering reflective of customer problems, and quality manufacturing. In two product lines they achieved over 85 percent of market share—nearly double the market share held when the effort first began.

Resources

Lewin, K. (1969). Quasi-stationary Social Equilibria and the Problem of Permanent Change. In Bennis, W.G., Benne, K.O., and Chin, R. (eds.), *The Planning of Change.* New York: Holt, Rinehart, and Winston, 235-238.

The "Analysis Form for Diagnosing the Change Process" is available from:
OHRD Associates
1208 Somerset Avenue
Austin, TX 78753

SYNECTICS TECHNIQUE

Purpose

Synectics is a structured method of creative problem solving. Combining linear and logical analysis with fanciful imaging exercises, Synectics draws on the full range of mental abilities of the team members. The result is greatly enhanced creativity in searching out courses of action, as compared to levels of creativity which emerge with conventional methods of problem solving.

Description

The Synectics Technique calls for:
- (a) a client with a problem and the willingness to take the primary responsibility for solving it,
- (b) a leader trained in conducting the process, and
- (c) a team willing to help the client.

The general format of the process is as follows:

1. The leader and the client briefly discuss the problem in private.
2. The leader introduces the client to the group and announces the problem as given. The leader asks the client to elaborate for the group by answering these questions:
   - What makes this a problem? Fill us in on the background.
   - What makes this a problem for you?
   - What have you tried or thought of already?
   - What help do you want from the team?
3. While the client answers the questions in Step 2, the team members listen and write restatements of the problem from their points of view, writing down goal/wishes. These are statements beginning with "How to . . ." or "I wish . . ." Team members then take turns sharing their goal/wishes with the group.
4. The client selects one or more of the goal/wishes, combining similar ones, and focuses the group's attention on one goal/wish

with which to begin. If the client wishes to limit the quantity of ideas, this is the time to do so.

5. Team members offer the client ideas for addressing the goal/ wish. They may build on each other's ideas. Quantity of ideas is encouraged unless the client has established a limit.

6. The client then selects an appealing idea and states three of the ideas's useful points. At this point, the client may express any major concerns about the idea's feasibility. Team members continue to alter the idea so as to keep the useful points and eliminate the concerns.

7. When an idea has been developed to the point that the client considers it a possible solution, the client says so.

8. The client commits to several next steps he or she will take to implement the possible solution.

9. Steps 4 through 8 are repeated until each of the selected goal/ wishes has been addressed.

The leader may take the group on "excursions" to gain fresh ideas and perspectives, especially during Steps 5 and 6. These exercises are playful and imaginative but serve several serious purposes. They breathe new energy into tired minds, break mind-sets, awaken senses, alter team members' perspectives, and make use of both brain hemispheres. New ways of looking at the problem emerge. Here are two examples of excursions:

(1) Team members examine pocket articles for "clues."
(2) Team members imagine that they are a part of the problem and describe that experience.

Synectics, properly used, often produces surprising and profoundly innovative approaches to problems. It is especially useful for ill-defined problems (also known as "fuzzy messes") and recurring problems (problems that won't stay solved).

One of the main strengths of this method can also be its main drawback: it's fun. In our culture, heavily influenced by the work ethic, there is a tendency to view work and play as opposites. By definition, play is fun. Therefore, there is a strong notion that work must not be fun. Most managers tend to frown on play in the workplace. The jovial mood of a Synectics group would strike most managers as frivolous, unseemly, and out of place. One good Synectics session disproves these notions and demonstrates that play, properly channeled, is profoundly productive.

Synectics depends on an open, permissive, anything-goes communication climate. This kind of climate in turn depends on two important factors: first, a trained and skilled leader, and second, a team of people willing to grant each other permission to speak freely, "immune from prosecution." A group of people who are accustomed to working together and have developed a healthy level of disclosure trust is required. There are exceptions, however. Synectics can work—

- with people who are creatively sophisticated (such as designers, artists, and entrepreneurs) although they may not know each other well;
- in settings where freedom of thought and expression are valued (such as most universities); and
- in situations where participants do not expect to cross paths again (such as conventions, training seminars, encounter groups.)

Example

A metropolitan training and development society used Synectics to upgrade its newsletter. The incoming communications chairperson, who served as editor for the newsletter, was anxious to please the membership by producing a good newsletter and equally anxious to shield herself from potential criticism. She knew that the membership wanted some fresh ideas and a "fresh look" for the newsletter, but felt she needed creative help from others if the publication was to be really innovative.

The editor prevailed upon an associate to round up a task force to "come up with creative ideas for improving the newsletter." The team members did not know each other well, but as training and development professionals they shared several key values which favored a Synectics approach. These included (1) a preference for open communications, (2) an inclination toward networking, and (3) a desire to help. The meetings were held on the campus of a nearby university. After some initial trust-building sessions the group rapidly developed a six-month plan for upgrading the newsletter.

The results were dramatic and surprised everyone involved. The creative exercises sparked a number of new ideas which none of the team members had thought of individually. The process made the client feel supported, and her choices in the process gave the group the direction needed for coming up with new and practical ideas. The client, who previously was anxious and uncertain, emerged confident, energetic, and appreciative of the new ideas provided by the team. The group members got their messages across to the client, felt good about succeeding, were surprised at how easy it turned out to be, and gained an appreciation for each other's strengths. The format of the newsletter was changed radically, the process for choosing articles to be published was improved and, as a result of several cost-saving ideas of the team, the cost of the publication was reduced by ten percent.

Resources

Prince, G.M. (1970). *The Practice of Creativity: A Manual for Dynamic Group Problem Solving.* New York: Harper and Row.

Rose, E. (1975). *Preparing for a Synectics Meeting.* Cambridge, MA: Synectics, Inc.

Other structured problem-solving methods:

Kepner, C.H., and Tregoe, B.B. (1965). *The Rational Manager: Systematic Approach to Problem Solving and Decision Making.* New York: McGraw-Hill Book Company.

Kepner, C.H., and Tregoe, B.B. (1981). *The New Rational Manager.* Princeton, NJ: Princeton Research Press.

Noller, R.B. (1977). *Scratching the Surface of Creative Problem Solving: A Bird's Eye View of CPS.* Buffalo, NY: D.O.K. Publishers.

QUALITY CIRCLES TECHNIQUE

Purpose

The Quality Circles method is a structured and formalized approach to group problem solving. It aims primarily at improving the quality of the team's product or service.

Description

The Quality Circles Technique was pioneered by the Japanese in the 1960s to upgrade their quality image. The phrase, "Made in Japan," had become synonymous with cheap, shoddy goods. The Japanese devoted many hours of rigorous research, testing, and experimentation to improve quality.

Quality Circles are small groups of people doing similar work. Circle members meet voluntarily and regularly to identify, analyze, and solve quality and other problems in their work area. The circles are usually formed in the following manner.

1. Top management decides to invest in a Quality Circles program.
2. A steering committee is formed to oversee the program.
3. A facilitator skilled in training and group dynamics is retained.
4. The facilitator recruits and trains circle leaders, often first-line supervisors.
5. Circle leaders recruit and train voluntary participants. The facilitator oversees this effort. Training includes skill development in:
    - Brainstorming
    - Problem identification and definition
    - Cause-and-effect problem analysis
    - Data collection and analysis
    - Consensus decision making
    - Oral presentation
6. Circles identify, analyze, and solve problems in their own work areas. A circle derives solutions and either implements them directly itself or (more typically) presents them to management for approval.

The advantages of a well run Quality Circles program are numerous. It contributes directly to improvement in the organization's product or service and to improving team members' skills as effective persons. In Japan, the latter receives the primary emphasis. This method builds assertiveness, oral communication, and problem-solving skills, and it provides employees an opportunity to directly influence their work environment. Such a program also tends to improve management-labor relations by creating two-way, task-oriented dialogue, giving labor some input into the management of the company.

Unfortunately, some Quality Circles programs in the United States have been so hastily carried out that the approach has picked up a bad reputation in some places. As a result, the term "quality circles" has been replaced by such euphemisms as "pride circles," "employee participation groups," "problem-solving groups," or "productivity teams."

Research shows that successful Quality Circles programs are characterized by these conditions:

1. The organization's management devotes much time to planning and study before committing to the program.
2. Management supports the program actively and visibly.
3. A functioning steering committee oversees the program, establishing objectives and guidelines, identifying departments or areas that could best use this approach, reviewing the program's progress, and promoting its expansion.
4. A skilled facilitator is assigned to the project full-time, to train circle leaders, nurture circles in the early stages, and coordinate and evaluate the program.
5. Participation in a circle is strictly voluntary.
6. Building team members' skills is emphasized as a major goal of the program.
7. Adequate training is provided to the facilitator, circle leaders, and circle members.
8. Teamwork is encouraged.
9. Circle leaders and members are given recognition for their participation and contributions.
10. Circles tackle problems in their own areas of expertise.

Example

In the early 1980s, an East Coast computer manufacturing firm decided to implement a Quality Circles program corporation-wide, calling the effort "Pride Circles." In one division, a facilitator was assigned to carry out the program, in addition to his full-time responsibilities. About a dozen circles formed and began working. Unfortunately, the facilitator did not have the time to guide and support the groups adequately. Within a year, all but two of the circles had disbanded in frustration.

Early in 1984, due to management's commitment to the approach, a new facilitator was hired on a full-time basis. She had extensive generalist training in adult education and organizational behavior in graduate school, as well as experience in public school teaching. She inherited responsibility for a program that had gained a bad reputation within the company, especially in the local division. Employees were reluctant to participate.

The new facilitator completed training at corporate headquarters, then went to work upgrading the training materials and recruiting circle leaders. She approached persons who had served as team leaders previously and persuaded several to try again. The presence of a full-time facilitator was a major selling point.

Circle leaders were given refresher training, while circle participants were recruited through posters, buttons, newsletter articles, and other publicity media. Ten circles formed and began to work.

A year after the new facilitator took over, the Pride Circles effort in the division boasted 21 working circles, involving 48 percent of the manufacturing department. One circle was composed entirely of production supervisors. Many professional employees were in the circles, usually in advisory capacities, and a group of research and development engineers began experimenting with circle methods in their design efforts.

Here are some highlights of Pride Circle accomplishments in the first year:

- A group of integrated circuit board quality control technicians achieved significant increases in their productivity by giving regular feedback to production operators and consulting with industrial and test engineers for their input.
- A group of assemblers arranged GED classes through a local community college, helping 29 assemblers earn high school diplomas while working full-time.

- Another group of assemblers designed a course in AC/DC electronics for test operators and took charge of recruiting students and scheduling classes.
- A group of assemblers, working with engineering, redesigned a process sheet which had become dysfunctional with the passage of time and changes in the work force. This improved the communication of production specification and led to sharp productivity gains which returned over 50 percent to before-tax profits.

Resources

Cole, R.E. (March, 1981). Japan Can But We Can't. Louisville, KY: I.A.Q.C. Conference Presentation.

Dewar, D. (1979). *Quality Circles: Answers to 100 Frequently Asked Questions.* Red Bluff, CA: Dewar Associates.

Ishikawa, K. (1968). *Quality Circles Activity.* Tokyo, Japan: Union of Japanese Scientists and Engineers.

Likert, R. (1961). *New Pattern of Management.* New York: McGraw-Hill Book Company.

Reich, R.B. (June 27, 1981). The Profession of Management. *The New Republic.*

Reports of Quality Control Circle Activities in Japan: 1980. Tokyo, Japan: The Union of Japanese Scientists and Engineers.

Yager, E. (October, 1979). Examining the Quality Control Circle. *Personnel Journal, 5,* 682-708.

NOMINAL GROUP TECHNIQUE

Purpose

The Nominal Group Technique (NGT) is a highly structured method for generating problem solving alternatives and arriving at a group decision. By involving all group members equally, NGT usually results in more and better ideas than are produced by brainstorming.

Description

NGT includes these carefully structured steps.

1. If the team consists of more than ten members, it is divided into groups of five to ten each. Each group appoints a recorder.
2. The team leader presents the problem or question to be explored. If the team is unfamiliar with NGT, the leader outlines the steps to be followed.
3. Team members *silently and independently* spend five to fifteen minutes listing their ideas. No discussion takes place.
4. Each group member, in turn, presents *one idea*. Each idea is listed on chalkboard or easel paper, so that the ideas are visible to all. This process continues in rotation until all group members have shared all their ideas. No discussion takes place during this process.
5. The floor is open to discussion, clarification, and evaluation. Each idea is discussed in sequence. No idea is removed from the list.
6. Each team member silently and independently rank orders the items on the list. These rankings are compiled by the leader. The ideas with the highest average rankings constitute the group's decision.

NGT controls several conditions that tend to inhibit the flow of ideas and evaluation in an interacting group. Dominant and high-status group members, who ordinarily would greatly influence the group's decision, exert less impact. Submissive or low-status members, who may be excellent sources of ideas, enjoy increased influence over the alternatives posed and the decisions made. The structure of the method heads off the natural tendency of interacting groups to converge too quickly on a decision. As with brainstorming, NGT precludes critical or evaluative remarks until all ideas are on the table.

The technique is especially helpful in the early stages of problem solving, such as selecting a problem, identifying issues, identifying resources needed, and finding and sharing facts. It is also effective with groups of persons unaccustomed to working together. It does not rely on disclosure trust as much as brainstorming does.

By involving everyone's input in a decision, NGT enhances commitment. However, commitment is not necessarily well served by rank-order voting. Consensus decision making is more characteristic of effective groups. The risk that minority opinions will be disregarded is clearly present when rank-order voting is employed.

The long periods of silence, the secrecy, and the prohibition of interpersonal communication sometimes have an effect of lowering group morale and may be taken as a sign of distrust. It is best, therefore, to use NGT sparingly in the life of a group that expects to work together for an extended time.

Example

A group of personnel and human resource professionals at a large manufacturing firm used NGT to generate ideas and priorities for the creation of a Human Resource Five-Year Plan. The group consisted of about 20 persons, including specialists and generalists from corporate headquarters, manufacturing plants, and field offices. All met as one nominal group. A senior personnel manager and a consultant conducted the exercise. The question in focus was: "What human resource goals and needs will be important over the next five years?" The ideas generated by the group filled one chalkboard and two easel pads. Despite a surprising amount of consistency in the themes sounded by group members, 27 distinct areas of need were identified.

Some interesting dynamics emerged during the discussion. Three or four of the most influential members were clearly uncomfortable with the process. This was particularly true of one person who usually used surreptitious means of control. On the other hand, many of the low-profile members displayed considerable energy and enthusiasm, in response to the broader-than-usual opportunities for participation.

After the rank-order voting was completed, the top three priorities became five-year goals: career planning and development, performance management methods, and comprehensive manpower development. Three task groups, one for each goal, formed to plan how to attain these goals. The process led eventually to a thorough evaluation of the company's human resources operation.

Resources

Delbecq, A.L., and Van de Ven, A.H. (1971). A Group Process Model for Problem Identification and Program Planning. *Journal of Applied Behavioral Science, 7*(4), 466-491.

Ford, D.L., and Nemiroff, P.M.F. (1975) Applied Group Problem Solving:
the Nominal Group Technique. In *The 1975 Annual Handbook for Group
Facilitators*. San Diego, CA: University Associates.

BROKEN SQUARES TECHNIQUE

Purpose

Broken Squares demonstrates the power of voluntarily sharing
information and resources in group problem solving. It also gives
participants direct experience with how competition for information and resources may interfere with accomplishment of a team
task. All team members must pay attention to the whole task in
order to solve the problem.

Description

1. Before the team session, make a set of materials for each group
   of five team members (see Figure 7.2).
2. Divide the team into groups of five. (Persons left over may act
   as observers, or you may simply adapt one set of materials for
   a group of less than five.)
3. Give each group a package of the materials and say: "In this
   package are five envelopes. Each contains pieces of cardboard
   for forming squares. When I give the signal to begin, the task
   of your group is to form five squares of equal size. The task will
   not be completed until each person has formed a perfect square
   of the same size as that held by others."

Directions for Making a Set of Squares. A set consists of five
envelopes containing pieces of cardboard which have been cut in
different patterns and which, when properly arranged, will form
five squares of equal size. One set should be provided for each
group of five persons.

To prepare a set, cut out five cardboard squares of equal size,
approximately 6 inches x 6 inches. Place the squares in a row and
mark them as below, penciling the letters a, b, c, d, and e. Enter
letters lightly so they can later be erased.

The lines should be so drawn that when cut out, all pieces
marked "a" will be of exactly the same size, etc. By using multiples

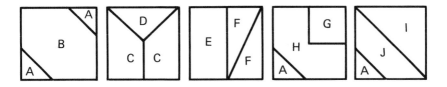

Figure 7.6. A Set of Squares.

of three inches, several combinations will be possible that will enable participants to form one or two squares, but only one combination is possible that will form five squares 6" x 6".

After drawing the lines on the 6" x 6" squares and labeling them with lower case letters, cut each square as marked into smaller pieces to make the parts of the puzzle.

Take five envelopes and mark each one with a letter: A, B, C, D, and E. Distribute the cardboard pieces in the five envelopes as follows:

Envelope A has pieces: i, h, e
Envelope B has pieces: a, a, a, c
Envelope C has pieces: a, j
Envelope D has pieces: d, f
Envelope E has pieces: g, b, f, c

Erase the penciled letter from each piece and write instead the appropriate envelope letter, as Envelope A. This will make it easy to return the pieces to the proper envelope for subsequent use when a group has completed the task.

Specific limitations are imposed during this exercise:

a. No member may speak.
b. No member may ask another member for a card or in any way signal that another person is to give him or her a card.
c. Members may, however, give cards to other members. Are the instructions clear?

Answer questions at this time. Then give the signal, "Begin working." Use a stopwatch to time the groups or use a clock or wristwatch and write down the starting and finishing times.

4. Enforce the rules while the groups work. Time each group on how long it takes to finish the task.

5. When all groups have finished the task, conduct a discussion. Use questions to probe the group's thinking and to stimulate communication, for example:

- How do you feel right now? Why?
- How did you like the exercise? What was the best thing about it? What was the worst thing about it?
- What was the smartest thing you saw someone in your group do?
- How did your group go about solving the puzzle?
- How did you communicate with each other?
- Did anyone get four squares done and have pieces left over that wouldn't make a fifth square? What did you do about that?
- What was the main thing you learned in doing this exercise?

For this exercise to achieve its purpose, it must be conducted as designed, and rules must be strictly enforced. No member may take a piece from a teammate. No member may point to a spot where a piece should go. The point of the exercise is to teach members to share resources without being asked. Be sure to time the exercise closely.

Example

Two large professional organizations were considering a merger; they had 6,000 and 8,000 members, respectively. After extensive study, they put together a steering committee to oversee the task of joining the two groups. Members were drawn from each organization. The members exhibited considerable rivalry for status and authority. This competition for power disrupted the group's efforts to achieve its purpose. A consultant helping with the merger conducted a series of exercises to show the inefficiencies created by competition among group members. Broken Squares proved to be a turning point.

After completing the task, the groups at first sat very quietly. Several members then discussed the frustration they felt in being prevented from seeking the resources they needed. Several participants described how difficult it was at first to offer resources (pieces) without being asked for them. The lowered levels of competitiveness and rivalry during the process were identified and discussed. The participants then began to talk about how they wanted to work together. A new norm of collaborative action began to form, replacing the old power-struggle with new problem solving norms. As a result, much of the group's energy and time were freed up, and the team was able to move on with the task of negotiating the details of the merger.

This example may not sound as dramatic as a Believe It or Not by Ripley. Nevertheless, the situation was as painful as Ripley's truths are hard-to-believe. The overall process of the merger took two years. When completed, however, it resulted in cost savings to members of approximately 45 percent and a significant increase in the quality of publications and the comprehensiveness of services provided to members. We know, as one of us was there!

Resources

Directions for the Broken Squares exercise are from the Leader's Guide to the CRM/McGraw-Hill Film, Team Building. The Guide was prepared by Barbara Schmidt Harrison. The Broken Squares Technique is originally from an article by Paul Sheets and Kenneth Benne in the *Journal of Social Issues*, Spring, 1948.

8

LETTING GO/MOVING ON

The Need for Closure

Groups that have reached a point where problem solving is a norm will experience a mixture of successes and failures. For the team which has achieved a holistic level of maturity, i.e., the team that has successfully journeyed through the stages described above, most experiences will be positive. Yet all teams, regardless of level of development, must learn how to let go of the past *to refocus energy on new goals* and daily plans for achieving them.

The Letting Go/Moving On experience involves two processes, the nature of which depends on the success or failure of the team's problem solving. When the team has achieved a goal, it celebrates its victory, both to give itself deserved feedback and to pave the way for new commitments. When the team has fallen short of its objectives, i.e., failed to let go of the defeat and to free energy for new commitments, it grieves.

What Is the Psychosocial Basis for Letting Go of the Past?

Talcott Parsons (1954) was an early writer on the significance of the letting go process and its function in the life and development of the team. Parsons views any type of goal-directed activity as consummatory. If a team is successful, during the process of goal achievement it psychologically "devours" its goal. Achieving a goal, then, leaves a void in the team's collective experience. Conversely, when efforts to reach a goal fail, there is unfinished business in the team's collective experience, which is also a void or loss.

A team expends an enormous amount of energy in trying to achieve a goal. The goal in fact serves to energize and focus the team's actions. This energizing continues as long as the goal is visible and efforts to reach the goal appear to be successful. So, when the goal is achieved or when failure is seen as inevitable, there is a sharp let-down of energy in the group.

During this let-down crisis, the team goes through a self-renewal or healing process. Celebrating and grieving are part of this process. During the rites of celebrating or grieving, the team (or the individual) is recuperating energy and creating the conditions for rest and making new commitments for future achievement.

What Enables the Team to Make New Commitments?

Teams that have learned to let go and move on are "metanoic" in their perceptions, which means "beyond mind" or having a transcendent vision. A metanoic team has a vision of what it can become. This vision is a meta-goal. The team which has a vision of excellence lets go of today's victories and defeats so that it can once more gain sight of the vision which propels it toward ever higher levels of excellence. When a team either fails to reflect on where it has been or becomes *preoccupied* with where it has been, it gets lost in its own processes and is unable to focus on the vision of what it is striving to create.

The metanoic team is impelled by this vision—this goal beyond a goal. Such teams are also impelled by the belief that they can create this vision through *results-focused activity*. By focusing on the vision, they are able to do the right thing right. The process of celebrating or grieving is a feedback experience that signifies success or failure. It also provides the basis for integrating new learning which helps orient the group toward the next goal. The remembrance of past achievements acts as an internal well of strength which sustains team members during times of failure. The past history of reinforcement from success also creates a *success expectancy*, which increases the probabilities of future success.

Team Health and the Process of Letting Go

Psychologists often use the term "balance" to refer to the process of letting go of the past to become free to focus on the concerns of the present. A mature person or team is able to maintain balance, which can be defined as the skill of investing energy in the right things. As an example of this concept, think of a person journeying from infancy to adulthood. As a child, he wants what he wants when he wants it, period! As he moves toward adulthood, he learns that he must often "delay gratification" of his wants, putting off short-term benefits. The person lets go of his need for immediate gratification. Sometimes we meet a big person who has not let go of this need. He acts impulsively and at times may even throw a tantrum if he fails to get his way. We can say that this person is out of balance. He has fixated on behaviors that were appropriate at an earlier age but are no longer appropriate.

Teams, too, must learn to let go of old business, for if they continue to identify with the past, they tie up energy that could be used to solve problems, be creative, and have fun today. Teams that become attached to their pasts instead of letting go develop unproductive behavior patterns. They stagnate, their interpersonal relationships get out of alignment, and their structures are not adequate to their mission. If we compare the productive team and the unproductive team, we see clearly what happens when a team fails to learn how to stay in the present and to focus today's actions on the vision which forms their mission. See Figure 8.1.

Celebration of Victories

First, celebration is a social process, one that brings people together for the purpose of sharing. Second, the get-together has a purpose—recognition of the victory, sharing enjoyment of the victory. When people assemble to celebrate, they talk about the victory, their contributions to it, the difficulties they had, and how they overcame these difficulties. This is the integrative aspect of the group learning process.

A second aspect of celebrating is having fun and relaxing. The team has just spent a great deal of effort in achieving an objective. Naturally, the team members will want to let go a bit and have some fun. Even in a convivial and relaxed atmosphere, people are doing some very serious work. They are discussing the past week's work, the successes they had as well as the failures. They are congratulating themselves for the good work they have done. They are preparing for the challenges that are coming, getting themselves

THE PRODUCTIVE TEAM	THE UNPRODUCTIVE TEAM
(1) has a clear purpose and a vision which embodies these purposes	(1) lacks a clear purpose and has vague ideas of why it exists
(2) develops harmonious interpersonal relationships so that people work well together toward a shared purpose	(2) ignores interpersonal relationships, thus creating disharmony among the people who are responsible for work and results
(3) develops a structure which reinforces and furthers the shared vision	(3) develops structures which are unrelated or even antagonistic to the expressed purposes
(4) is open and regularly assesses its functioning relative to its goals and purposes	(4) is closed and rarely if ever assesses its functioning relative to its purposes
(5) is adaptive, able to change when change is needed.	(5) is unadaptive, holding on to unsuccessful patterns.

Figure 8.1. Characteristics of Productive Versus Unproductive Teams.

"psyched" so that they can work with the same level of enthusiasm and commitment to excellence that enabled them to succeed last time.

A third aspect of celebration is providing feedback and reinforcement to those people who made the success happen. People need to know that they are valued both for their expertise and just because they are who they are. Celebration allows the team to purposefully and systematically provide each person on the team with feedback about their contribution to team success and about their importance to the organization. This type of feedback is an important source of *recognition* that motivates people to work even harder.

Levels of Celebration. There are three levels of celebration. Each must be recognized and given an opportunity to take place.

At the basic level, there is the "cell experience," when the smallest subunit within the team gathers to enjoy success. At a higher level are celebrations of the whole team. At the most comprehensive level are those celebrations of the total system. These collective experiences bring the whole system together around the shared vision. They communicate to people that they are vital players in a process resulting in the success of the total system. Effective managers see the need for celebration at each level and make sure people have ample opportunity to participate.

Grieving as a Letting-Go Process. So far we have discussed only the positive aspects of letting go and moving on. But sometimes teams fail to reach hoped-for goals and objectives. And, just as it is natural and useful to celebrate victories, it is also natural and useful to grieve over losses. When teams (and people) fail to grieve over their losses, their creative energy is tied down in repressing negative feelings. Over time, they become so completely identified with the failure (loss of esteem) that they become failures. Grieving is the process by which the team accepts its defeat, experiences the sadness associated with the defeat, lets go of the sadness, and renews its commitment to excellence.

Some managers do not feel comfortable expressing so-called "negative" feelings. They inhibit their expression of disappointment and the loss of self-esteem that is associated with a failure experience. In doing so, a manager makes it more difficult for the team to get reinvolved in positive, goal-directed activity.

What happens when the team does not "process" its setbacks? Think about what happens when a feeling is repressed. We know that feelings denied expression often emerge in the form of potentially destructive symptoms. Thus a team that has failed but has repressed the feelings of frustration and sadness associated with failure often shows signs of depression (e.g., lowered morale, a lack of energy, lowered productivity, absenteeism, etc.). The energy associated with the anger and disappointment sap the team's creative energy, so the team adopts basic assumption mental states and its essentially inactive.

What Are the Stages of Grieving? The grieving process has five predictable stages (see Kubler-Ross, 1969, 1974):

1. People deny the significance of the loss or failure. They pretend that it really is not important.

2. People move on to the stage of bargaining. They try to excuse the failure.

3. Bargaining does not work and gives way to a stage in which anger predominates. People feel cheated and frustrated about the loss. They may try to find a scapegoat on whom to pin the blame for the failure. Their anger is directed toward this individual or group.

4. After discovering that anger will not make things right, people become depressed. They recognize that they have indeed failed, and depression is a reaction to this loss.

5. Finally comes acceptance. People admit to the failure and their contribution to it. Now the team is ready to deal with the failure and to discover new modes of behavior, ways that will allow them to succeed and to avoid similar future setbacks. With acceptance the team is ready to re-engage itself in goal directed activity.

What Happens When the Manager Inhibits the Grieving Process? Managers who fail to allow the grieving process are, in effect, creating an unproductive team. The team becomes paralyzed by guilt, lacks confidence in its ability to succeed, distrusts its members, and is unwilling to be responsible. Table 8.2 illustrates the differences between the team that learns how to deal with failure and the team that does not.

How Can the Team Leader Promote the Positive Resolution of Failures? The team leader can act as a catalyst to bring about the positive resolution of failures. First, he must learn to deal with his own experiences of failure. He must understand that failures and setbacks are the realities or price of success, that to win you must be willing to risk failing. This positive attitude tells the team members that it is okay to take positive risks for the purpose of achieving excellence.

Second, the team leader must learn how to recognize and accept failures within the group. Accepting failure doesn't imply that you are condoning or encouraging failure. It simply signifies that you recognize that failures will sometimes occur and that the best way to deal with them is to acknowledge them and seek positive alternatives as soon as possible.

WHEN THE MANAGER HELPS THE TEAM GRIEVE	WHEN THE MANAGER BLOCKS THE GRIEVING PROCESS OF THE TEAM
1. The team learns to accept responsibility for its actions.	1. The team learns to blame and find a scapegoat for its failures.
2. The team feels OK about itself.	2. The team becomes discouraged.
3. The team feels free to express a wide range of feelings.	3. The team is afraid to express feelings and denies them.
4. The team's members "own" their feelings.	4. Team members blame others for the feelings they experience.
5. Team members feel a sense of cohesion and belonging.	5. Team members feel alienated from the group.
6. The team learns to focus itself on results.	6. The team gets off into hidden agendas and other symptoms.
7. The team learns to monitor its functioning and to make changes when needed.	7. The team refuses to assess its functioning and is resistant to change.

Figure 8.2. Grieving and Non-Grieving.

Third, the team leader needs to be able to express a wide range of feelings. He also needs to encourage and give people permission to express a wide range of feelings within the team environment. When people can express their feelings without fear of embarrassment or rejection, they become more open. See Figure 8.2.

It is important that the leader avoid blaming people for failure. Instead, he should help the team focus on what went wrong and on how to correct the situation. When team members are openly attacked for failures, they become increasingly reluctant to express their concerns openly.

Grieving takes time. People need time to share their concerns and feelings about the failure experience. On the other hand, it is counterproductive to allow people to "wallow" in their feelings. Thus, the manager needs to help the team move toward positive action as soon as this is possible. After each team member has expressed his concerns, it is time to evaluate what went wrong and to discover positive alternatives to the situation.

Feelings follow action. People feel depressed when their actions fail to produce what they hope for and feel good when their actions succeed. Having failed and grieved, the team that moves on and experiences positive actions finds the pain of previous failures soon reduced.

References

Homans, G.C., (1950). *The Human Group.* New York: Harcourt, Brace, and World.

Kubler-Ross, E. (1969). *On Death and Dying.* New York: The Macmillan Co.

Kubler-Ross, E. (1974). *Questions and Answers on Death and Dying.* New York: Collier Books.

Parsons, T. (1954). *Essays in Sociological Theory.* New York: Free Press.

CLOSURE ACTIVITY TECHNIQUE

Purpose

This activity is designed to give the team a sense of closure at the end of a project, successful or unsuccessful. It provides team members an opportunity to express and let go of feelings generated by their involvement in the group's work.

Description

The Closure Activity Technique takes 30 to 40 minutes and can be used with a team of any size.

1. Have each team member choose a partner.
2. Pass out to each member a copy of the closure booklet.
3. Go over the instructions with the team (see Figure 8.3). If the team is using this exercise to let go of a failure, each ground rule is particularly important. One of the guidelines, "Own your own feelings," means to admit that your feelings are your own personal reactions to what has happened, and that nobody

This booklet contains ten open-ended statements to which you are to respond to express your reactions to the project you have just completed and to prepare you for the next project.

You and your partner will take turns reading aloud from the booklet and responding to the items you read. One of you will respond to even numbered items, the other will respond to the odd numbered items.

Opportunities are provided for you to openly and honestly discuss your feelings about the project. Keep in mind that you:

- can pass on any item,
- should be willing to take risks,
- should try to give here and now responses,
- should own your feelings and reaction,
- should be open and accepting of your partner's statements.

One feeling I have about the project just completed is . . . .   (1)

If this experience were a movie, its title would be . . . .   (2)

The thing I enjoyed the most was . . . .   (3)

The highlight of the experience for me was . . . .   (4)

Something I learned about myself was . . . .   (5)

Something I learned about the other people on the team was . . . . . .   (6)

Something I learned about you was . . . .   (7)

If I could do it all over again I would . . . .   (8)

One thing I regret not having done is . . . .   (9)

Before we go I would like you to know . . . .   (10)

Figure 8.3. Closure Booklet.

made you feel that way. It means to accept your feelings and the responsibility for dealing with them appropriately.

4. Allow team members about 20 minutes to take turns and share responses with their partners as instructed. Update the group every five minutes or so on time remaining.

5. Convene the group and briefly discuss the activity and task they are letting go. Questions like these may help guide the discussion:

   • Does anyone have any comments on the activity we just completed—any reactions to share?

   • What were some of the movie titles you came up with?

   • Anger and resentment are perfectly legitimate feelings. Sharing these feelings openly gives us an opportunity to reach new understandings. Another choice is to forgive and forget. The worst thing we can do as a team is choose neither and bottle up those feelings because they will return to haunt us. If anyone has feelings of anger or resentment, please speak up. Tell us how you're feeling and why.

   • Do any of you have any regrets you would be willing to share with the team?

   • Do any of you have any appreciations you would like to express to other team members?

When a team is celebrating a success, this activity is fun, boosts morale, and helps draw team members closer. If the team is mourning failure, this exercise provides an opportunity to look on the bright side and face up to responsibility. Be prepared for sorrow and do your best to comfort those people who show sadness openly. Be prepared for fireworks. Steer the team away from blaming and recriminations, and focus on openly settling the issues. Look for a way for everyone to win.

Example

A five-member task group in a research and development division took on the task of developing project management guidelines. The division had experienced a number of problems with product quality control, low morale among its members, and a decline in market share.

The group realized that even though theirs was a "rational" task to develop a project management model, many negative feelings needed to be dealt with. Several product managers were harboring anger over poor group performance in the past. A number of product managers were also resisting setting clearly defined production goals, out of fear that the goals would not be met and that this would further lower the confidence and morale of the division's workers.

When the group completed a concept paper for the new management model, they decided to introduce it to the division's product managers in a full-day workshop. The workshop was designed as a series of problem solving group activities. The Closure Booklet was used early in the day to process team member's feelings about the division's past problems and to clear the way for moving forward with the new management model.

During the exercise a number of product managers expressed anger and frustration over the inadequacies of previous project management procedures. The participants also had a discussion about goal setting and the importance of taking risks in striving for excellence in future performance. By sharing negative feelings in a permissive group atmosphere the participants became better able to accept past failures; they felt more free to express their feelings and to move on with new goals for the future. As a result of this experience the managers as a group were able to accept the new guidelines with renewed enthusiasm and to communicate positive attitudes toward future division goals to the people they supervised. Over the next six months, division morale improved dramatically, product quality problems were resolved, and the division's products were making steady progress in regaining the company's former share of the market.

A TOAST FOR THE VICTORS TECHNIQUE

Purpose

This activity aims to provide an opportunity for the team to acknowledge victory, focusing on each member's contribution to a shared achievement. It also shifts the emphasis from celebration to preparation for near- and long-range goal setting.

Description

The exercise is simple, appropriate for a team of any size, and can be done in 15 minutes.

1. The leader explains the purpose of the exercise, and everyone takes a cup or glass, imagining it filled with the victory or success just achieved.
2. The leader offers a toast, for example, "Joe, I toast your determination, which is an inspiration to me, and will be an asset in future projects." Each toast should give recognition for individual contributions to the team's success and should affirm the importance of that person's contributions to future goals.
3. If the group is small (12 people or fewer), its members may be invited to propose toasts to each other for the whole team to share in, with each person receiving at least one toast, or they may be encouraged to mix and mingle, offering their toasts to each other on a one-to-one basis. The latter approach works better for teams of more than twelve.

Example

This activity was used to celebrate the end of a team-building project in a property management company. A number of technical and interpersonal problems had been identified, and the team set out to find and implement realistic solutions to these problems. Each problem was assigned to a project task group charged with assessing and solving the problem. Each team was successful in resolving the problem assigned to it, but individual contributions to the team process had not been recognized or acknowledged.

At a predetermined time, the team met to review the work of the task groups and to express appreciation for individual contributions to the team effort. The Toast for the Victors process served to deepen the commitment of each individual to the long-term future goal of improving company productivity.

Interestingly, without this opportunity for celebration, problem solutions which were developed by discrete subunits would not have been shared with the group as a whole. The entire team would not have shared in the acknowledgement of individual achievements, and solutions would not have been "bought into" by various group factions. Problems which otherwise would have resurfaced were dealt with in this celebration, and interpersonal relationships were strengthened, enabling the team to more effectively address new problems.

PAYDAY TECHNIQUE

Purpose
Here is a creative way for team members to measure their own and each other's performance in contributing to a success or failure experience. It both provides practice in giving and receiving feedback, and helps in letting go of the past.

Description
Payday requires about an hour.
1. If the team numbers more than eight, form smaller groups. (Several groups may participate simultaneously in the same room.) Have each group sit together in a circle, with an empty chair in the center.
2. Give each team member a blank check and an envelope.
3. Review with the team the goals they recently did or did not attain.
4. Have each member evaluate his own performance in striving to attain the goals and write himself a check for up to $100, according to his self-evaluation. If he contributed little of value, he should pay himself only a small amount. If he feels he contributed a great deal, he may pay himself up to $100. Each member writes out his check (keeping the amount secret for the moment), places it inside the envelope, seals the envelope, and writes his name on the outside. Each group collects its own envelopes in a paper bag.
5. Give each team member enough index cards for his group.
6. Explain that the next step is to give and receive feedback. You may want to review briefly the guidelines for constructive feedback (See Chapter 6, the section titled, "How Do You Give Feedback?").
7. An envelope is drawn from the bag. The team member whose envelope is drawn goes to the chair in the center of the circle.

8. The other members each take an index card and write in large numbers how much they would pay him. When everyone has done this, they reveal their cards simultaneously.
9. The teammate in the center of the circle then reveals his "paycheck," which reflects his self-evaluation.
10. The group discusses these questions:
    1. What did the individual do to earn his pay (positive contributions)?
    2. What could he have done to increase his earnings?
    3. How does his self-evaluation compare with the group's evaluation?

    The person in the middle comments on this feedback.
11. Repeat Steps 7-10 for each team member.
12. Convene the entire group for a short discussion.

    These questions are suggested for focusing the discussion:
    - What did you learn about yourself?
    - What did you learn about the group?
    - What changes do you think you will see in how this team functions?

Team members may feel discomfort in putting dollar values on their own and each other's efforts. Emphasize that this is simply a vehicle for gauging effectiveness and a springboard for discussion. Hurt feelings for individuals given low ratings is a risk in this exercise. A person who rates himself low, for instance, may be wishing for high ratings from the others. Team members have an opportunity to raise and discuss important interpersonal issues that would otherwise consume the group's energy and undermine future efforts. It is essential that the one in the center of the circle receive support and reassurance that he is a valued team member; what is in question is his behavior as a team member and not his worth as a human being.

Example

Payday was used by a product improvement team which had been working together successfully for several months in a paper products company. The team had met its initial short-term product improvement goals and was ready to start work on a new set of problems. The team leader had noticed a decline in group energy in recent weeks, however, as completion of the first set of objectives drew near. He talked with several members of the group, and discovered that the "let-down" in group energy was due largely to several of the workers feeling that they had contributed a lot to the project without having not been adequately recognized for their individual accomplishments. In reviewing the team's work, the leader realized that he had not provided any opportunity for formal recognition of contributions by individual team members.

The Payday experience paid off in unexpected ways. Most of the members of the group received a good deal of supportive feedback and positive recognition for their accomplishments, which helped to energize the group for the new tasks at hand. At the end of the exercise the team got into an unplanned discussion of the group's work, with several members stating that the opportunity to work with the other members of the team was a high point in their careers. This interaction helped the group to experience personal recognition and to "let go" of the work which was already completed; they moved onto new tasks with enthusiasm and an unprecedented level of team cohesiveness.

Resources

Burning, R.A. (1975). Payday: A Closure Activity. In Pfeiffer, W., and Jones, J.E. (Eds.) *The 1975 Annual Handbook for Group Facilitators.* San Diego, CA: University Associates, Inc.

REFLECTIONS TECHNIQUE

Purpose

This activity is a way for the team to let go of the past by reflecting on successes and failures of the past week.

Description

Reflections takes 30 to 40 minutes and will work with a group of any size.
1. Have each team member divide a standard sheet of paper into four equal sections (see Figure 8.4).

REFLECTIONS	
Highlights of the week:	Do unto others:
Plans I am making:	If I had only:

Figure 8.4. Reflections Worksheet.

2. Explain the purpose of the exercise, assuring members that the worksheet is for their own use, and that they can choose which of their responses to share and which to keep to themselves. Encourage them to "pull out all the stops" and express themselves fully in filling out the worksheet. Have some fun with it.

3. In the upper left section, team members jot down the highlights, personal or team-related, from the past work week.

4. In the upper right section, team members write down their reflections about interactions with other team members, positive and negative, and thoughts about how to make these relationships more positive and less negative.

5. In the lower left, team members jot down their plans for team activities in the week approaching.

6. In the lower right section, team members complete the sentence "If only I had . . ." with as many regrets, small and large, as they can think of.

7. Each team member chooses a partner, and shares responses, discussing how things can be made better through their own personal efforts. The following guidelines may help here.
   - You can pass on any item.
   - Take at least a few small risks.
   - Focus on the here and now.
   - Own your feelings and reactions.

- Be open and accepting of your partner's statements.
- Ask questions to probe and clarify; do not criticize.

8. Conduct a short discussion with the whole group. Here are suggested questions:
    1. Would anyone care to share with us some of your highlights from last week?
    2. How about plans for the coming week?
    3. Does anyone have anything to say to the whole group? Is there anything you would like for us all to know?
    4. Does anyone have a funny moment to share? What was the most amusing thing that happened last week?

This simple, low-risk exercise is an excellent way to let go of success or failure and focus energy on the present and the future. It touches on all the resentments, regrets, and appreciations that must be expressed in order to let go and puts team members in control of the risks they will take.

Example

Reflections was used to conclude weekly team building training sessions in a medium sized utility company. The objective of each session was to deal with a specific issue affecting the operations of the company, e.g., a lack of communication among field offices, or a lack of openness among executives. After dealing with the problem, each team member completed this instrument to describe where he had been, what he had discovered, where he was going, and how he was going to get there.

Discussions among the team members revealed that the process helped team members to reach closure on past accomplishments (and failures) and to focus more clearly on future work of the team. The section in the exercise where team members reflect on their interpersonal interactions proved to be the most dynamic part of the process; several group members took advantage of the exercise to clear up misunderstandings or to resolve conflicts with other members of the team. The improved communication among team members helped "clear the air" for the team to work more harmoniously and effectively toward group goals.

DISCOVERIES TECHNIQUE

Purpose

Discoveries is a letting-go tool that focuses team members' thinking on what they learn about themselves.

Description

Discoveries takes about 30 to 45 minutes and is used at the end of a team meeting.

1. Pass out or post the eight sentence stems listed in Step No. 3, and have team members prepare to copy them.
2. Explain the purpose of the exercise. Assure team members that they will choose which responses to share and which to withhold. Encourage them to be candid with themselves and to have some fun with it.
3. Allow the group 10 to 15 minutes to jot down responses they think of to these eight sentence stems:

    I learned that . . .
    I was surprised that I . . .
    I remembered . . .
    I found it hard to believe . . .
    I was saddened that I . . .
    I enjoyed . . .
    I never knew . . .
    I plan to change . . .
4. Have members choose partners to share responses, taking turns going first. Instruct them to follow these discussion guidelines:
    - You can pass on any item.
    - Take at least a few small risks.
    - Focus on the here and now.
    - Own your feelings and reactions.
    - Be open and accepting of your partner's statements.
    - Ask questions to probe and clarify; do not criticize.
5. Convene the whole team again and allow an opportunity for anyone who desires to share any thoughts, feelings, or incidents with the group.

Self-awareness is an essential building block for effective teamwork. The sentence stems in this exercise tap a broad range of personal growth issues. It is a very useful, simple tool for probing within. It is especially helpful in dealing with failure experiences, where people tend to place blame on others or on outside factors. It also increases team members' ability to be honest with themselves and to realistically take *personal responsibility* for improving.

Example

Discoveries was used as a closure activity for team development training in a large manufacturing firm. By causing the team members to recall new concepts and skills and to recount how they felt about the training experience, the process helped link what they had learned to recent conflicts between management and labor. The exercise increased team members' awareness of new discoveries about themselves and the impact their behavior had on others in their work units. Because the Discoveries technique is simple and straightforward, engages both cognitive and affective learning processes, and ends with the participant planning for the future, it is a very effective procedure for reaching closure on training sessions. It is flexible enough to be used in virtually any type of learning situation.

AWARD CEREMONY TECHNIQUE

Purpose

Award Ceremony offers a humorous and creative way for the group to appraise its performance and the contributions of its members to a team success or failure. In the process, team members receive valuable feedback.

Description

Award Ceremony is appropriate for 12 or fewer group members. For groups of five or under, the exercise lasts about 20 minutes a member. Larger groups should allow about 10 minutes per member. Proceed as follows:

1. Explain the purpose of the activity. Encourage the team to have fun with it.

2. If the group consists of six or more members, form two sub-groups of equal size.
3. Give each person an instruction sheet (see Figure 8.5) and as many 3" x 5" cards as there are people in their group. (You may wish to make construction paper and other art supplies available as well.)

You are to receive an award for your contribution to the recent success of the group. When your turn comes, leave the group for 15 minutes and create an award you believe you should be presented for your contribution to the group's success. While you are silently reflecting on this award, your group will be creating an award to be presented to you when you rejoin the group in a few minutes.

When you return to the group, your teammates will show you the award they have created for you. You are to show the group the award you believe you deserve. Then you will all discuss the similarities and differences in the awards.

Figure 8.5. Award Ceremony Instruction Sheet.

---

4. Have one member of each subgroup leave the room for 15 minutes. During this time, the absent member dreams up and constructs an appropriate award. Meanwhile, the group creates and makes an award for the absent member.
5. When the member returns, the group presents him with the award they have designed, along with an explanation of why they feel it is appropriate.
6. The member then reveals the award as designed and explains the basis for it.
7. The group then discusses the similarities and differences between the two awards and specific actions or events that led up to the awards. (This discussion should take about five minutes.)
8. Repeat Steps 4-8 until each team member has received an award.
9. Convene the team as a whole and discuss the total Award Ceremony experience. Use questions like these:

1. How do you feel right now? Why?
2. Has this exercise been helpful to you personally?
3. What kinds of changes would you hope for in the way we work together as a team?
4. What was the funniest thing that happened today?
5. What is the best thing about what we have accomplished so far as a team?

Humor is invaluable in breaking up tensions and makes a negative feedback package more palatable. This exercise can be especially useful in dealing with failures if the group dares to have fun with it. In the process, team members find that they are accepted by the others, their follies and all, and are challenged to do some soul-searching as well. In celebrating success, this technique provides recognition and congratulations, but also opens the door for some good-natured ribbing, helping to keep egos under control.

Example

Award Ceremony was used as a closure activity by productivity improvement teams in a large electronics manufacturing company. In one of these teams, the focal person of the exercise was a new employee of the company who was not able to contribute much to the goup goals, due to his lack of experience in the organization. Perhaps to compensate somewhat for his lack of experience, he had arrived at most of the team meetings with a box of pastries from a popular local bakery. In this exercise, the group presented him with a "Just Desserts" award, "for contributing excellent pastries and little else to the work of the team." His award for himself was a "Group Process Enabler" award, "for helping to create a human climate where co-workers could open up and talk more freely with each other."

In comparing the two awards the team learned something about this member's self-perception in regard to how he fit in with the group. Where they had seen his contribution of pastries as a kind of apology for being the "new kid on the block," they realized during the exercise that he had in fact made a real and positive contribution to the group climate. His initial reaction to the "Just Desserts" award was negative; at first he felt that it was unfair, but he quickly realized, from the jovial way they presented the award, that they meant it to be taken as constructive criticism.

In processing this exchange, the team made a number of suggestions about how this member could contribute more to team goals in the future. As each team member described ways that he could better work with the group, several participants learned ways that they themselves could improve their own performance on future projects.

ANNOTATED BIBLIOGRAPHY
OF PERIODICALS

Culbert, S.A. (1970). Accelerating Laboratory Learning Through a Phase Progression Model for Trainer Intervention. *Journal of Applied Behavioral Science*, Jan. - March, 6, 21-38.

The author conceives of six phases in development of a group. These are (1) developing a climate of trust, (2) exposing individual differences, (3) exchanging perceptions of others, (4) individual problem solving, (5) group problem solving, and (6) review and evaluation of learning. He describes trainer intervention designed to accelerate progress through these phases.

Greiner, L.E. (1973). What Managers Think of Participative Leadership. *Harvard Business Review*, March - April, 111-117.

Greiner, a professor of organizational behavior at the Harvard Business School, surveyed 318 managers to determine (1) what concrete behaviors managers associate with participative leadership, and (2) whether managers feel that participative practices are the most effective. He found that the managers surveyed were much in agreement on what constitutes participative leadership. In addition, seven of the ten behaviors considered most participative also appeared on the managers' lists of the ten most effective managerial practices. The article provides a simple operational definition of participative leadership and managers' thinking on keys to effective management.

Harvey, J. (1974). The Abilene Paradox: The Management of Agreement. *Organizational Dynamics, 3*, 63-80.

Many conflict situations are actually created by a failure to realize that everyone agrees. The author points out that failure to manage agreement is a major source of organizational dysfunction. The author terms this phenomenon "the Abilene Paradox," and provides clues for identifying when a conflict is actually an agreement, as well as ways to intervene and correct the problem.

Kirkwood, W.D., and Wilson, J. (1981). Leadership Strategies for Successful Meetings. *Supervisory Management*, Oct., *26*, 2-9.

This article provides a good basic guide to the chairperson's role in planning and carrying out worthwhile meetings. In addition to principles of preplanning, skills in responding to group members during meetings are discussed. The reader is also introduced to several well developed techniques for structuring meetings so as to stimulate information sharing and creative problem solving.

Lewin, K. (1947). Frontiers in Group Dynamics: Concept, Method, and Reality in Social Science: Social Equilibria and Social Change. *Human Relations, 1*, 5-41.

The noted field theorist presents his notion that human interactions take place in the context of a system. The system at any given moment is in a state of equilibrium between opposing forces. This conception led to the development of force field analysis as a tool for diagnosing and planning change.

Lewin, K., Lippitt, R., and White, R.K. (1939). Patterns of Aggressive Behavior in Experimentally Created "Social Climates." *Journal of Social Psychology, 10*, 271-99.

The authors report on a series of experiments involving groups of boys led in authoritarian, democratic, or laissez-faire manners. They found that groups with authoritarian leaders tended to be either very hostile or very apathetic, as compared to the democratic groups.

Miles, R.E., and Ritchie, J.B. (1971). Participative Management: Quality Vs. Quantity. *California Management Review, 13,* 48-56.

In a survey of 381 managers in a West Coast firm, the authors found that a manager's satisfaction with his or her boss was a function of two variables: (1) the frequency with which the boss consulted the manager in reaching decisions (in other words, the quantity of participation), and (2) the boss's confidence in the manager. Of the two variables, the latter was slightly more important in influencing the manager's satisfaction with the boss. The article also helps debunk three common alibis for failing to include subordinates in decisions.

Odiorne, G.S. (1978). A Management Style for the Eighties. *University of Michigan Business Review, 30,* March, 1-6.

The author, a professor of management at the University of Massachusetts, offers his informal speculations concerning the way in which business management will have to change in the 1980s. Based on major changes occurring in the 1970s the author identifies ten different trends, most of which have proved true in the seven years since the article was written. The article provides useful perspectives on why the workplace is changing and how.

Prince, G.M. (1969). How to Be a Better Meeting Chairman. *Harvard Business Review*, Jan. - Feb., 88-98.

The author, an authority on creativity in group problem solving, offers some unexpected suggestions for chairperson strategies. The article offers considerable insight on the interaction between the group leader and the group members, and offers seldom-mentioned but profound pointers on how to stimulate creative thinking in meetings.

Sashkin, M. (1984). Participative Management Is an Ethical Imperative. *Organizational Dynamics*, Spring, 5-22.

A professor of industrial and organizational psychology at the University of Maryland summons extensive research evidence to support two propositions:

(1) "Participative management, properly implemented, is clearly effective in improving performance, productivity, and employee satisfaction." (p. 6)

(2) "Participative management . . . fulfills the three basic human work needs: . . . autonomy, . . . meaningfulness, and decreased isolation." (p. 11)

He marshals further evidence that "when the three basic work needs are frustrated by organizational conditions, employees are both psychologically and physically harmed" (p. 14). Participation, therefore, becomes an employee's right, and an ethical responsibility of management.

ANNOTATED BIBLIOGRAPHY OF BOOKS AND MONOGRAPHS

Beckhard, R. (1969). *Organization Development: Strategies and Models.* Reading, MA: Addison-Wesley Publishing Co.

The author of this short book defines organization development as "an effort (1) planned, (2) organization wide, and (3) managed from the top, to (4) increase organization health and effectiveness through (5) planned interventions in the organization's processes, using behavioral-science knowledge" (p. 9). The author was ahead of his time, so that this book still rings with great clarity and relevance today. It concisely covers such topics as (1) strategies and tactics, (2) culture change, (3) managerial strategy change, (4) job design, (5) the role of the pilot project in spreading change, (6) communication and influence, (7) conditions for failure and success in interventions. Finally, the author predicts future trends in organization development with profound and surprising accuracy.

Bennett, T.R. (1980). *Planning for Change: A Looking-into-Leadership Monograph.* Fairfax, VA: Leadership Resources Inc.

In a 16-page booklet, the author condenses much of what is known about how to effectively plan and implement change. The author presents a few rules of thumb, and covers topics such as force-field analysis, major processes involved in change, typical sources and types of resistance, and effective and ineffective ways to overcome resistance. Finally, the author provides an eight-question planning guide for carrying out change. Like other Looking-Into-Leadership monographs, this is an excellent starting point in understanding this topic.

Berne, E. (1964). *Games People Play.* New York: Grove Press.

The father of Transactional Analysis defines an interpersonal game as "a series of complementary ulterior transactions progressing to a well defined predictable outcome" (p. 48). He then lists and describes many such games. This can aid in understanding group members whose behavior follows a pattern that appears on the surface to be self-defeating.

Bion, W.R. (1961). *Experiences in Groups and Other Papers.* London: Tavistock Publications.

The author explores the basic assumptions people make about the groups to which they belong, and the group mentalities that arise from these assumptions. Three group mentalities are identified in particular. One is the dependent group, whose purpose is to be sustained by the leader. Another is the fight-flight group, which exists to defend against some threat, by fighting or running away. The third is the pairing group, whose purpose is unity leading to some new entity.

Bradford, L.P. (ed.) (1961). *Group Development.* Washington, D.C.: National Training Laboratories.

This is a collection of articles written by leading contemporary group process experts. Topics include group dynamics, the role of the individual, how to get results from a group, how to diagnose group problems, functional roles of group members, hidden agendas, decision making, and so on, along with very useful short guides to key group processes.

Brown, D.S. (1980). *Authority and Responsibility: A Looking-into-Leadership Monograph.* Fairfax, VA: Leadership Resources Inc.

In this 18-page booklet, Brown examines five common (but false) assumptions about responsibility and authority, and discusses the two-sided nature of both of these phenomena. He points out that conditions necessary for authoritative communication and the subordinate's latitude for choice in responding. Finally, he offers eight new and more realistic assumptions in place of the five flawed ones.

Charrier, G.C. (1965). *Cog's Ladder: A Model of Group Growth.* (Unpublished paper at Proctor and Gamble Co.)

This work suggests that there are five stages of group maturation: (1) politeness (getting acquainted, sharing values, etc.), (2) goal setting, (3) power (competing for influence), (4) cooperation (constructive, open-minded work, accepting individual differences), and (5) esprit de corps (unity, cohesion, and high morale).

Gibb, J.R. (1978). *Trust: A New View of Personal and Organizational Development.* Los Angeles: Guild of Tutors Press.

The author argues that "when trust is high, relative to fear, people and people systems function effectively." He conceives of trust as the key to self-discovery and to intimacy, and presents and develops a four-phase theory (called the TORI Model) of trust development.

Janis, I.L. (1972). *Victims of Groupthink: A Psychological Study of Foreign Decisions and Fiascos.* Boston: Houghton Mifflin.

Groupthink is defined as a group pathology in which group members suppress individual judgments in the service of preserving group cohesion. Usually this is because the group is under prolonged or intermittently acute stress, feels a need to present a united front against outside dangers (actual or potential), and senses the dissenter as a threat to its singleness of purpose and thus a threat to its power. This book can help in diagnosing and guarding against this destructive phenomenon.

Kiefer, C.F., and Senge, P.M. (1984). Metanoic Organizations. In Adams, J.D. (ed.) *Transforming Work.* Alexandria, VA: Miles River Press.

The authors describe the power of a shared vision in stimulating organizational effectiveness. This shared vision imparts a sense of purpose, brings individuals into alignment, empowers people to take control of their environments, and helps strike a balance between reason and intuition. The style of the article is scholarly and intellectual. It may provide a useful perspective on the organization in which you work.

Lippitt, G. (1967). *Organization Renewal.* Reading, MA: Addison-Wesley Publishing Co.

A prestigious expert in the field of organization development presents a textbook on the subject, emphasizing the organization's capacity and resources for growth and self-renewal. Renewal is seen as the process of tackling needed changes so as to produce and maintain an adaptable, mature, and effective organization.

Lippitt, G.L., and Seashore, E. (1980). *Group Effectiveness: A Looking-into-Leadership Monograph.* Fairfax, VA: Leadership Resources, Inc.

In a 12-page booklet, the authors condense much of what is known about how people work together effectively in groups. Drawing on behavioral research and practical experience, the authors present four basic principles of group behavior, eleven characteristics that characterize effective groups, ten basic concepts about group life, three levels of group activity, twelve leadership functions necessary to a healthy and productive group, four typical issues on members' minds, and an informal questionnaire a group can use to monitor its own health. Like others in the Looking-Into-Leadership series, this monograph is an excellent starting point in understanding this topic.

Mink, O., and Mink, B. (1975). *Developing Effective Work Groups.* Austin, TX: OHRD Associates.

This is a workbook or training manual containing about 75 pages of tools, techniques, concepts, models, and lecturettes aimed at building cohesive, openly communicating work teams. Examples are the Menninger Morale Curve, FIRO-B, Johari Window, interpersonal contracting, trust, group health, leadership functions, guidelines for useful feedback, force field analyses, films and discussion guides, the helping process, and conflict resolution. Since it is organized around the same six-phase model of group development as this book, it makes a practical companion for training purposes.

Mink, O., Schultz, J., and Mink, B. (1979). *Open Organizations.* Austin, TX: Learning Concepts, Inc., and LaJolla, CA: University Associates.

The authors present their open organization model, based on the principles of unity, internal responsiveness, and external responsiveness. The book offers tools and techniques for a step-by-step approach to clarifying the organization's values, studying its strengths and weaknesses, setting goals, building open communications in work units, improving decision-making, developing management, and evaluating progress. The authors offer inspiring new insights into organizations as open systems.

Rubin, I., Plovnick, M., and Fry, R. (1977). *Task-Oriented Team Development.* New York: McGraw-Hill Book Co.

This is a training manual, organized into eight modules. Each module takes the group about three hours, and can be conducted with or without a professional trainer. Modules include tools, concepts, and exercises aimed at assessing team functioning and diagnosing problems, identifying the team's mission, clarifying individual roles, making and keeping agreements, resolving conflicts, guiding decision making, developing leadership in group members, identifying and reshaping group norms, and setting and monitoring group goals. This book is useful for teams that will be working together on a long-term basis.

Schmidt, W.H. (1980). *Styles of Leadership: A Looking-into-Leadership Monograph.* Fairfax, VA: Leadership Resources, Inc.

The author identifies five styles of leadership which differentially divide decision-making authority between the leader and the group. The effective leader makes use of all five styles as appropriate. The author identifies forces in the leader, in the group members, and in the situation which influence the choice of leadership styles. He argues that participative or "member-centered" leadership is more likely to improve motivation, decision-making, morale, individual skills, and adaptability of subordinates.

Schutz, W.C. (1958). *FIRO: A 3-Dimensional Theory of Interpersonal Behavior.* New York: Rinehart.

The author presents his theory that people need to give and receive inclusion, control, and affection. He reviews the research supporting the reasonableness of supposing these are interpersonal needs, and compares them to biological needs. He discusses a survey called the FIRO-B, which measures individual characteristics regarding these needs. Compatibility of group members based on their FIRO-B scores is explored. This book will introduce you to a well-traveled tool useful in understanding group functioning.

This, L.E. (1980). *The Art of Listening: A Looking-into-Leadership Monograph.* Fairfax, VA: Leadership Resources, Inc.

This 16-page booklet summarizes much of what is known about the listening process and how to improve it. Topics covered include statistical data on listening and speaking speeds, eight phases of every communication event, steps to better listening, a self-assessment questionnaire for identifying strengths and weaknesses as a listener, and seven exercises for increased listening skill. Like other Looking-Into-Leadership monographs, this is an excellent starting point in understanding this topic.

This, L.E. (1980). *Interpersonal Communication: A Looking-into-Leadership Monograph.* Fairfax, VA: Leadership Resources, Inc.

In a 10-page booklet, the author summarizes much of what is known about interpersonal communication. Key topics covered are the information space model, major factors affecting communication, guidelines for improving, and some useful exercises. Like others in the Looking-Into-Leadership series, this monograph is an excellent starting point in understanding this topic.

Smith, P.B. (1980). *Group Processes and Personal Change.* London: Harper and Row.

The author, in a review of group therapy research, finds that the two essential behaviors necessary to bring about maximal behavior change in another person are support and confrontation. Without support, confronting another person with negative feedback will produce a "fight or flight" response, unless the confronter has power over the confrontee. In that case, confrontation without support will produce mere conformity as long as the powerful confronter is present, but no real behavior change.

INDEX